Michael Davitt
New Perspectives

Edited by
FINTAN LANE
and ANDREW G. NEWBY

IRISH ACADEMIC PRESS
DUBLIN • PORTLAND, OR

First published in 2009 by Irish Academic Press

2 Brookside
Dundrum Road
Dublin 14, Ireland

920 NE 58th Avenue, Suite 300
Portland, Oregon,
97213-3786, USA

This edition © 2009 by Irish Academic Press
Individual chapters © contributors

www.iap.ie

British Library Cataloguing in Publication Data
An entry can be found on request

978 0 7165 3042 8 (cloth)

Library of Congress Cataloging-in-Publication Data
An entry can be found on request

Printed in Great Britain by the MPG Books Group, Bodmin and King's Lynn

Contents

List of Abbreviations

BL	British Library
DP	Davitt Papers
NAI	National Archives of Ireland
NLI	National Library of Ireland
NLS	National Library of Scotland
NYPL	New York Public Library
PRO	Public Record Office
PRONI	Public Record Office of Northern Ireland
QUB	Queen's University Belfast
TCD	Trinity College Dublin

Notes on the Contributors

Paul Bew is Professor of Politics at Queen's University, Belfast. His publications include *Land and the National Question in Ireland, 1858–82* (1978), *C.S. Parnell* (1980), *Conflict and Conciliation in Ireland, 1890–1910* (1987), *Ideology and the Irish Question: Ulster Unionism and Irish Nationalism, 1912–1916* (1994), *John Redmond* (1996) and *Ireland: The Politics of Enmity, 1789–2006* (2007).

Thomas Davitt is a grandson of Michael Davitt and a Catholic priest, with the Vincentians (Congregation of the Mission), based in Dublin.

John Dunleavy is an Oxford-based local historian, who has taught and researched widely on nineteenth-century education and about Davitt's time in Lancashire. He is the author of *Michael Davitt and Haslingden* (1983), *Haslingden Catholics* (1987) and *Davitt: Exile and Exiles* (1996).

Fintan Lane is the author of *The Origins of Modern Irish Socialism, 1881–1896* (1997) and *In Search of Thomas Sheahan: Radical Politics in Cork, 1824–1836* (2001). He is co-editor of *Politics and the Irish Working Class, 1830–1945* (2005) and *Essays in Irish Labour History* (2008), and editor of *Politics, Society and the Middle Class in Modern Ireland* (2009).

J.J. Lee is the Director of Glucksman Ireland House and Professor of History at New York University. His publications include *The Modernisation of Irish Society, 1848–1918* (1973) and *Ireland, 1912–1985: Politics and Society* (1989).

Elaine McFarland is Professor of History at Glasgow Caledonian University. Her publications include *Protestants First: Orangeism in Nineteenth-Century Scotland* (1990), *Ireland and Scotland in the Age of Revolution* (1994), *John Ferguson: Irish Issues in Scottish Politics* (2003) and (as co-editor) *Scotland and the Great War* (1999).

Owen McGee is the author of *The IRB: The Irish Republican Brotherhood from the Land League to Sinn Féin* (2007).

Laura McNeil is Assistant Professor in History at Elms College, Massachusetts. She graduated with a PhD in History from Boston College (2002), with a thesis entitled 'Land, Labor and Liberation: Michael Davitt and the Irish Question in the Age of Irish Democratic Reform, 1878–1906'.

Laurence Marley was the first holder of the Michael Davitt Fellowship and graduated from NUI, Galway in 2005 with a PhD in History. He is the author of *Michael Davitt: Freelance Radical and Frondeur* (2007).

Patrick Maume is a researcher with the *Dictionary of Irish Biography*. His publications include *'Life that is Exile': Daniel Corkery and the Search for Irish-Ireland* (1992), *D.P. Moran* (1995) and *The Long Gestation: Irish Nationalist Life, 1891–1918* (1999).

Andrew G. Newby is Senior Lecturer in History at the University of Aberdeen, and Adjunct Professor in European Cultural and Area Studies, University of Helsinki. He is the author of *The Life and Times of Edward McHugh: Land Reformer, Trade Unionist and Labour Activist* (2004) and *Ireland, Radicalism and the Scottish Highlands, 1870–1912* (2007).

Alan O'Day was a Senior Fellow in History at Greyfriars Hall, University of Oxford and is Senior Visiting Fellow at the Institute of Irish Studies, QUB and Visiting Professor at TCD. His publications include *The English Face of Irish Nationalism* (1977), *Parnell and the First Home Rule Crisis* (1986), *Irish Home Rule, 1867–1921* (1998) and *Charles Stewart Parnell* (1998). With D. George Boyce he has co-edited five volumes on modern Irish history, the most recent being *The Ulster Crisis, 1885–1921* (2005).

Pauric Travers is President of St Patrick's College, Drumcondra, and the author of *Settlements and Divisions: Ireland, 1870–1922* (1988) and co-author (with Donal McCartney) of *The Ivy Leaf: The Parnells Remembered* (2006).

Preface

Michael Davitt (1846–1906) is often hailed as one of the pre-eminent figures of nineteenth-century Irish history, remembered in particular as 'the father of the Land League'. For various reasons, however, historical research on Davitt has been erratic and scarce. As early as 1908, when writing his celebratory account of Davitt's life and work, Francis Sheehy-Skeffington railed against the promotion of the individual over ideals:

> These are days when a great man is forgotten almost before he is buried – unless his greatness consisted in skilled exploitation of his fellow-creatures, in which case his memory will be preserved by costly and ugly monuments.[1]

Though intended as a reference to the 1880s cult of Parnell, Sheehy-Skeffington also warned that:

> Davitt himself must not posthumously fall victim to a similar misconception. There seems little danger of this today, it is true; the present position of Irish affairs is remarkable for the extent to which Davitt's ideals have already been forgotten.[2]

However, apart from Sheehy-Skeffington, only M.M. O'Hara's *Chief and Tribune* (1919) made any major attempt to cover Davitt's career in the decades after his death, and there was a clear disparity between the extent of writing on the 'Chief' (Parnell) and the 'Tribune' (Davitt). It was the centenary of Davitt's death in 1946 that marked the beginning of a new stage in his historiography. A stamp was produced celebrating the role he played with Parnell in creating the Land League, but it was also at this point that Theo Moody began to plough through the huge volume of personal papers and diaries now known as the 'Davitt Papers', culminating in several important articles and, in 1981, the publication of *Davitt and Irish Revolution*. The importance of this work is unquestioned, and yet it only covers Davitt's life until 1882 – after which time, Moody concedes in his conclusion, he pursued an important career as 'nationalist, labour leader, democratic reformer, humanitarian, and internationalist'.[3] Nevertheless, *Davitt and Irish*

Revolution dominated the historiography of Davitt's life for over a quarter of a century, and it is the purpose of this collection of essays to supplement, challenge and revise Moody's work – to highlight areas of Davitt's life, work and travels which have remained in the background and to reassess Davitt's position in Irish history and popular imagination.

The essays that appear in this volume are revised versions of papers that were originally presented at the Michael Davitt Centenary Conference, held in St Patrick's College, Drumcondra, Dublin, on the final weekend of May 2006 – the centenary of Davitt's death. The first meeting of the conference committee had been held four years earlier, as various interested scholars had not only recognised the need for an event similar to that which had marked the centenary of Davitt's birth in 1946 (and 150th in 1996), but also – vitally – the emergence of a new wave of writing and research on Davitt. Eighteen years had passed between Moody's *Davitt and Irish Revolution*, and the publication of Carla King's succinct *Michael Davitt*, which despite its brevity signalled the emergence of a new generation of 'Davitt scholars'. Carla King's editing of not only Davitt's own *Jottings in Solitary* (2003), but also eight volumes of his other writings (2001), has provided the inspiration for many scholars and authors to undertake new research on Davitt's life and importance, and much of that work is reflected in these pages.

The collection proceeds thematically, but with a sense of chronological coherence, and opens with the personal journey of Davitt's grandson, Fr Thomas Davitt, in attempting to construct a personal image of a grandfather he never met. J. Joseph Lee then presents an appraisal on Davitt's life 'of such variety, such controversy and, indeed such improbability', arguing that, for all the causes that he espoused, popular memory in Ireland continually recalled Davitt the nationalist above all else.

Stepping outside of Ireland, into the Irish communities of northern England, John Dunleavy describes the way in which Davitt's early years in Lancashire shaped his later thought and actions, especially his attitude towards education. Alan O'Day then places Davitt in the context of two other Irish leaders – Butt and Parnell – reflecting on their very different ideas of what form should be taken by an independent or 'home rule' Ireland. Paul Bew and Patrick Maume take this further by highlighting the complex, often divisive relationship that Davitt had with the people of Ireland, and Parnellites in particular.

One of the three epithets given to Davitt by Sheehy-Skeffington was that of 'labour leader' and, despite the overwhelming focus on the Land League years in the historiography to date, Davitt's position in the development of the labour movement in Britain has received significant attention. This is not the case with regard to his interaction with the working class and labour movement in Ireland. Fintan Lane's chapter in this volume deals with Davitt and Irish labour activists, and it reveals a much more complicated, even problematic, relationship with Irish labour leaders and the working class than has been previously recognised.

Among the celebrations of Davitt's life that took place in 2006, one area of controversy appeared to be the continuing debate over his links with the fenian movement, especially later in life. Owen McGee tackles the issue of Davitt and Irish republicanism, from his arrest at Paddington station in 1870 through to his effective retirement from public life at the end of the nineteenth century.

McGee notes that one area in which Davitt felt uncomfortable was with the development of an 'exclusively Catholic' 'Plan of Campaign' in 1886, and Pauric Travers' article on education again highlights that Davitt supported an educational system in which 'rights of all faiths' were guaranteed. This may have brought him into open conflict with the Catholic bishop of Limerick, among other clerical luminaries, but it also helps to connect his later life with the formative years described by John Dunleavy – of a young lad imbued in a non-denominational, technical education.

As a labour advocate, agrarian reformer and also, as time went on, as a nationalist, Davitt enjoyed a considerable degree of popularity among sections of the Scottish population. Two chapters deal with these links, with Andrew Newby arguing that Scottish enthusiasm for Davitt was well reciprocated, as it gave Davitt and his supporters a forum in which to air more radical social ideas during the 1880s without necessarily appearing to challenge the hegemonic Parnellites. Elaine McFarland examines more deeply a possible source of Davitt's interest in Scotland, a personal friendship with Belfast-born Protestant John Ferguson. In investigating the comparisons and contrasts between the lives of these two men, the chapter also highlights the sheer diversity of national, class and religious identity within the Irish community in Scotland, of which Ferguson was an acknowledged leader, during the later Victorian era.

Rounding off the collection are two accounts that reflect on Davitt's entire career and its legacy. Laurence Marley gives an account of the difficulties which Davitt faced, especially after the dissolution of the Land League, in giving his full commitment to any individual cause or party, leading some contemporaries to suggest that 'Davitt's cosmopolitanism was his undoing'. Laura McNeil's final chapter examines some of the ways in which competing interests have fought over Davitt's memory. Again, it might be argued that Davitt was enigmatic, or simply a man of extremely broad interests, but political squabbles in his name were again commonplace in 2006, as differing groups on the political spectrum claimed direct lineage.

The breadth of research on Davitt is, in many respects, merely a reflection of the diverse range of interests held by the man himself. As will be seen, this collection presents new writing on Davitt's personal and early life; his connections – personal or intellectual – with various politicians, nationalists, labour activists, clerics and others; or subsequent folk memory or use of Davitt's life and career in political rhetoric to the present day. All of the contributors have their own reasons – personal, academic, or a mixture of both – for pursuing research into Davitt's life and career, which in itself gives some indication of the sheer breadth, geographically and politically, of Davitt's interests. Similarly, the fact that events commemorating Davitt's centenary were held in places as disparate as Dublin, Straide, Haslingden, New York and Portree highlight his role as a 'guiding light' for the Irish diaspora and other communities around the world which either benefited from his attention or saw in themselves a parallel to the Irish peasantry with which he was so strongly identified.

It should be noted that the articles contained within this book are very much intended as stand-alone works. As a result, there may be internal debates between the various authors and, indeed, it is possible that the same important piece of information about Davitt appears on more than one occasion. As editors, we have attempted as far as possible to standardise style, but not to construct a single overarching narrative of Davitt's life, activities or reputation, or to constrain authors by denying them the use of facts or quotations that appear in other essays.

It remains to thank the large number of people who helped to make the 2006 Dublin conference a success, and who have contributed to the publication of this set of essays. The organising committee comprised Carla King, Brendon Deacy, Máirtín Ó Catháin, John Dunleavy and the editors of the current volume. Many other academics, politicians and performers contributed hugely to the success of the conference, and we would like to extend our gratitude, therefore, to Andy Irvine, Kathleen Smith, Joe Ryan, Hasia Diner, Anthony Jordan, W.J. McCormack,

Justin Keating and Mary Robinson. We were also fortunate to have the administrative support of Maura Sheehan and the staff of St Patrick's College, Drumcondra. Several of the speakers at the conference also participated in a four-part RTÉ radio show on Davitt's life, *Discussing Davitt*, which was presented by Kevin Whelan and produced by Cathal Póirtéir. Audio recordings of this series have been archived by RTÉ and made available via the Internet; they can be accessed (January 2009) at: www.rte.ie/radio1/discussingdavitt/1093964.html

Those who contributed financial or other support towards the conference and the publication of this book include St Patrick's College, Drumcondra; Fáilte Ireland; and the Dublin Convention Bureau. Thanks also to Lisa Hyde and the staff at Irish Academic Press for their assistance and patience. We are grateful to the board of trustees, Trinity College Dublin, for permission to use quotations from the Davitt Papers.

Most of the essays contained within this book were produced before the recent explosion in digitised, searchable newspapers and other printed material from the nineteenth century. Forthcoming generations of writers, scholars, graduate students and others will benefit from increased access to new resources, leading to new elements of Davitt's life being scrutinised, and well-known aspects of his career being reassessed. We hope, and anticipate, that by the bicentennial of Davitt's birth in 2046, his place in Irish history will be as contested as it has been in the century since his death, but considerably better researched.

Fintan Lane
Andrew G. Newby

NOTES

1. Francis Sheehy-Skeffington, *Michael Davitt: Revolutionary, Agitator and Labour Leader* (London, 1908), p. vii.
2. Ibid., p. 279.
3. Theodore W. Moody, *Davitt and Irish Revolution* (Oxford, 1982), p. 547.

CHAPTER ONE

Getting to Know Grandad: A Family Perspective on Michael Davitt

THOMAS DAVITT

Everyone has four grandparents. I knew three of mine and, from early childhood, was conscious that the fourth was missing; my father's father had died nearly a quarter of a century before I was born. There were photographs of him in the house. They showed him with a beard, making him different from my other grandfather, who had only a moustache. He did not come up much in conversation and I cannot recall when it first struck me that I was the grandson of a famous historical person. My father would not have wanted any of us to stress that, anyway. The only other fact that I remember from earlier childhood is that, when going into town by tram along Lower Mount Street, the house in which he died, a former nursing home, was pointed out to me. Also, at some stage, my father showed us 'Land League Cottage' in Ballybrack, where my grandparents lived after their marriage in California and where my father was born.[1]

The period of the Land League was part of the Irish History course for the Intermediate Certificate but as the course covered about eight centuries of Irish history and the same of European, the Land League got rather skimpy coverage in class. I did not go on to take History as a subject for the Leaving Certificate and thus my knowledge of the Land League stayed at Intermediate Certificate level. This was only remedied when my father brought my late elder brother and myself to a lecture in the Mansion House by Professor T.W. Moody, of Trinity College Dublin, on 25 March 1946, the centenary of my grandfather's birth.

History, indeed, did not form a component of my Arts degree, and my university and seminary studies gave me enough to do without taking on any systematic study of my grandfather's place in Irish history. Also, since I grew up in what is now known as Dublin 4, the whole agricultural background of the Land League period was alien territory to me.

After ordination I was appointed to teach in Castleknock and, at this point, I had to teach History at Intermediate Certificate level. That was when I began to take a real interest in my grandfather. I have to say, however, that I became far more interested in Michael Davitt as a person than in his role as an important historical figure. I tried to discover more from my father, but as he was only twelve when his father died his recollections were limited. His father was away from home a lot, often for long periods, but even when he was at home in Dalkey my father said that he was a 'distant' parent. On the other hand, he used to take my father and his elder brother Michael for walks along the Vico Road, and he told them that he liked that stretch of road so well that after his death he might haunt it. This was an interesting item in my construction of an image of my grandfather, and I always think of that when I am on the Vico Road.

Other small details helped to develop the image. Radio Éireann, as it was then called, was to transmit a radio programme on Michael Davitt, and they consulted my father as to what sort of an accent the actor portraying his father should use. The producer was unsure whether to get the actor to use a Mayo accent or a Lancashire one; my grandfather had grown up in Haslingden from the age of five. My father told them that his father had neither of those accents, and that his accent could really be styled 'neutral'. I do not recall the actual broadcast and it may be that I was away at school on the day.

Some years later, in the late 1950s, I met a man who had returned to Dublin after many years in South Africa. As a child he had lived in Dalkey and, along with other young children, he used to follow my grandfather into Dalkey post office to watch him, a one-armed man, writing telegrams with his left hand. Details like that helped me to see him as a person rather than as an historical character.

My grandfather's eldest sister Mary married in Lancashire a man named Cornelius (Neil) Padden, and they emigrated to Scranton in Pennsylvania. When my grandfather realised that he would probably be arrested for his fenian activities he persuaded his parents to follow them, which they did, together with their other two daughters. Ann had married a man named Edward Crowley from Cork and the other daughter, Sabina, known as Sib, never married. My father sometimes spoke of his Aunt Sib, and claimed, apparently from first-hand knowledge, that she had an unpleasantly shrill voice! I presume she must have visited Ireland, unless on one of the three occasions when his mother brought the family to Oakland, California they stopped off in Washington where she lived. My father, indeed, was brought to America three times before he was ten years old.

In the mid-1960s I was studying at Fordham University, New York, and I contacted several of my American relatives, Paddens and Crowleys, including some first cousins of my father whom he had never met. Some of these relatives remembered my grandfather and from them I heard first-hand memories of their Uncle Michael, supplementing what I had heard from my father. In 1965 Professor Theo Moody was on study leave in Princeton. We arranged to meet in New York. This was the first time I had met him since his 1946 lecture in the Mansion House. From conversations with him, the picture of my grandfather continued to fill out.

A SENSE OF PLACE

I have always found, when trying to build up a picture of somebody from the past, that it is very helpful to visit places associated with them and especially to get inside buildings in which they had lived or worked, or at least to look at such buildings from the outside. I have been to Straide, where he was born, many times. I have looked at 'Land League Cottage' in Ballybrack and 'St Justin's' in Dalkey, the last house in which he lived.[2]

Visits to England, naturally, have also been useful in constructing a personal history of my grandfather. I first visited Haslingden in Lancashire on my own, when I was helping in a nearby parish one summer. He grew up there, and I saw the commemorative plaques in the parish church and elsewhere in the town. I was invited to go over there in 1996 for the celebration of the 150th anniversary of his birth, and again in March 2006. I have looked at Dartmoor prison from the outside, and whenever I am in Paddington station in London I try to visualise the moment of his arrest, between the arrival platform and the entrance to the Underground in Praed Street. At that time he had been lodging in 35 Millman Street, but when I went to look for the house I discovered that it was no longer there. The whole row had been a victim of either the Blitz or the developer. The same was true when I went to see 67 Battersea Park Road, where the whole family had lived while he was an MP.

My work for the religious congregation of which I am a member has meant that I have been to the United States many times and I have used these occasions, whenever possible, to get on my grandfather's tracks. He met his future wife, Michigan-born Mary Yore, in Oakland, California, and later married her there. After the accidental drowning of her mother, her father married again, and Mary was sent over to an aunt, Mary Canning, and her husband in Oakland; they were childless.[3] Before my visit to Oakland I was told by my father that the house where my grandmother grew up is no longer extant. I recently learned, though, that this information was incorrect, and that one of my Dublin cousins had her photo taken outside it not too long ago. I visited St Francis de Sales' church in which the nuptial Mass was celebrated. The church, which was unfinished at the time, was being built as a gift to the parish from my future grandmother's aunt, who was married to a builder. When Oakland later became a diocese this church became the cathedral. When I visited it I photographed the commemorative plaque, located in the entrance. Written in Latin, it mentioned that the church was the gift of Mr and Mrs Canning. I heard that the church has since been damaged in an earthquake, but I do not know to what extent.[4] I met a first cousin of my father, on his mother's side, Dr Robert Yore, a dentist, in whom I saw a great family likeness.

In the eastern United States, I have been on several occasions to Manayunk, Philadelphia, where my grandfather's mother, Catherine (née Kielty) died. She owned two adjacent houses on Main Street, which are still extant. I also visited her grave in the cemetery beside St John the Baptist church, though the present building is a replacement of the one she had known. My grandfather's father, Martin, had died earlier in Scranton, and I visited his grave in the cathedral cemetery there. In October 2000 I was at a symphony concert in the Concert Hall of the Academy of Music in Philadelphia. My interest was divided between listening to Hilary Hahn playing the Brahms violin concerto and trying to picture my grandfather speaking from the same platform on 16 December 1878.

In New York, I once went looking for the building that had housed the office of the Land League, 40 Washington Square, only to discover that it had been replaced by a modern university block. In October 2001, I had a few days in Cape May, New Jersey. My grandfather chose Cape May as a holiday destination in summer 1878, rather than the more popular Atlantic City, where many of his friends and relations from Manayunk were staying, but whom he wanted to avoid. He wrote this in a letter to John Devoy, on 16 August, and continued:

[M]y time would be occupied in useless confab with every blath-
erumskite I would come across. I'll get on very well here as
nobody knows me.[5]

He spent his time bathing in the Atlantic, walking, writing, and going
to dances and other evening entertainments. He wrote 'bathing', not
'swimming', leading me to ponder the ability of a one-armed man to
swim.

Before going on to deal with the diaries I will say something here
about another matter which I later investigated in a different manuscript in Trinity College Dublin. In the mid-1960s, when living in
New York, I made several visits to my American relatives, as I mentioned earlier. On one visit, possibly to the Crowleys, I was shown an
album in which each page had a printed set of questions, to which
guests were asked to write in their answers. One of the questions was
'Who is your favourite poet?' My grandfather wrote 'Wordsworth'. I
mentioned this later to my father and he said he did not recall his
father having any interest in poetry, and said he probably wrote down
the first poet's name that he thought of. Being a bit of a fan of
Wordsworth myself I was rather disappointed at that. I gave no further thought to the matter until 2003, when Carla King's edition of
my grandfather's *Jottings in Solitary* was published. In her
'Introduction', Dr King refers to his love of poetry and mentions
some of the poetry transcribed in *Jottings*, but which she had to omit
from her edition in order to adhere to the Classics of Irish History
format, the series in which her edition was published.

Having read that, I went back to Trinity to read the manuscript pages
that Dr King had omitted. *Jottings in Solitary* is written on foolscap
pages, only one side being used. However, on the reverse of pages 21
to 34, except for the reverse of page 30, are transcribed several poems.
These reverse sides are all, except for the reverse of pages 32 and 34,
dated 'Sunday, Oct. 2nd, 1881'. Many of them have headings such as
'Quotations &c', 'Things worth scribbling', 'Things worth remember-
ing'. There are poems in English, Latin, German, French, Italian and
Spanish. Sometimes the same poem is written in two languages.

What are we to make of this? If he knew all these pieces by heart,
why did he write them out? If he had them in a book or books of his
own, again why would he transcribe them? My guess would be that
he had temporary access to a multilingual anthology, something like
Maurice Baring's *Have You Anything to Declare?* of half a century
later, and transcribed them because he had the book only on loan.[6]

How well did he know any of these languages in 1881? The way in which the poems are written suggests to me a very careful transcription. There is a complete transcription of the well-known Latin hymn *O Deus Ego Amo Te*, generally ascribed to St Francis Xavier. In the left-hand margin is a literal English translation, in less careful script. I think this is almost certainly his own version. On the following page is a version in Spanish, headed 'Supposed to be the original of the preceding'. Then there is an English version, at the end of which, in brackets, are the words 'Own translation'.

I was once, for some reason which I do not now recall, going through with my father a magazine from around 1900. In it there was an advertisement for a language course – French, I think – and perhaps Linguaphone, on recorded cylinders. There was an illustration of the machine, with a tube ending in ear pieces rather like those of a stethoscope. When my father saw this he remembered that his father had owned something similar. In one folder among his papers there is only a single sheet, written on both sides, headed 'My 36th Birthday, March 25th 1882'. In the middle of a paragraph on the reverse he inserted a question in French: *Laquelle voulez-vous?*

FAMILY LIFE AND THE DAVITT DIARIES

Thus, for all of my 'fieldwork', it was only when I began to investigate his letters and diaries that I really felt that I was getting to know granddad, and for the remainder of this chapter I would like to share some of my personal gleanings from these important sources.[7] These are extracts which might not necessarily have attracted the attention of the many academic historians who have used the diaries, but which have been very important in my search for Davitt, 'the man'.

In 1981 Professor Moody published his long-awaited book, *Davitt and Irish Revolution, 1846–1882*. In preparing this book he had all my grandfather's letters and diaries on loan from my aunt, my father and my uncle. This meant that we, the next generation of the family, did not have the chance to see this material until after the publication of the book in 1981, when the diaries, letters and other documents were given to Trinity College Dublin by my father, and so became available to researchers. I cannot say exactly when the cataloguing and so on was completed and the material made available in the Manuscripts Department of the TCD library, but I had made up my mind that I would go in there and have a look at the diaries some day. Time passed quickly and it was not until 1996 that I actually did so.

The 150th anniversary of my grandfather's birth was 25 March 1996, for which various celebrations were organised. I was living in Rome at the time and I received an invitation from a committee in Haslingden to participate in their celebrations there and to celebrate Mass in the parish church. Needless to say, I accepted the invitation and enjoyed the occasion. It provided me with the necessary stimulus to contact the librarian in TCD and arrange to see the diaries during my summer holidays from Rome. Thereafter, I returned regularly to the TCD library.

My grandfather was not a consistent diary keeper; there were many years when he did not keep one, and even when he did there are many blank pages. I made several visits to TCD and copied out various pieces from the diaries. Unlike many historians, I was not looking for political entries but for personal and family ones, all the time trying to get to know better what sort of a man he was.

In one diary he had filled in the blanks on one of the first pages and gave his height as 5'11" and his weight as 11 stone. This seems rather light for a man of almost six feet, but we have to remember he was without the weight of one arm.

Although much attention has focused on my grandfather's political life, it seems clear that he often grew tired of life 'on the road' and yearned for relatively simple domestic pleasures. I will include here extracts from his diaries in 1886, and juxtapose them with some from 1888, after his marriage to Mary Yore. On 8 August 1886 he was in Buffalo, New York, and registered in the hotel as Mark Davidson in order to avoid journalists. On the 28th he wrote in the diary:

> Am sick & tired of this everlasting speaking on the one eternal topic. O for the end of it!

In some other places, he refers to his lectures and speeches as 'spouting'. His entry for the 31st is:

> Left for Chicago. Journey of a day & night. Bad as such long journies [sic] are they are infinitely preferable to the task of addressing meetings. Yet, horror of horrors! I have a lecture tour before me with a prospect of 50 or 70 speeches! A year in Portland would be a more preferable programme.

Portland refers, of course, to the prison. His second imprisonment was there, from February 1881 to May 1882, and was much less severe than his first imprisonment in Dartmoor, from 1871 to 1877. (When on such journeys he often made comments in the diary on the scenery he noticed from the train, and also on city parks, gardens and

similar places. Later, when married and living in Ballybrack, he made
several diary entries about his gardening activity there, which I will
mention in due course.) On 5 November he wrote from Wisconsin:

> Hell & Furies. Meeting in Oshkosh <u>last</u> night & no Michael
> Davitt! The idiots who organised meeting have not sent me a sin-
> gle line to inform me in any way about meeting. I have Nov. 5 in
> my engagement list …

I could imagine my father writing or saying something like that! Amid
the stress of the 'Plan of Campaign' and the home rule crisis, my
grandfather was clearly becoming jaded with public life. And yet,
1886 ended on the highest of notes. His final entry for that year, 30
December, is written diagonally across the whole page:

> Married at Oakland today
> Hurrah!

The joy expressed on his wedding day seemed to continue into married
life, and I will now highlight some of the extracts which can be found
during my grandfather's second year as a married man, 1888. One
thing I observed in the winter and spring was his continued interest in
gardening:

13 January:

> A day's gardening! Reminds me of Portland, only present
> 'warder' is much more lenient. Wish could devote few hours
> every day to this delightful exercise. Would soon get strong
> enough to undertake more work in the political field.

15 January:

> Musical evening. One of the many which have delighted my life
> since 30 Dec. 1887.[8] How I could enjoy an existence that would
> divide itself into – gardening in the morning – attending to cor-
> respondence and doing some literary bread-and-butter work in
> the afternoon, and then enjoying 'mine own fireside' in the
> evening, listening to Verdi & Rossini and the other musical mas-
> ters rendered by a most loving & thoroughly devoted little wife.[9]

21 January:

> Bought twenty-six kinds of flower seeds at McKenzie's yesterday.

McKenzie's was a seed merchant's shop on what is now Pearse Street; I remember it.

5 February:

> At home gardening all day.

The next day's entry, 6 February, also concludes '... then gardening all day'. Music and theatre also seemed to give him pleasure. On 15 February he crossed to England, and on arrival in London where do you think he went? To see *Puss in Boots* at Drury Lane. He returned from London on 26 February and wrote:

> Reached home weary & sick. Brought back severe cold.

On 17 August he records the birth of his first child:

> She is to be called Catherine Mary after my own dear mother and hers. Her birth occurring within the octave of the Assumption Mary will also be appropriate. It is also Mrs Canning's name and that of my eldest sister.

In fact, she was always called Kathleen. Mrs Canning was his wife's aunt, who had brought her up in Oakland, California, as I mentioned earlier.

Jumping forward eight years, he has an entry for 15 August 1894. He says that after a jaunting car chase to Donnybrook to get a doctor he just caught the 2.45 train and got back with the doctor to Ballybrack five minutes before the birth of his fourth child and second son, my father. From Donnybrook he and the doctor probably went down Ailesbury Road and caught the train at Sydney Parade, where this new-born son would take up residence forty years later. The following Sunday he recorded in his diary the new arrival's baptism:

> May the little fellow's life be as calm and painless as mine has been troubled, and full of suffering.

At Christmas that year, he wrote:

> Weather most mild or warm for this time of year. Pansies & Primroses in bloom out of doors as if it were April or May. All shrubs budding as if it were in early Spring instead of mid-Winter. Many roses still in bloom on my bushes.

The final excerpts I have chosen relate to the last months of my grandfather's life, beginning with this extract from 30 December 1905:

Nineteen years married today. So many years of domestic sunshine, save death of Kathleen & our own political trials, troubles and disillusionments.

His eldest child, Kathleen, had died ten years previously at the age of six and a half, probably from pneumonia.[10] On New Year's Eve he wrote:

Our little Domestic Republic of St Justin's bade farewell to Old Year and greeted young 1906 in my study. Rosary repeated.[11]

His entry for St Patrick's Day 1906 is:

Home. Mass. Day fine & warm. Called on Dentist Phillipson, 1 Upper Fitzwilliam St. To call on Monday 26th at 1 o'clock.

Eight days later was his birthday, 25 March:

60th birthday. Cold, snowing, frosty air. Two walks. Reminiscences – nine of these occasions happened in prison. How many more or how few more?? Better not to know, perhaps. Visit from Father Dawson.[12]

His wondering how many more birthdays he was to have is not the first reference which I came across to his awareness of the ageing process. He had mentioned it earlier in a rather unexpected context. On 30 September 1894, he recorded:

Climbed Croagh Patrick. Find I am not as young as when I did this feat before, five years ago. Well, one must begin to grow old sometime.

His comment that it was, perhaps, better not to know how many or how few more birthdays he was to have is interesting. In fact, he would not have any more, and would be dead nine and a half weeks after writing that entry in his diary. On St Patrick's Day, noted above, he referred to his seeing his dentist. That is where the trouble started.[13] He saw the dentist again on the 26th, the day after his birthday:

At Dentist Phillipson's. These old ruffians of stumps extracted by the American hypodermic injection process. No pain, only slight sick feeling arising from the injection.

He was back with the dentist on 2 April:

Dentist Phillipson 10 A.M.

The following day he has a few memos in the diary, the last entries except for a large star in red ink on 30 April. I do not know the significance of that, or even whether he himself put it there. The earliest reference I have found to his illness is in a letter his wife wrote to the editor of the *Freeman's Journal*, which was published on 15 May. She says her husband received a letter the previous day from San Francisco, describing the earthquake. The fact that it was his wife who wrote to the editor would indicate that Davitt was ill.

Two days later the same paper reported that he was in the Mount Street private hospital for another operation. The reference is to 'another' operation, because a month previously, on 16 April, Sir Thornley Stoker (president of the Royal College of Surgeons of Ireland) operated on him to remove an abscess in his jaw from which the two teeth were extracted in March.[14] The day after his death the *Freeman's Journal* gave an account of his illness:

> About the end of March Mr Davitt consulted a dentist in the city regarding his teeth, and on that occasion had one tooth extracted. A few days afterwards he returned and had two more teeth removed by the same gentleman. Leaving the dentist it is said that Mr Davitt proceeded to the National Library and, as stated, he spent two hours there [...]. It is thought he contracted a chill on that occasion which led to the formation of an abscess in the jaw from which the teeth were removed [...]. Blood poisoning seems to have been already developed.[15]

A medical bulletin was issued from the Mount Street private hospital on 18 May:

> Mr Michael Davitt was attacked some weeks ago by severe sceptic inflammation of his lower jaw, which resulted in an extensive abscess and destruction of a limited portion of the bone. An operation was done for the purpose of evacuating the portion of the bone. This was successfully accomplished and the septic condition has since diminished. Mr Davitt's rest is disturbed by a troublesome cough, but in other respects he has improved. There is no reason why he should not make a thorough recovery, but his convalescence must be tedious and will involve rest for some time.

> Signed W M'D A Wright, Joseph O'Carroll, W Thornley Stoker.

Despite their optimistic prognosis, he died less than a fortnight later, around midnight on 30 May. I have always thought it somewhat ironic that when my grandfather was suffering from fatal blood poisoning the surgeon who tried to save him was Thornley Stoker, brother of the author of *Dracula*.

All my life I have been familiar with the Lafayette copy of an American photograph of 1904 or 1905 by Prince, of Washington, the one which my father said showed his father as he remembered him. More recently I have become re-acquainted with the portrait by Sir William Orpen from 1906 – that shows the man I would love to have known. Orpen recorded that my grandfather had said to him: 'Don't take any side, just live and learn to try to understand the beauties of this wonderful world.'

NOTES

1. The name 'Land League Cottage', of course, is no longer on the building.
2. The name has since been switched to the house next door.
3. Incidentally, her father lost his second wife and then married for the third time. He had no children by either his second or third wives, sparing my generation a possibly complicated set of relatives.
4. Editors' Note: The old cathedral referred to here was indeed destroyed by the Loma Prieta earthquake in 1989. It has been replaced by the Cathedral of Christ the Light, which opened in September 2008.
5. Theodore W. Moody, *Davitt and Irish Revolution 1846–82* (Oxford, 1981), p. 227.
6. Maurice Baring, *Have You Anything to Declare?* (London, 1937).
7. Davitt diaries, 1886, 1887–8, 1894, 1906; Davitt Papers ,TCD.
8. He wrote 1887; the 7 was corrected in pencil to 6. 30 December 1886 was his wedding day.
9. 'Little' here is probably not meant in a patronising sense; Mary Davitt was a short, slightly-built woman.
10. See Laurence Marley, *Michael Davitt: Freelance Radical and Frondeur* (Dublin, 2007), p.115.
11. 'St Justin's' was the name of his house in Dalkey, as I mentioned earlier.
12. He has two question marks after 'How many or how few more'. When I saw the name 'Father Dawson' I presumed that he was a local priest, but when I looked in the *Irish Catholic Directory* for 1906 I found that there was no diocesan priest of that name in Dublin, and only four priests with that surname in Ireland. In the index to my grandfather's papers in TCD, there is mention of a photograph of 'Fr Dawson, St Lawrence Mission, Greenock, Dec. 1894'. I think it reasonable to presume that the two Fr Dawsons mentioned are one and the same person. Greenock is in the diocese of Paisley in Scotland, so I contacted the diocesan archivist. Fr Bernard Joseph Dawson was born in Tullow, Co. Carlow, in 1855 and was ordained in Scotland in 1883. He was stationed in St Lawrence's, Greenock, from 1892 to 1898. The year on the photograph is 1894. It seems likely that this is the man in question, but I have no idea what the connection with my grandfather might be, or why he kept the photograph. But the fact that Fr Dawson called on him on his birthday, and that the mention in the diary is merely 'Visit from Fr Dawson' would seem to indicate that he was a close friend.
13. Editors' Note: Francis Sheehy-Skeffington, in 1908, was at pains to highlight the link between Davitt's dental troubles and the 'hand of the English government'. He wrote: 'One of the teeth thus removed was the stump of one which had been broken during Davitt's imprisonment by a brutal and careless warder who acted as prison dentist. The broken remnant of a tooth gave Davitt trouble all his subsequent life, and it was its extraction that killed him at last. The hand of the English Government, so relentlessly hostile to the fearless patriot all through his life, is thus distinctly, though distantly, traceable in the manner of his death.' Francis Sheehy-Skeffington, *Michael Davitt: Revolutionary, Agitator and Labour Leader* (London, 1908), p. 263.
14. *New York Times*, 17 May 1906.
15. *Freeman's Journal*, 31 May 1906.

CHAPTER TWO

Michael Davitt: An Appraisal

J.J. LEE

Essaying an overview of a life of such variety, such controversy, indeed
such improbability, as that of Michael Davitt poses a daunting challenge. Born in Straide in Mayo in 1846, his family evicted from their
few acres in 1850, he grew up in the mill town of Haslingden in
Lancashire, where he acquired a lasting sympathy for wage-workers.
Ever grateful for the generosity of a Wesleyan benefactor who funded
four years' schooling for a Catholic boy when his right arm was amputated at the age of 11 after being mangled in a mill machine, he would
deplore religious antagonism for the rest of his life and preserve an
affectionate memory of his Wesleyan school teacher that would be
warmly reciprocated down to his own death.[1]

His fenian activities earned him a sentence of fifteen years' penal
servitude in 1870 and a vile existence in Millbank and Dartmoor jails,
before his release, on a ticket of leave, in December 1877, an experience that would lead to a passionate life-long commitment to penal
reform. His return to Ireland in 1878 catapulted him into public
consciousness; he was one of four fenians who received a tumultuous
reception in Dublin on their release, thanks to a high-profile campaign for amnesty led by Isaac Butt. He soon played so crucial a role
in elevating to national level the land agitation that began in his native
Mayo in 1879 that he would be christened Father of the Land League,
established to resist landlord rent demands in the face of feared
famine. So rapidly did his fame precede him that already on his
American fundraising tour of 1880, the *Washington Post* could greet
his arrival with the simple headline 'Michael Davitt's Reception' and
the *New York Times* later headed a column 'Michael Davitt in
California'.[2] The most socially radical of the Land League leaders, and
the inspiration behind the Ladies' Land League, he was rearrested and
imprisoned in Portland prison in England from February 1881 to May

1882, isolated from the events in Ireland that culminated in the 'Kilmainham treaty'.

His revulsion at the Phoenix Park assassinations of Burke and Cavendish on the day of his release led to his break with the fenian organisation, faithful though he remained to the fenian ideal of Irish sovereignty. But the atrocity also effectively subverted the possibility of his sustaining further agitation for social reform once Parnell opted to wind down the agrarian agitation to concentrate on home rule. He further undermined his own position when, inspired by his reading of Henry George, he espoused land nationalisation instead of peasant proprietorship in 1882. His contention that the Land League slogan, 'the land for the people', actually meant all the people, and not simply the current tenants, proved politically ill-judged. It reflects his extraordinary public stature that he could enjoy any public role again after embracing a proposition that the tenantry, as well as virtually the entire political class, found so heretical. Although he had to agree to refrain from making a public issue of what he would later call 'the superstition'[3] of peasant proprietorship – and many of his ambitious ideas for social regeneration under Land League auspices remained still-born[4] – he would continue to play an active role in the public life of Ireland and the Irish diaspora for the rest of his life.

With home rule on the horizon, he launched his own newspaper, *Labour World*, in London in September 1890, to promote social reform internationally as well as nationally, only for it to flounder the following May in the maelstrom of the Parnell split. Davitt would play a central role in that split, using the paper to become the first prominent Irish nationalist to declare against Parnell's leadership after the revelations of the Divorce Court in November 1890. Although a reluctant MP, he held seats in 1892–3 and from 1895 to 1899. Happier outside parliament, he played an important role in the success of William O'Brien's All for Ireland League after 1898, and remained active in the reunited Home Rule Party from 1900 until his death in 1906, just as he was contemplating launching a new socially radical newspaper, the *Irish Democrat*. He combined his activities in Ireland with travel throughout the Irish diaspora in Britain, America, Canada, Australia and New Zealand, and with visits to Palestine, the Boer Republics and Russia. Numerous condolences from abroad, as well as the massive range of obituaries in foreign papers, testify to his international standing.

UNIFIER OR SPLITTER?

Picking a rapid route through so multilayered a career inevitably risks distortion. However, Davitt himself summarised the lessons he purported to have drawn from a tempestuous life shortly before his unexpected death, in response to criticism from the *Nationist*, an 'Irish-Ireland' newspaper:

> My idea of an Irish-Ireland is an Ireland as politically independent as we can make it; with all her people well educated, in Gaelic and in English, and in as many other languages as they wish to learn; cultivating every available acre of Irish soil, and exporting millions of what we can spare from our own needs, to England, or to any other country, and receiving in economic exchange all the useful and needful articles we require ... and I will tell you how I would not work to create this Irish-Ireland: I would not attack ... Mr John Redmond as if he were a worse enemy than Mr James Bryce; or declare that Mr John Dillon did not belong to Irish-Ireland because his constituents elect him to Parliament; or waste energies denouncing 'politicians' which could be better employed in teaching Gaelic or in popularising home-made necessaries; or try to persuade your readers that Irish National Sentiment was first discovered or invented a few years ago by the Gaelic League ... I welcome all serviceable movements for Ireland ... the little philosophy I have picked up in a varied life's experience teaches me that while most movements are short-lived, Ireland is to live on for ever; and if we of to-day want to do more for her freedom and happiness than those who have laboured and sacrificed for her liberty before we were born, we will not make the fatal mistake of thinking and of acting as if each of us in our little circle or League possessed, alone, the true virtue of spotless patriotism, and were walking and working on the only possible road that could lead to the gateway of an Irish nation.[5]

'We will not make the fatal mistake' sounds like a manifesto for 'inclusiveness' among Irish nationalists. Nor was this tone false or forced. An Irish speaker, he could cherish both Irish and English, just as he could be a patron of both the Gaelic Athletic Association and Glasgow Celtic. For all his differences with individual nationalists, fenians or home rulers, he could envelop them all in his concept of service to Ireland. A driving force in uniting the various fenian, home rule and agrarian factions in the Land League, his massive 1904 work, *The Fall of Feudalism in Ireland*, breathed an inclusive tone in displaying remarkable – for an instinctive fenian – magnanimity towards the memory of Daniel O'Connell: 'Ireland has never produced a greater man than O'Connell.'[6] Even if one may suspect this was partly meant to put Parnell in his place, then he was notably fair to Parnell too, despite the bitterness of the split. His will of 1904 breathed the same spirit of conciliation[7] as his editorial refusal in 1890 to publish a letter in his *Labour World* 'because it is calculated to raise controversy, when we have resolved not to be factionalists, or to encourage dissension in any organisation – political, social or athletic, working for Ireland'.[8] But who decided who was 'working for Ireland'? The very next month his would be the first Irish nationalist voice to demand Parnell's resignation. Davitt, in London editing his newspaper when the judgement of the Divorce Court was announced on 17 November 1890, observed the full blast of non-conformist reaction. He decided to go public in the *Labour World*, on 22 November, with the demand that Parnell step aside temporarily as party leader 'although I know what it will cost me in abuse and other ways'.[9]

He would learn he didn't know the half of it. He grossly underestimated the cost of a struggle that he later complained privately 'has broken down my health and left me, financially, all but ruined'.[10] His stance alienated not only parliamentary Parnellites but many fenians who rallied to Parnell, and whatever credit he accumulated with the clergy was largely squandered by his politically injudicious criticism of clerical influence in education. Yet his reasoning was clinically logical in terms of existing Home Rule Party policy. The choice, he concluded immediately, lay 'between Parnell and Ireland'.[11] It was in Britain that 'Home rule is to be won or lost'[12] and 'every sane politician in the country knows that without the co-operation of the party led by Mr Gladstone, Home Rule is impossible for years to come.'[13] By 6 December the tone had sharpened against 'Mr Parnell's shameful conduct' as well as 'political mistakes'.[14] In the next issue, of 13 December, he threw down the gauntlet in a direct personal challenge to Parnell.

Why did his position harden so much over these three weeks? Under the heading 'Lie Boldly and Lie Often', he claimed that Parnell had attacked him in Cork, and sought to take over the Irish Democratic Labour Federation (IDLF), despite his having originally opposed the idea when Davitt promoted it in January 1890[15] – though Davitt's role in founding it was disputed[16] – and 'on leaving Cork Mr Parnell's carriage was surrounded by a crowd, who groaned for Davitt, "the place hunter" and cheered for Mr Parnell', provoking the outraged Davitt to respond with the ominous threat that at the imminent by-election, 'Mr Davitt will meet his libeller face to face in Kilkenny.'[17] It was a rapid escalation from his initial proposal that Parnell step aside temporarily as party leader. Davitt, with his fastidious, not to say prickly, sense of personal honour, was already seething from a sense of personal no less than political betrayal because the explicit assurances he believed he had received from Parnell (that he would emerge unscathed from the divorce case rumbling for the previous year) had turned out to be misleading. Now the die was cast. Not only would he criticise Parnell, he would now oppose him personally on the hustings. That sections of organised labour should be pitched against himself, far more sympathetic to working-class interests than Parnell, was the unkindest cut of all for him. What Davitt saw as Parnell's cynically opportunistic twisting of what he regarded as his own organisation – the IDLF – against him stoked the vehemence of his response. In Davitt's mind now, Parnell had not only stolen another man's wife; he had stolen his natural constituency away from himself. That Parnell versus O'Shea had become not only Parnell versus home rule but Parnell versus Davitt, helps to explain the fury of his assault.[18]

Davitt's handling of the whole divorce issue can be criticised on tactical grounds; nevertheless, it is difficult to accept the views of Archbishops Croke and Walsh, who 'were agreed that had silence been observed in the immediate aftermath of the divorce verdict, a reasonable compromise might have been negotiated. Davitt, said Croke, though substantially right, was as usual precipitate.'[19] Perhaps the archbishops were correct. However, it seems improbable. What could constitute 'a reasonable compromise' in the circumstances? And 'negotiated' with whom? With Parnell? Parnell, so flexible on other issues, was utterly inflexible on the issue of his leadership. For him the only 'reasonable compromise' was no compromise.

It was easy to forget from the perspective of Clonliffe and Thurles that there was another main party involved – the non-conformist support base in Britain of Gladstonian home rule. The archbishops were thinking only of Irish nationalists observing silence, as if the issue were a purely Irish matter. However, non-conformist leaders had immediately demanded Parnell's resignation on news of the divorce verdict, and the non-conformist vote was generally held to be crucial to Gladstone's ability to carry home rule. The apparent assumption of Catholic clergy, as of so many later writers, and even scholars, that only Catholics cared about marital matters and that Protestants were indifferent to sexual behaviour, has diverted attention from the non-confirmist value system. The redoubtable Hugh Price Jones had already asserted in the *Methodist Times* on 20 November that if the Irish sought to ignore such immorality, they would show themselves unfit for any type of government except military despotism.[20] Davitt, familiar with non-conformist culture from his school days, was more alert to this than the archbishops. While one cannot discount a possible accumulated personal resentment against Parnell, he could easily have felt that in the circumstances he had no choice but to go public to try to avert impending disaster when the Home Rule MPs seemed paralysed into a refusal to face inescapable reality.

Davitt's attitude reflected his loyalty to causes rather than personalities. His electoral judgement in 1890 was almost certainly correct, for 'at least in the short term, it was the reaction in England which was decisive',[21] But if he could well claim that his proposal was the only way of averting a split, whatever the immediate modalities, if Parnell refused to face reality, and that he merely wished to provide a sense of direction to salvage as much as possible from the inevitable crisis, nevertheless his critics might ask who was the factionalist now? His attitude alienated many, and almost certainly diminished the political role he might have subsequently played, however prominent he remained on the national stage. Matthew Kelly cogently suggests that 'were it not for his position during the split, Davitt would have been ideally placed' to act as a unifying influence, but also notes the observation from a decade later that 'some of the old Parnellites, who embrace some of the staunchest physical force men, are slow to forget the bitterness of his animosity towards them in the years of the "split" and are slow to trust him again.'[22] As with his bewildering espousal of land nationalisation, it reflects his enormous moral stature that he held any ground at all after offending so many priests, Parnellites and fenians in one direction or another by his stance on the split. Politically he got the worst of all worlds out of it. 'You are not near as objectionable to Parnellites – or to Priests – as I am,'[23] Davitt told William O'Brien in 1899, in rueful recognition of how maladroit he must have been to have managed to make enemies of such improbable bedfellows, to say nothing of many fenians.

The Parnell split made his desire to avoid faction impossible to achieve, but even as inclusive a response as his letter to the *Nationist* in 1906 could be evasive enough beneath the tone of sweet reasonableness – for he chose to overlook the more substantive point raised by the *Nationist*, an intellectually alert paper for which he himself had 'considerable regard'.[24] The *Nationist* complained that Davitt's speeches in

England on behalf of Labour during the general election of 1906 trusted too much in the English working class to achieve Irish independence, arguing that it would be time enough to foster relations with English workers when Ireland was independent. It charged Davitt with behaving more like a trade unionist than an Irish nationalist, and 'a trade union is not a nation'.[25] The overall tone was more rueful than hostile, and it claimed, precisely because of the high esteem in which it claimed to hold Davitt, that 'We earnestly wish that Mr Davitt would come to Irish Ireland. He could then become in reality an Irish leader.'[26] Davitt's response evaded this central question. It was an article of faith for him that the British masses would atone for the domination of the British classes over Ireland. 'We who know the working men of England, Wales, and Scotland so intimately,' he insisted at the outset of the Parnell split, 'are confident they will support Home Rule.'[27] It did not require Anglophobia from the *Nationist* to conclude that the confidence he reposed in British working-class support for Irish nationalist demands was, at the very least, premature.

Davitt, then, despite his genuine desire to the contrary, could be not only a unifier but also a splitter. This could be seen charitably as his suffering the fate of the ecumenicist, who is shot at from many angles by more single-minded guardians of their true faiths. However, it also meant that his ideological position often created enemies of the causes he championed. There are still depths to be explored here – and contradictions to be resolved, if indeed they can be.

CELTS, PEASANTS AND EMIGRANTS

Although *The Fall of Feudalism in Ireland*, Davitt's great apologia *pro vita sua* of 1904, served many purposes, it was essentially a hymn to the two categories to whom it was dedicated: 'the Celtic peasantry of Ireland, and their kinsfolk beyond the seas'. This dedication reflected a number of recurring features of Davitt's thinking, for both 'Celtic' and 'peasantry' were important – if loosely conceived – categories for him.

Davitt chose his title partly to establish a relationship by semantic suggestion between the 'land revolution' in Ireland and the mainstream of European revolutionary history as seen through the prism of the French Revolution. Feudalism did not exist legally in Ireland; the 'Seigneur and the serf' of Fanny Parnell's 'Hold the Harvest', were symbolic terms. Davitt too used the term more in a symbolic than a technical sense to describe the total structure of 'this despotic social and political ruling power' in Ireland. It was 'by aid of this empire' that the landlord class had 'seized all the spoils of conquest – land, government, law, authority, patronage, and wealth'.[28] He drew on the term in a manner reminiscent of its use in popular French parlance on the eve of the Revolution, as a derogatory term for denouncing the whole structure of society. He himself tended to focus more on imperialism than on feudalism as the ultimate enemy, for his feudalism was a function of imperialism.

Many an incongruity lurks within *The Fall of Feudalism*, as was scarcely avoidable in a combative 700-page book composed at high speed in the interstices of numerous other demands on his time. The most glaring incongruity exposes an abiding challenge to his concept of politics, perhaps a factor in his relative political failures: the tension between his image of the 'leader' and the 'people'. Having begun his Preface by talking about 'the story of an Irish movement which sprang without leaders from the peasantry of the country',[29] within a page he finds himself talking about how 'men of the Irish race, scattered by eviction and the evils of unsympathetic rule in Ireland to all parts of the earth, were "enlisted" in the final struggle for the soil and rule of the Celtic fatherland, under Mr Parnell's superb leadership',[30] and further noting how 'in a combative organisation which at one period of its existence numbered more than half a million of members',[31] 'every leader and prominent member from Mr Parnell downward' was imprisoned.[32] Some 700 pages later, he feels it unfair to finish the narrative without listing several other leaders in Ireland and the United States.[33] Indeed, he is sufficiently sensitive from the outset to the obvious objection that his belief in the 'masses' jarred with his references to his own role, to feel obliged to concede that:

> The personal mention is, I regret, introduced in a few of the chapters of my story more frequently and more prominently than is agreeable to the feelings of the writer. Silence or omission in this respect would, however, only convey the suggestion of a mock modesty. It would invite the less charitable imputation of an unreal and affected self-effacement.[34]

Yet, however much the book revolves around the personalities of Parnell and himself, his democratic impulses required him to envelop the leaders in a model of political activity that extolled the qualities of the plain people – not the faithful few, but the faithful many – in his own act of faith:

> This ceaseless Irish warfare of practically passive resistance

against the strength of the British empire in Ireland will com-
pare, in an endurance of penalties, in triumphs over defeats, and
in a tenacity of dauntless protest against the decrees of conquest,
with any struggle ever waged by a civilised race for the recovery
of its land and freedom.[35]

Professor T.W. Moody, the late doyen of Davitt scholars, rightly concluded that, 'For a book written in less than a year, it is a miraculous
performance'[36] – all the more so, one might add, for being written without a research assistant or ghost writer (a fact that Moody would have
taken for granted, but which few academics nowadays, much less public figures, would even contemplate). Anne Kane adds further depth in
concluding that 'unlike many accounts of historical events written by
participants, Davitt's work is sufficiently multidimensional to allow
numerous generations of scholars to mine it for new insight using current models of analysis.'[37] These accolades are even more remarkable in
that the *Fall of Feudalism* was not written in tranquillity; it was a
weapon to rally the faithful to sustain the struggle for independence. In
his conclusion, 'A future racial programme' – racial, of course, does not
mean racist, but is used in the normal sense of the time – he asks:

> Why should we be denied, as a people, the freedom which has
> made the small nations of Europe peaceful, prosperous and pro-
> gressive. We have committed no crime against mankind or civil-
> isation which should deprive us of these blessings.[38]

The virtues of 'small nations' constitute one of the stock themes of his
political faith. 'Small nations,' he asserts, 'have been the truest pio-
neers of progress, and the best promoters of the arts and sciences, in
the evolution of society, from the middle ages to the present day.'[39]
Contrary to then widespread emphasis on empire as the inevitable
organisation of the future, he argued that:

> Nationhood is not a decaying but a growing force, and is gaining
> new vitality in Europe. It will be found that the principle of nation-
> ality, rooted as it is in the very foundations of human society, will
> grow stronger and more virile as education and enlightenment
> spread among the people, while imperialism, with its tendency to
> military rule, crushing taxation, and constant provocation to wars,
> will breed the diseases of its own decay and downfall. In Great
> Britain, parliamentarianism or imperialism must die. They cannot
> live together. The growth of military power, increasing arma-
> ments, aggressive politics which provoke international disputes,

expeditions for the subjugation of so-called savage races, all mean a constant danger to social peace and to true progress, with increasing taxation upon those who looked at parliamentary government as the best protection for their trading interests and liberties. Imperialism is necessarily impatient of constitutional control, and will not always submit to its restraining influence.[40]

Whatever the core of truth in this mode of thought, he remained oblivious to the danger, natural enough for one who had spent years in English jails, that it could lead to indulgent verdicts on England's rivals, especially Germany – which he insisted on perceiving as a cluster of small states, credulously assuming the validity of the constitutional mirage instead of recognising the iron reality of Prussian dominance.[41] Even more could it lead to indulgent verdicts on small peoples in direct conflict with the British empire, above all the Boers. Indeed, much of the *Fall of Feudalism* was written under the influence of the second Anglo-Boer War of 1899–1902, whose impact pervades his later writings. He resigned his seat in parliament in 1899 in declared outrage at the treatment of the Boers, declaiming that he would prefer to see Ireland continue in bondage if the price was their defeat. Though he can hardly have been unaware that Salisbury's government was unlikely to immediately confront him with so agonising a choice, the sentiment, nevertheless, was in keeping with Davitt's character. When he decided to go to South Africa to report on the war – securing commissions from the *Freeman's Journal* in Dublin and Hearst's *New York Journal* – the ultimate result of the two months he spent there in 1900, and of his further reflections, was the 600-page *Boer Fight for Freedom*, published in 1902. Consisting of war reporting by a virtually 'embedded reporter' on the Boer side, with no attempt at balance – perhaps indeed, Donal McCracken suggests, revealing little of 'what he really thought' – it falls far short of his best work, even if it still ranks as 'an impressive book which no historian of the war can ignore'.[42]

Even had circumstances permitted him to visit the British side – and given his bitter hostility to the war, safety considerations alone would have counselled against[43] – it is highly unlikely that his reporting or reflections would have been any more balanced. He shared the view widespread in Ireland, and frequent in Europe and even Britain itself, that the Boers were another small people falling victim to the predatory impulses of a British capitalist/imperialist juggernaut. Although his attribution of the origins of the war mainly to the machinations of London financiers seems highly questionable in the light of recent

archival research,[44] it was widely shared at the time. Davitt's sentiments were not exceptional, though the vigour with which he
expressed them was. One is even tempted to speculate that it may be
that this second Anglo-Boer War came as an emotional release for
him, partly reflecting the subliminal instincts of a repressed fenian.
Here he could give vent to fundamental feelings he felt it necessary to
keep suppressed on Irish matters. The Boers were doing what he
would have loved to have done, but British command of overwhelming violence in Ireland made it impractical.

Whatever the explanation, he could henceforth barely mention the
war without exploding into paroxysms of fury at this other example of
English hypocrisy, against which he had already raged, not least in
expressing his horror at the slaughter of the wounded and of innocents
by Kitchener's army at Omdurman in 1898.[45] This horror was now
exacerbated by the slaughter of wounded Boers at Elandslaagte.[46] His
contempt for the 'concentration camp' policy of the British, and for
what he saw as their fraudulent excuses – in contrast to his apparent
belief in the axiomatically honourable behaviour of the Boers – allows
for little variation or subtlety of tone. Whatever the reason, here there
is little hint of sympathy for the plight of native peoples that he had
expressed in his attitude towards Ashanti, Maoris and Australian
Aborigines.[47] Here will be found no echo of the slogans paraded on the
placards for the Irishtown meeting of 1879 that launched the movement out of which the Land League would emerge, and which purported to embrace the 'kraals of Kaffirland' as well as 'the cabins of
Connemara' as victims of the 'invader', much less of his own sympathy
for the Zulus at the time.[48] He may have felt that blacks in southern
Africa were treated no better by British than by Boers, and that the
black leaders in British-dominated territory were blind to put their trust
in British goodwill – as, indeed, time would cruelly confirm.[49] He may
too have been seeking to use his unqualified expressions of support of
the Boers, and opposition to Britain, as a way to position himself as a
link between the United Irish League and the fenians,[50] on the model of
the original New Departure. However, in other circumstances, it would
be very surprising if he had not found something to say about the dehumanising treatment of blacks by the Boers. It was as if nothing should
be allowed tarnish the escutcheon of Boer nobility of character, even by
one who had not shrunk from expressing severe strictures on racist attitudes elsewhere.

His columns on his next assignment from Hearst – testimony to his
international standing as a journalist – to report on the Kishinev

pogrom in Tsarist Russia in 1903, would reach an august American audience. Although Davitt could be caustic, from his social perspective, on the alleged influence of London financiers, not least Jewish ones, in driving Britain to war in South Africa to grab the diamond and gold riches of the Boer Republics, the sufferings of the Jews of Kishinev not only moved him to denounce the barbarities perpetrated on them, but to embrace Zionism in the conviction that the only safe haven for Jews would be their own national homeland in Palestine. His reports, which he collected and expanded in book form, so impressed the Jewish Publication Society in the US that they distributed *Within the Pale: The True Story of Anti-Semitic Persecutions in Russia* to leading public figures from the president down.[51] Although Davitt had already strongly opposed threatened labour discrimination against Jews in Ireland long before Kishinev, the sufferings of the Russian Jews probably further inspired his passionate public condemnation of the boycott of Limerick Jews in January 1904 and he explicitly referred to them in his letter to the *Freeman's Journal* about the Limerick situation.[52]

Davitt can sound remarkably contemporary in his thinking. This is especially true when he ponders the potential of the diaspora – the idea of mobilising 'the sea-divided Gael' in Ireland's interests:

> The Irish race have a place in the world's affairs of today that is incompatible with the position which Ireland occupies as a kind of vegetable patch for selfish imperial purposes. We are fully 20,000,000 of the world's population, and though four-fifths of these reside out of Ireland, they are potential factors, neverthe-less, in the political fate and fortunes of the country from which a rule of stupidity and race hatred drove their progenitors away.[53]

Yet, this pride also jostled with a recurring fear that emigration was draining its best to the US so much that Ireland at home would wither from inanition.[54] However, he could propose no realistic solution, though he did later indulge the hallucination of the instant prosperity brought on by a putative home rule regime after 1908 attracting Irish-American investment to Ireland. This could not be investment in software or in pharmaceuticals, of course, but rather in the distinctly less promising – retrospectively, at any rate – field of peat production. Nevertheless, the idea of American investment, though already mooted in the 1880s, still has a visionary ring about it.[55]

THE ULSTER QUESTION

So, in the event, does his ambition to reassure Ulster unionists that they had nothing to fear from home rule. Intensely though he despised and hated landlordism, he was more relaxed about the Anglo-Irish once landlord power was curbed – as it largely was by the time of the Wyndham Act of 1903 – however vigorously he denounced that Act as excessively generous to landlords. However, he recognised that, with landlordism effectively neutered, Ulster unionists had superseded the Anglo-Irish as the major obstacle to home rule. Moreover, the prospects of a Liberal victory at the next general election were brightening with Liberal by-election victories from 1902 and, with it, the prospects for home rule. But Davitt was under no illusion about the depth of Ulster unionist hostility, having witnessed at first hand as an MP the tenacity with which their representatives fought Gladstone's second Home Rule Bill in 1893, and his mind began to turn to the practicalities of reconciling Ulster unionists to a home rule administration.

The decade after the defeat of the second Home Rule Bill was scarcely conducive to thinking about how a home rule Ireland might function. However, now that a putative Liberal victory made it seem practical politics once more, one of his last writings was a sketch of what it might be like. Though he has relatively few earlier references to Ulster unionists, this reflected circumstances rather than inclination. In the years of the first and second Home Rule Bills of 1886 and 1893, he sought to address issues raised by Ulster unionists. As early as 1887, his mind was thinking along the lines of a left/right division superseding a nationalist/unionist one in a home rule Ireland.[56] And with home rule putatively achieved in his dream world of Liberal revival, he thought he saw a chance of realising, through the Protestant working class of north-east Ulster, his long-cherished dream of realigning Irish politics around social as well as national issues. His scenario envisages a situation in which the first prime minister of a home rule Ireland, Sir John Waterford (obviously John Redmond, as in the draft, thinly disguised, like all his nominees, behind a verbal veil), under a putative Home Rule Act of 1908 had won the confidence of Ulster unionists by 'the generous policy pursued towards the Protestant minority'.[57] In particular, Waterford assuaged the fears, 'real or imagined', of unionists that they would not be treated impartially,[58] by using the RIC to suppress Catholic demonstrators protesting against an Orange march in the mixed town of Warrenpoint.[59] Though he heaped praise on Waterford's moderate and judicious leadership of the transitional government coalition based on his National Conservative Party, they nevertheless lost office in the putative 1910 general election because a left/right divide abruptly superseded a nationalist/unionist one following the introduction of universal suffrage.[60]

Nevertheless, apparently so anxious was Davitt to extend conciliatory hands all round, he had the Speakership first being offered to 'Colonel N. Surrender, of North Armagh, as a mark of esteem towards a one-time fierce opponent of Home Rule; but was declined'[61] – even in so apparitional a mode, Davitt retained sufficient wit to permit a fleeting flash of realism intrude by having Col. Saunderson refuse, thus allowing Edward Blake (Edward Toronto) to be unanimously elected.[62] It is easy to dismiss as a mirage Davitt's vision of the break-up of the home rule and unionist blocks in favour of a broad left/right divide, with the new National Democratic Party, supported by Progressive Unionists and an Independent Labour Party, defeating Waterford's Conservatives, supported by other, presumably non-progressive, Unionists. Among the improbable assumptions on which this scenario was based was that a constitution would be based on adult suffrage, female as well as male.[63]

Equally a mirage, it may be thought, was his attributing this victory to 'the general enthusiasm for national and practical education that had been created through the labours of the Gaelic League',[64] 'a great boom in Irish manufacturing industry' due to the aforementioned American investment,[65] and public support for a 'National' rather than a 'Catholic' university.[66] Education was a passion for Davitt, reflecting the importance he attached to his own formative years. His proposals in March 1906 (anticipating, incidentally, much of Patrick Pearse's criticism of the National Board of Education) included a national 'Council of Education' of ten members to overhaul national school books, which should be compiled 'with due and direct relation to the industrial commercial life, and the economic and social conditions of our country, its history and its geographical individuality'.[67] His proposed membership of this council reveals another aspect of his inclusivist impulse: Dr Mahaffy and Dr Finlay (Religion and Morals), Dr George Sigerson (History and Philosophy), Prof. Hartley (Science), Sir Horace Plunkett (Economics and Agriculture), Douglas Hyde (Gaelic and Linguistics) and Stephen Gwynn (Literature).[68] This is a plausible line-up of the best minds. Transcending religion, ideology, personal relationships and bureaucratic self-interest, it was also highly doubtful as a practical possibility.

The number of potential obstacles in the way of a rapid realisation of Davitt's dream, whether in education or in his broader social vision, must leave one highly sceptical of his notion of a home rule parliament divided along a left/right axis. Despite what may be thought about the impracticality of his proposals, his remarks are instructive in relation to his dedication in the *Fall of Feudalism*; it is to the influence of the Irish in the British empire and, above all, in the US – 'the kinsfolk beyond the sea' – on the politics of their adopted countries that he attributes the putative British decision of 1908 to grant this degree of home rule.[69] On the other hand, the 'Celtic peasantry' of the *Fall of Feudalism* dedication got rather short shrift compared with the rising urban voters, whose representation would be sharply increased in a constituency revision (following the granting of universal adult suffrage), precisely 'to prevent a peasant element from asserting a dominant class-power in the new rule of the country'.[70] Davitt's role in the Land League, and his genuine detestation of landlordism, can disguise the fact that he was in reality much more a townsman than a countryman. Most of his life was spent in towns and cities, in Ireland and abroad. For all his efforts to link economic growth to agriculture, it was no accident that he quite failed to realise the incompatibility of his intellectual commitment to Free Trade, with his policy commitment to reducing emigration by fostering tillage, a policy doomed to failure in Irish climatic and soil conditions in normal circumstances. It was not inappropriate that his last public address should be in support of town tenants.

SPECULATIONS

There was nothing necessarily final about any of Davitt's policy positions. His vision of a home rule Ireland, implausible though it might be, suggests a mind still open to alternative ways of arriving at his ultimate goal of Ireland's 'absolute freedom and independence'. Acknowledging the reality of overwhelming British command of potential violence through its superior military power, the young fenian had become a stepping-stone man of the head, if not of the heart. But the stones were still for stepping, not for standing still. Davitt embraced home rule as a staging post on the journey towards his ideal, without ever rejecting in principle the right of the conquered to repay the conqueror in his own coin – if they had enough of the coin to do so: 'On his deathbed, he was explicit that he did not recant his connection with Fenianism and its objects.'[71] An emotional man, he had a long memory. On his deathbed too, he directed that his corpse be waked in Clarendon Street church – the only Catholic church in Dublin that would accept the corpse of his fellow prisoner, and fellow fenian, Charles H. McCarthy, who dropped dead in his presence at a reception breakfast for the released prisoners on 15 January 1878, the second morning after their return to Dublin.[72]

His putative policy steps should not be deduced solely from his specific historical references. However much inspiration Davitt drew from his image of the Irish past, he preserved immense flexibility in how he harnessed this image as a guide to immediate policy prescriptions. Consistent though his ultimate aspirations remained, Davitt's mind was far too probing, too open to new possibilities, to be slotted into historically prescribed pigeonhole categories. There is always a danger of plucking from a long career those aspects that are deemed to appeal most to current taste. A man of such passionate feeling, and such active pen and tongue, will leave a record of millions of words, inevitably giving many a verbal hostage to fortune. Neither counsel for the prosecution nor the defence would find any difficulty stringing together a series of quotes to convey very different impressions of the 'essential' Davitt. However, the historian has to contextualise every quote to arrive at a genuinely historical verdict.

In reconstructing the influences that moulded his personality and character, one must sift carefully – and necessarily speculatively – the impact of his early experiences. However, we cannot read the consequences from those as if in a straight line. Many another who suffered so searing a series of experiences might well have crumpled beneath them, their humanity blighted for life. Davitt instead became a prison reformer, devoting his first book to reflections on the system. The memory of eviction and of famine, often recalled around the Haslingden fireside, left an indelible impression that would fuel his hatred of any system that allowed the exercise of arbitrary power by one human being over another. From his early childhood days, when he was determined to go to work to help out his family, he combined a strong will with a desire to serve, perhaps even a self-sacrificial impulse. Learning to cope with losing an arm – not least with the daily Dartmoor routine of stone-breaking while one-handed – may have steeled him in the belief that sheer willpower could overcome the most daunting challenges.

The gospel of self-help inculcated in his Wesleyan school days may have been a further factor in his becoming 'self-reliant almost to the point of fanaticism'.[73] For a crusader for worker solidarity, he could lay enormous emphasis on self-help and on sturdy independence of spirit. His prison years reinforced this – however much they woke his compassion for prisoners subjected to dehumanising behaviour – and his contempt for a mindset that could clinically devise such behaviour.

Moody, citing as a prime example his willingness to fight for private ownership of farms despite his faith in land nationalisation, reflected that:

> Davitt's weakness as a political leader lay in his diffidence, his modesty, his rooted disinclination to force opinions down the throats of others, his capacity to appreciate his opponent's point of view ... this intense desire to be of service to his fellow men predisposed him to work for objectives that seemed possible of attainment even though they fell far short of his ideals.[74]

The conundrum then is how to reconcile the diffident Davitt with the decisive Davitt, the Davitt of deference to the early Parnell with the Davitt of defiance of the even more domineering later Parnell. If he was too prone to defer, how did he project, at least for some, the image of belligerence? Was occasional vehemence of expression confused with inherent pit-bull aggressiveness? Or was the overall problem that while as an ideologue he was too forthright, as a politician he was too conciliatory?

Davitt's penetrating portrait of Parnell in the *Fall of Feudalism* leaves us with much to ponder about his own personality and value system:

> Magnanimity or gratitude he had none. His mind had few if any generous impulses, and was barren of all faith except a boundless belief in himself. Here he possessed the fanaticism of the zealot and made a fatalistic confidence in his own destiny the dominating idea of his political career. He frequently quoted two lines of Shakespeare which inculcated fidelity to one's self as the rule of existence. Herein lay the secret of his pride, and the vulnerable spot in Achilles's heel. A fanatical cult of one's own ego untempered by a little human heresy borrowed from the wisdom of the serpent, if not from any higher moral source, is very apt to beget infidelity to the nobler duties and obligations of life, and thereby to injure or to isolate the idol of self-worship.[75]

Even if Davitt proceeded immediately to add that 'these faults in the human portraiture of Parnell are but like the wart on Cromwell's face', the evaluation could be taken to mean that – for Davitt – leadership has its duties as well as its rights. At least, it may be considered a counter-portrait to Davitt's own self-image.

Wherever his preternatural willpower derived from, it enabled him to overcome several horrendous challenges. That willpower did not seek gratification in the domination of others, but, rather, was channelled more into basic devotion to causes rather than personalities. That was the essence of his conflict with Parnell in the saga of the split. There was a deep irony in this. Parnell had pronounced that the way to treat an Englishman was to 'stand up to him'; Davitt regarded Parnell as 'an Englishman of the strongest type', even if one 'moulded for Irish purposes'. It was when he deemed that Parnell no longer represented Irish purposes that, in the end, he stood up to him. In Davitt, in this mood, Parnell then met a strength of will as adamantine as his own; it was now Parnell who found himself being stood up to. Despite the ample testimony that Davitt was sweet-natured in personal relations, on a platform, or with pen in left hand, he could sometimes be ferocious, even when preaching conciliation and inclusiveness, seeing his critics as not only politically misguided but as morally deficient as well. There is a sense in which, temperamentally, if not doctrinally, Davitt was himself cut from non-conformist cloth, and his pursuit of Parnell during the heyday of the split had something of a remorseless Roundhead crusading fervour to it.

Moody concluded that 'perhaps there is nothing more extraordinary about him than this: that he fought neither for money nor for power.'[76] Money certainly not, for he was usually short and could have earned far more had it been his prime concern. More power he would certainly have liked, which leaves the question of why he nonetheless deferred frequently to others. Yeats recorded, after meeting Davitt around 1898, that he did not find him a natural politician at all.

> Davitt suggested to me a writer, a painter, an artist of some kind, rather than a man of action ... One felt he had lived always with small, unimaginative, ineffective men whom he despised; and that perhaps through some lack of early education, perhaps because nine years' imprisonment at the most plastic period of his life had jarred or broken his contact with reality, he had failed, except during the first months of the Land League, to dominate those men ... I think he shared with poet and philosopher the necessity of speaking the whole mind or remaining silent or ineffective. [77]

It is indeed possible that in a free country he might never have been a politician. There may be something to be said for a people to be occasionally subjected to external threats, and to know they can resist daunting odds. One may come out the far side of the test with a deeper and prouder sense of self. However, for the already conquered to be subjected year after year, generation after generation, over several centuries, to control by the conqueror, even a conqueror as civilised as the corrupting power of domination over others ever allows a conqueror to be, threatens to shrivel the spirit and perspective of the conquered. The issue of how to preserve wider human sympathies in a culture of resistance, while all the time condemned to futility by the conqueror's overwhelming command of violence, presents a corrosive challenge for the conquered.

Part of the price to be paid for resistance to conquest is the obsession with politics that tends to dominate all other considerations. Davitt himself lamented, as he trundled yet again on another tour across America, that he had to devote his life to politics, to the endless circuit and circus of public performances, when his ideal day consisted of reading in the morning, gardening in the afternoon, and listening to his wife, who had a fine operatic voice, singing in the evening. A voracious reader, his love of books followed his footsteps all his days from the Mechanics' Institute in Haslingden to the National Library in Dublin. In Haslingden too, he soaked in the words of the visiting Chartist lecturer, Ernest Jones, just as later he devoured the pages of, among others, Herbert Spencer, John Stuart Mill and, above all, Henry George. However, he also read in history to a degree exceptional even among the public figures of a reading age. The manner in which he blended his reading of leading social thinkers with immersion in history in general, and Irish history in particular, to a degree unusual among his contemporaries, would repay further research.

He tried as best he could to live the life of a free man in a free country instead of remaining the prisoner of a public sphere whose boundaries were decreed by the conqueror. Few in his generation can have combined so active a public role with such a desperate attempt to live a normal life and pursue so wide a range of intellectual interests while committed to the politics of resistance. He may have been the most intense reader among Irish public figures. It is no accident that his will actually mentions his library, as if it were a prized possession. A compulsive writer as well as reader, his presentations, if not always convincing, are certainly compelling. His was one of the most potentially reflective and constructive of Irish energies to have been diverted from their natural path in devoting their lives to the effort to roll back the conquest, physical and mental.[78]

The cascade of condolences on his death from around the Irish world, at home and abroad, and indeed from many British friends, bears witness to both a public and private respect for a man whom Archbishop Croke had earlier called 'the noblest Roman of them all'. Nobody is on their oath on condolences, but two tributes from political opponents, one Anglo-Irish, one Ulster unionist, reflect sentiments widely expressed. John Shawe-Taylor had met him only once, but 'his absolute sincerity of purpose and devotion to Ireland made an impression which time can never efface'.[79] An Enniskillen unionist, a JP, paid tribute to

> ... a patriot with whom I differ strongly on some national questions of importance, but one of whose probity, honour, loftiness of sentiment and nobility of character I had the highest admiration. Unselfish to the last degree, self-sacrificing for the good of others, pure in his conception of duty, and unyielding in the cause of right, Mr Davitt always impressed me as a grand and strong character, and made of me a life-long friend ...[80]

Few born into a smallholding of Davitt vintage in Mayo, however fortuitous the spiral that would sweep him onwards and upwards, would write so much, organise so much, or attempt to improve the lot of so many, in Britain as well as in Ireland. Moody's verdict was that, 'In his endless fight against oppression, in his devotion to truth and justice, in his courage, his constancy, and his disinterestedness, his stormy life has a unity and a moral grandeur seldom to be found in the annals of politics.'[81] One may be sceptical if any public figure – or indeed private one – could deserve such an encomium. Nevertheless, tactical though Davitt could be – and he could be highly tactical – and by no means incapable of dissimulation, the core of Moody's valedictory verdict remains valid, for perhaps the most noteworthy thing of all about Davitt was that striking though he was as a public figure, he was even more remarkable as a human being.

However, the crowds that poured spontaneously – for he had requested a private funeral – onto the Dublin streets and into Clarendon Street church to pay their respects do not seem to have been there primarily to pay tribute to the prison reformer, labour organiser, champion of women's equality, denouncer of anti-Semitic atrocities, advocate of educational opportunity, general crusader for the downtrodden, much less the author, or even artist, manqué, but simply because, behind the innumerable array of causes he championed, in Frank Sheehy-Skeffington's reluctant acknowledgement – for Sheehy-Skeffington himself would have wished it otherwise – 'he was, first and last, a rebel against English rule'.[82] Most in the Ireland of his day would probably have held that to be the highest accolade one could pay an Irishman. That was, in the Ireland of his day, his triumph. That it was this, in the Ireland of his day, that had to be his triumph, was also his tragedy.

NOTES

1. TCD, DP, MS 9658, Mary Hall to Mrs Davitt, 17 May 1906. See also Mary Hall to Mrs Davitt, 3 August, 1906.
2. *Washington Post*, 24 May 1880; *New York Times*, 20 September 1880.
3. *Labour World*, 19 October 1890.
4. Carla King, 'Introduction', in Carla King (ed.), Michael Davitt, *Jottings in Solitary* (Dublin, 2003), pp. xx–xxi.
5. Michael Davitt, 'Mr Davitt and Irish Ireland', *Nationist*, 8 February 1906.
6. Michael Davitt, *The Fall of Feudalism in Ireland, or, the Story of the Land League Revolution* (London & New York, 1904), p. 35.
7. 'Michael Davitt's Will', 1 February 1904, published as the final entry in Carla King (ed.), *Michael Davitt: Collected Writings, 1868–1906* (Bristol, 2001), vol. 2. [Hereafter cited as King, *Collected Writings*]
8. *Labour World*, 19 October 1890.
9. Davitt to Archbishop Walsh, 20 November 1890, quoted in Emmet Larkin, *The Roman Catholic Church in Ireland and the Fall of Parnell, 1888–1891* (Chapel Hill, 1979), p. 212.
10. Davitt to Archbishop Walsh, 8 December 1891, quoted in Larkin, *Roman Catholic Church in Ireland*, p. 288, n. 90.
11. Davitt to Archbishop Walsh, 20 November 1890, quoted in Larkin, *Roman Catholic Church in Ireland*, p. 212.
12. *Labour World*, 22 November 1890.
13. Ibid.
14. *Labour World*, 6 December 1890.
15. Laurence Marley, *Michael Davitt: Freelance Radical and Frondeur* (Dublin, 2007), p. 104.
16. *Irish Times*, 13 December 1890.
17. *Labour World*, 13 December 1890.
18. Much remains to be disinterred about the relations between national and labour politics at this time, but, for suggestive leads, see Emmet O'Connor, *A Labour History of Ireland, 1824–1960* (Dublin, 1992), p. 53; Fintan Lane, 'Rural labourers, social change and politics in late nineteenth-century Ireland', in Fintan Lane and Donal Ó Drisceoil (eds), *Politics and the Irish Working Class, 1830–1945* (Basingstoke, 2005), p. 134. Also, see Fintan Lane, 'Michael Davitt and the Irish working class' in the present volume. I am most grateful to Dr Lane for providing me with a copy of his paper.
19. Marley, *Davitt*, p. 111; Donal McCartney, 'From politics to history: The changing image of Parnell', in Donal McCartney and Pauric Travers, *The Ivy Leaf: The Parnells Remembered – Commemorative Essays* (Dublin, 2006), p. 158.
20. Marley, *Davitt*, pp. 116–17.
21. Conor Cruise O'Brien, *Parnell and his Party* (Oxford, 1957), pp. 287–94; Pauric Travers, *Settlements and Divisions: Ireland, 1870–1922* (Dublin, 1988), p. 51.
22. Matthew J. Kelly, *The Fenian Ideal and Irish Nationalism, 1882–1916* (London, 2006), p. 160.
23. Kelly, *Fenian Ideal*, p. 161, n. 167.
24. Marley, *Davitt*, p. 127.
25. *Nationist*, 1 February 1906.
26. *Nationist*, 1 February 1906.
27. *Labour World*, 6 December 1890.
28. Davitt, *Fall of Feudalism*, p. xvii.
29. Ibid., p. xi.
30. Ibid., p. xii.
31. Ibid.
32. Ibid., p. xiii.
33. Ibid., pp. 713–16.
34. Ibid., pp. xiii–iv.
35. Ibid., p. xii.
36. Theodore W. Moody, *Davitt and Irish Revolution, 1846–82* (Oxford, 1981), p. 550.
37. Anne Kane, '*The Fall of Feudalism in Ireland*: A guide for cultural analysis of the Irish Land War', *New Hibernia Review*, 5, 1 (2001), p. 140.
38. Davitt, *Fall of Feudalism*, p. 722.
39. Ibid.
40. Ibid., pp. 722–3.
41. Ibid., p. 722.
42. Donal P. McCracken, *MacBride's Brigade: Irish Commandos in the Anglo-Boer War* (Dublin,

1999), p. 155.

43. For concerns about his safety even closer to home, see Carla King, 'Michael Davitt, Irish nationalism and the British empire', in Peter Gray (ed.), *Victoria's Ireland? Irishness and Britishness, 1837–1901* (Dublin, 2004), p. 128.

44. See Iain R. Smith, 'A century of controversy over origins', in Donal Lowry (ed.), *The South African War Reappraised* (Manchester, 2000), pp. 23–49.

45. TCD, DP, MS 9651/14, *Saint John Bull*, p. 2.

46. Michael Davitt, *The Boer Fight for Freedom* (New York, 1902), reprinted in King, *Collected Writings*, vol. 6, pp. 135ff.

47. Michael Davitt, *Life and Progress in Australasia* (London, 1898), reprinted in King, *Collected Writings*, vol. 5, pp. 33ff, 383ff, 396ff; Eugenio Biagini, *British Democracy and Irish Nationalism, 1876–1906* (Cambridge, 2007), p. 326.

48. Moody, *Davitt and Irish Revolution*, p. 289.

49. Christopher Saunders, 'African attitudes to Britain and the empire before and after the South African War', in Lowry, *South African War*, pp. 140–9.

50. Kelly, *Fenian Ideal*, pp. 160–1.

51. Hasia Diner, 'Michael Davitt: Irish nationalism, the pogroms, and American Jewry', unpublished lecture delivered at the Michael Davitt Centenary Conference, Dublin 2006. I am most grateful to Professor Diner for providing me with a copy of her lecture.

52. *Freeman's Journal*, 18 January 1904.

53. Davitt, *Fall of Feudalism*, p. 724.

54. See esp. 'Ireland's appeal to America', *Denvir's Monthly Irish Library*, March 1902, reprinted in King, *Collected Writings*, vol. 2.

55. Thomas N. Brown, *Irish-American Nationalism, 1870–1890* (Philadelphia & New York, 1966), p. 168.

56. Marley, *Davitt*, p. 94.

57. Michael Davitt, 'The Irish National Assembly', *Independent Review*, April 1905, reprinted in King, *Collected Writings*, vol. 2, pp. 1, 2, 14.

58. King, *Collected Writings*, vol. 2, p. 3.

59. Ibid.

60. Ibid.

61. King, *Collected Writings*, vol. 2, pp. 14–15. Davitt and Saunderson had 'a grudging respect' for one another; see Alvin Jackson, *Colonel Edward Saunderson: Land and Loyalty in Victorian Ireland* (Oxford, 1995), pp. 99–100.

62. Davitt, 'National Assembly', p. 15. Edward Blake had staunchly supported the party in its darkest financial days: Davitt, *Fall of Feudalism*, p. 673. See also Margaret A. Banks, *Edward Blake: Irish Nationalist, 1892–1907* (Toronto, 1957), pp. 337–8; Biagini, *British Democracy*, p. 157.

63. Davitt, 'National Assembly', p. 14.

64. Ibid., p. 1.

65. Ibid., p. 10.

66. Ibid., p. 16.

67. TCD, DP, MS 9651/11, p. 6.

68. Ibid., p. 5.

69. Davitt, 'National Assembly', pp. 12ff.

70. Ibid., p. 14.

71. T. W. Moody, 'Michael Davitt, 1846–1906: A survey and appreciation, Part III,' *Studies*, vol. 35 (December 1946), p.438.

72. Moody, *Davitt and Irish Revolution*, p. 190; F. Sheehy-Skeffington, *Michael Davitt* (Dublin, 1908), p. 213.

73. Moody, 'Michael Davitt, 1846–1906: A survey and appreciation, Part III,' *Studies*, vol. 35 (December 1946), p. 438.

74. Moody, 'Michael Davitt, 1846–1906', p. 438.

75. Davitt, *Fall of Feudalism*, p. 658.

76. Moody, 'Michael Davitt, 1846–1906', p. 437.

77. W.B. Yeats, *Autobiographies* (London, 1955), pp. 356–7.

78. See Marley, *Davitt*, p. 287.

79. TCD, DP, MS 9658, Condolences, John Shawe-Taylor to Mary Davitt, 3 June 1906.

80. TCD, DP, MS 9658, Condolences, J. Trimble to Mrs Davitt, no. 237.

81. Moody, 'Michael Davitt, 1846–1906', p. 438.

82. F. Sheehy-Skeffington, *Michael Davitt: Revolutionary, Agitator and Labour Leader* (London, 1967 edn), p. 213.

CHAPTER THREE

Michael Davitt in Lancashire

JOHN DUNLEAVY

On 2 July 1889, George Poskitt, the proprietor of a school near Manchester, penned a letter to his former pupil, Michael Davitt, suggesting that the time had come for him to set down his impressions of his life and education in the Lancashire town of Haslingden, where he had resided between 1850 and 1870. Whether Davitt acknowledged the letter is not known, but we do know that on that very same day he was preoccupied with other business. He was in London, attending the Royal Courts of Justice, where a Special Commission, decreed by parliament, was engaged in the task of inquiring into the truth or otherwise of the allegations against himself and most other leading members of the Irish national movement. The allegations charged that they had been engaged in a vast conspiracy to effect Irish independence by the use of force. The case against Parnell and his colleagues rested on a series of letters published previously by *The Times* under the heading 'Parnellism and crime'. Appointed in 1888, the commission would sit for over a year, issuing a report early in 1890 that largely exonerated Parnell and his associates from the charges. The case had appeared to founder at an early stage when the letters forming the basis for *The Times* allegations were found to be fabrications, while the forger-in-chief, Richard Piggott, fled the country, committing suicide in a Madrid hotel room. Many assumed the matter was at an end, *The Times* and government case seemingly in ruins; but it was not to be. The Thunderer's reputation was at stake while Lord Salisbury and his colleagues were intent on discrediting the national movement.[1]

There is no doubt that public interest in the hearings waned after the dramatic exit of Piggott, but the commission ploughed on into the summer, enjoyed a three-month recess and resumed its deliberations in October. Overall, the commission sat for 117 days, some 98,000 questions were put to 450 witnesses, and the proceedings taxed the energies of the finest legal talent in the country. Parnell attended only a few sessions, while Davitt was rarely absent. Sir Charles Russell, QC, assisted by Herbert Asquith (the future prime minister) represented Parnell, Davitt choosing to represent himself. His own examination, followed by cross-examination, began on 2 July and extended over three days. Davitt's speech to the commission, a trenchant defence of the Land League, occupied three days in October. Some contemporaries regarded these allegations as putting the Land League under scrutiny; others maintained it was the Irish national movement that was in the dock; while others agreed with Sir Charles Russell that the whole Irish nation was on trial. Thus, in the face of such a challenge, Davitt perhaps could have been forgiven for failing to act on his former teacher's suggestion at that time, devoting all his waking hours and energies to the hearings.[2]

Davitt had already received requests for an autobiography. In 1881, during his second term of imprisonment, he drew up some notes that would have been useful for his life story, while in the 1890s he composed further notes that might have been intended for an autobiography, but he never completed the task. Of his published works, however, the *Fall of Feudalism in Ireland*, an account of the 'land war' years, was based on much of the material he had collated for his defence before the Special Commission in 1889.[3] Poskitt, by contrast, urged Davitt specifically for an account of his younger days in Haslingden, focussing on his life and working experiences. Had Davitt chosen to act on this advice, then there is no doubt he would have produced a useful story, especially if he had been able to consult Poskitt on matters of detail, the latter having enjoyed a lengthy residence in the area and being possessed of a vast fund of local knowledge. As Poskitt reminded Davitt, their acquaintanceship went back some thirty years, and the intervening period had witnessed great changes. Poskitt would have been aware of Davitt's earlier learning and might have elucidated some details there. Michael regarded his father, Martin, as his first teacher, while his mother, who made no pretence at book learning, was said to have been possessed of a keen natural intelligence.[4]

THE IRISH IN HASLINGDEN

There were a number of schools, both proprietorial and voluntary, in Haslingden when the Davitts first arrived in 1850. The nearest Catholic mission, St James the Less at Rawtenstall, was directed by Fr Thomas Unsworth. The mission maintained an elementary school for the children of the congregation, and there was a Sunday school where Christian doctrine was supplemented by secular subjects. The Education census for 1851 recorded two Catholic Sunday schools in the Haslingden union registration district.[5] One of these may well have been at Haslingden, where there had been a Mass station, or centre, for some years. On the establishment of a separate Catholic mission at Haslingden in 1854, Fr Thomas Martin opened a day school. Davitt was among the pupils, for in later life he would recall his ordeal of submitting to the discipline exerted by Mr Burke, head of what he termed a 'spelling purgatory'. But he could only have attended the mission school for a matter of months, for at the age of nine he found work in a cotton mill at Ewood Bridge.

Poskitt would have been as well placed as anyone to prompt Davitt, should he have fallen in with the proposal to record his Lancashire reminiscences. He had arrived in the town in 1849 – a year ahead of the Davitts – on his appointment as head of the Wesleyan day school. He found an old market town undergoing change socially, economically and politically. The mood of the town was decidedly conservative, its geographical location on a spur of the Pennines having inhibited the pace of industrial development in comparison with neighbouring towns. Set at approximately 900 feet above sea level, Haslingden had never had the benefits of water transport, lacking a canal or a navigable river, while the railway completed in 1848 was set in a valley below the town. Local government was archaic, though in 1834 the town had become the centre of a Poor Law Union while a Local Board of Health was to be established in 1875. The magistrates, drawn from the minor gentry and Anglican clergy, were predominantly Tory in their outlook. The town possessed a variety of churches and chapels, reflecting the diversity of religious belief to be found here. Although some domestic trades were still functioning, mechanisation of the textile industry (cotton mainly, though there were a few woollen mills) meant that what would later be termed the industrial revolution had become a reality. As industry grew, the demand for labour rose, and thus offered the prospect of work to families such as the Davitts.[6]

The earliest description of the Irish community in Haslingden comes from 1855, when Fr Thomas Martin, charged with the task of building the Catholic mission, estimated the size of his congregation to be around 1,000.[7] Many, though by no means all, were recent arrivals from Ireland, their livelihoods dependent on their daily earnings. The textile trade provided work for men, women and children, and it was not unusual for all the members of a particular family to be employed in the same mill. While Irish women and children found work in the mills, their men folk frequently sought other occupations. Many Irishmen found employment in the stone quarries, and they were numerous in the construction trades. Others, determined to be mobile and independent, became hawkers, Haslingden being regarded as the ideal centre for such traders as it was located in the middle of a radius of larger, faster-growing towns. Initially, the Catholic mission was obliged to utilise rented property for use as a chapel and school, though within five years of his appointment as rector, thanks to the generosity of his congregation and external donors, Fr Martin had the satisfaction of building a church. Some years later a school was built, and these two buildings represent the earliest visible evidence we have of the Irish presence in Haslingden. Progress of the mission, and the district generally, suffered a severe check in 1861 following the outbreak of the American Civil War. As imports of raw cotton dwindled, short-time working and frequently lengthy spells of unemployment became a feature of Lancashire life. The local Irish, many of whom had left their native country during the potato famine, now faced destitution again as a consequence of what came to be known as the cotton famine.[8] A significant number migrated to districts where work was more readily available. Fr Martin estimated the size of his congregation to be 1,400 in 1861; three years later he reckoned something like 350 had gone elsewhere.[9]

Poskitt's curiosity about Davitt's Haslingden connections appears to have been shared by many. The local press was partly responsible for this. When Davitt was arrested in 1870, for instance, the *Accrington Times* reported the fact and dwelt on his antecedents, while during his imprisonment stories about his treatment found their way into local journals. Following Davitt's release, his subsequent part in the 'land war' was followed with keen interest locally, Haslingden Irishmen forming themselves into a branch of the Land League (Davitt branch) – the term still employed by Haslingdonians when describing the Irish club. Over the following years there were occasions when the Davitt association was evident, notably in 1883 when he was the recipient of an illuminated address from the local Irish community; and in 1886 when he declined to stand as the local Liberal/Home Rule parliamentary candidate but played an active part in the Gladstonian Liberal cause in the fiercely contested general election of that year. Poskitt not only followed Davitt's career from the public prints, but corresponded with him and met him occasionally. In view of all this, it seems a great pity the two were not able to find the opportunity to collaborate on what promised to be an enlightening joint account of life and work in Victorian Lancashire compiled by master and pupil.[10]

DAVITT'S EARLY LIFE AND EDUCATION

Davitt's introduction to the textile industry came in 1855, when he was nine. He found work as a piecer, assisting a mule spinner in a mill at Ewood Bridge. He stayed only a month, the spinner declining to pay him the promised half-a-crown. Later he found work at another mill, where he was engaged in the card room, a position he left after the tragic death of his friend John Ginty. Despite this fatality, Davitt nevertheless found work in the card room at another mill at Baxenden. This modern mill was owned and managed by John Stelfox, who hailed from Cheshire, and was yet another indication of the burgeoning cotton trade. One day, when tending the carding machine, Davitt attempted to disentangle a skein, and in so doing his right arm became trapped in the machinery. The arm was so badly lacerated that it had to be amputated some days later. This put an end to Davitt's employment in textiles, and he now faced the daunting prospect of trying to make a livelihood relying on the use of one arm.[11]

Ironically, the accident opened up new opportunities for Davitt, opportunities which would set him apart from most of his contemporaries, for he was able to resume his full-time education at the town's Wesleyan school. Davitt entered the school at an auspicious time, for it had become the first institution in the town to be recognised by the government for grant aid purposes. The success of the school owed much to the commitment to education of the Wesleyan community, and the skills apparent in George Poskitt, who had directed the school since 1849. Poskitt had been inducted into the profession by taking a full-time course at the Glasgow Normal Seminary, which at the time was still under the supervision of its influential founder, David Stow. Stow was motivated by what he saw as the 'deficiency in the moral economy' of modern urban society. Whereas in rural society moral values could safely be left to parents, Stow considered morals in the city to be in decline, urban centres having become nothing less than 'nurseries of vice'. His system of moral training was formulated to fill up this wide and important gap in the 'Godly training' of youth. This is where Poskitt was introduced to the craft of teaching. Stow insisted there was a difference between mere instruction and what he termed 'training'. 'Teaching [he maintained] may be considered as the implanting of principles – training as the exercise of the principles' – education in its widest sense, including both moral and intellectual development. 'Training,' Stow continued, 'was a highly skilled craft, awakening thought, stimulating and directing enquiry and evolving the energies of the intellect.' Stow had no faith in the prevailing monitorial system, such as had been developed by Bell and Lancaster, arguing for what he termed 'the sympathy of numbers', pupils being drilled and answering in chorus. He also urged the practice of 'picturing out', presenting verbal pictures which may stimulate the child's imagination. He held that by using simple terms and ideas within the range of the pupil's experience, he can be 'made to perceive as vividly as the mental eye as he would real objects by the bodily eye'. But learning was not confined to the classroom, for provision must be made for recreation. The Haslingden school had a playground, what Stow called the 'uncovered school room', where recreation was considered part of the curriculum.

It was in the 'uncovered school room' that Davitt discovered that while Poskitt was scrupulous in making sure his teaching would not offend the beliefs of other denominations, it was not possible to insulate the school entirely against sectarian feeling. Davitt later recalled how he was obliged to champion the cause of the papacy occasionally in the yard, Pope Pius IX being assailed by Garibaldi and the forces of Italian unity at that time. The school day began with prayer, followed by scripture taught by Poskitt. On his first day in school, Poskitt suggested Michael might like to be excused from attending. The following day, Michael reported that his father felt he ought to attend the scripture class, and he evidently learned a great deal there. In 1885, after visiting the Holy Land, Davitt wrote to Poskitt to the effect that the scenes he had described years earlier were still as clear in his mind as when he first heard of them in Haslingden – a gratifying testimonial for any teacher. Davitt never stinted in praise of his old school or his teacher, telling a Haslingden audience in 1883 that the lessons of Christian morality he had imbibed there had informed his public life and actions ever since.[12]

LANCASHIRE AND THE MECHANICS' INSTITUTES

Davitt spent four years at the Wesleyan school. When he left at the age of fifteen he had had the benefit of a more formal and effective education than most of his contemporaries, yet employment opportunities for amputees were limited. He was fortunate to find a sympathetic employer in Henry Cockroft, who combined the role of the town's postmaster with that of a printer. As Cockroft would later explain, he initially employed Davitt as an errand boy, as a preliminary to becoming a postman. But in the congenial atmosphere of the post office, Davitt demonstrated that he was capable of performing a number of tasks. He was drawn to the print section at an early date, and despite his handicap was able to set type and prepare formes for the press as well as any other apprentice. Davitt shared a number of interests with his employer, including a growing love of poetry. Both were to have poems published during the 1860s, Cockroft's appearing in the Tory *Bacup and Rossendale News,* while Michael's were welcomed by the editor of the ultra-nationalist *Universal News.*

Cockroft was clearly a man of some learning and when one of his sons showed promise as a musician he determined to secure the best education for him, sending him to Berlin and Leipzig. Although the hours of work at the post office were long, Davitt clearly thrived in that environment, becoming virtually a member of the family and permitted to address Cockroft as 'Dad'. His growing absorption in the Irish cause seems not to have caused concern to Cockroft, for it was while he was at the post office that Davitt was drawn into the fenian movement. Press accounts of the sectarian unrest, the so-called Murphy riots, that affected Lancashire during 1867–8 cannot have gone unnoticed by the postmaster, Davitt being referred to by the local weekly as the 'young man who has made himself conspicuous in these disturbances'. As the tensions subsided, Davitt chose to submit his resignation to Cockroft, announcing his plan to become a commercial traveller. In bidding his employee farewell, a remark attributed to Cockroft suggests he guessed at Davitt's real intentions: 'If you turn out as good a man as you are a boy, you'll be a great man for Ireland.'[13]

Throughout his period with the Cockrofts, Davitt chose to pursue his love of learning. Printed material became more widely available with the repeal of the Advertisement Tax in 1853, which had been framed by some as 'taxes on knowledge'.[14] Davitt was able to indulge his fondness for reading by joining the local Mechanics' Institute. The nature of these agencies for further education was not always understood, something that still presents a problem for some modern scholars. The institutes were voluntary bodies set up to offer education beyond the level then available in elementary schools. The Haslingden Institute consisted of a library and newsroom, and promoted classes and lectures, mainly in the evenings. Lacking public funding, it was dependent on donations and subscriptions. The management of the institute was vested in the directors, who were drawn from the larger donors. It was this body that ensured the founding aims were observed, and Haslingden was no exception in prohibiting the teaching and discussion of 'sectarian theology, socialistic views, and principles of infidelity'. Yet critics at the time frequently alleged the institutes were 'nurseries of radicalism', or even worse, and should be avoided. The principal officer at the Haslingden Institute was Dr John Binns. Born in Sunderland and of Quaker stock, Binns settled in the town shortly after qualifying as a surgeon and espoused a variety of reform issues, such as street lighting, public health and temperance. Following the failure of the free library campaign, he threw himself into the plan for a mechanics' institute, and proved to be the moving spirit there for a considerable period. He insisted the mission of the Mechanics' was not to offer elementary subjects such as A, B and C but that it was to go further, into the sciences such as chemistry, mechanics and drawing. A former Chartist, he became a friend and adviser to the fledgling cooperative movement, and later went on to found the Haslingden Liberal Association. Binns was one of the new Liberal magistrates appointed in Lancashire following Gladstone's electoral victory in 1868. While numerous Haslingdonians differed from Binns in many respects – his penchant for change was not to the liking of the conservative elements – there was little in his activities of which Davitt would have disapproved.[15]

Mechanics' institutes were criticised for other reasons, one of the most frequent complaints being that they regularly promoted social activities such as popular entertainments and seaside excursions at the expense of serious learning. Sir James Kay Shuttleworth was one of a number of educationalists to address these complaints. In an attempt to make the local institutes effective educationally, he formed a federation in east Lancashire employing trained teachers, and introduced annual examinations to test the attainment of pupils. He anticipated that the improvements effected in the district would be emulated in other parts of the country, and he clearly hoped for government funding for institutes in the absence of donations or subscriptions, but it was not to be. In one respect his east Lancashire scheme found emulators in that regular classes and examinations, such as those of the Society of Arts and the Lancashire and Cheshire Union, became more commonplace, though what amounted to one of the most novel and promising innovations of the Victorian period found only limited support.[16]

Kay Shuttleworth was drawn to the problems of the institutes in the 1850s, having realised that while Britain had demonstrated its ability to produce manufactured goods cheaply and in abundance, the next step was to make improvements in design and quality, otherwise foreign competitors would forge ahead.[17] The development of these institutes, it was felt, would be the ideal way to take on this work, which some described as a second industrial revolution. With a few exceptions, however, the plan was not realised. Far too many of the

students attending the institutes had an imperfect elementary education, joining evening classes usually upon the realisation that there was
a serious deficiency in their primary schooling. Davitt's name appears
among the subscribers to the Institute, but if he enrolled for any of the
taught courses, it would seem he never completed them. His name
does not appear among those awarded certificates, suggesting he was
content to utilise the newsroom and library where, he would claim
later, he had first read the history of Ireland.[18]

DAVITT AND HASLINGDEN

Davitt's residence in Haslingden extended over a twenty-year period,
or one third of his life. In the long weary years of his imprisonment,
he clearly regarded Haslingden as home, since he knew no other.
Once free from prison, for a time at least, he envisaged returning to
Haslingden, hoping to persuade his sister Sabina to return from the
States to act as housekeeper-secretary. From his speeches and writings
he always revealed a debt of gratitude to Haslingden and its people, a
number of whom he kept in contact with. Although he spent a great
deal of time and energy on the Irish land question, he never forgot his
industrial experience in England. Later in life he was always prepared
to collaborate with others in efforts to secure legislative measures to
alleviate the worst aspects of industrial life, notably in respect of securing compensation for victims of industrial accidents. He tried, with less
success, to convert the enfranchised English workers to the home rule
cause, arguing that self-government would ensure prosperity in
Ireland. Instead of travelling to England in search of work, and competing against English labour for jobs, Irish people would be content
to stay at home. Home rule, he liked to say, was a labour question, but
not all were persuaded by this argument.[19]

On his arrest in 1870, many for the first time came to realise the key
position Davitt held in the fenian movement. The authorities believed
that they had neutralised most of them in the wake of the events of
1867, but Davitt, although he played a modest role in the abortive
Chester Castle raid, slipped through the net. Yet his name began to
appear in the local press more frequently, usually in respect of Irish
functions in Haslingden, when he invariably occupied the chair. It
seems the police had underestimated his importance, or failed to appre-
ciate that many involved in the amnesty movement were fenians.[20]

Davitt was fortunate in that he came to live in Haslingden when
facilities for education were improving. From his papers we can learn

more about his views on education, compiling what was effectively a treatise on the subject during his incarceration in Portland prison in 1881.[21] Like many of his contemporaries he had great faith in the power of knowledge. While welcoming the extension of popular education in Ireland, he deplored the inadequate funding allocated to the schools and the failure of the national system to address the need to provide an education in what was primarily a rural, agricultural country. As a former Mechanics' student he cannot have been unaware that in England similar concerns were aired occasionally at the failure of education there to link science and technology with the national system. Despite this, Davitt felt that Ireland should emulate the English model, calling for a network of educational institutes. Essentially he wanted something on the lines of the Lancashire mechanics' institutes adapted for Irish purposes. These establishments, Davitt claimed, had conferred great benefits on the wage earners of northern England. Nevertheless, he overlooked the fact that there was a huge gap between what the institutes aimed to be and what was actually achieved. While technical subjects and science may have been envisaged by the promoters, lack of funds meant most institutes could afford only theoretical courses. James Kay Shuttleworth, who did much to try and revitalise the institutes but remained keenly aware of the lack of adequate funding, admitted a command of English was necessary for pupils to succeed, irrespective of the subject chosen. With few exceptions, revenue at the disposal of the English institutes was inadequate to allow anything beyond this. It was only later in the nineteenth century, when government devoted funds to higher education, that technical schools became a reality.[22]

CONCLUSION

Davitt's childhood and youth were not easy. The Davitts, having been domiciled in the west of Ireland for generations, on their arrival in Haslingden had to make the transition to living and working in the heartland of industrial England. By attending the Wesleyan school Davitt received the finest formal education the town had to offer, but his home tutoring by his father, along with the experience of business he gained while in the employment of Henry Cockroft, and his membership of the Mechanics' Institute, proved to be equally significant in his formation. His concern with education would continue for the rest of his life. The New Departure, for instance, usually dismissed as nothing more than a merger of the physical force men with the home rulers, was much more than that. Davitt was able to remind the Parnell

Commission that reform of popular education was among the original aims of the New Departure and occupied a place in the programmes devised by the Land League's successor bodies. His own personal commitment was impressive. Two of the chapters, or lectures, in his *Leaves from a Prison Diary* are concerned not just with elementary schooling but with education in its broadest sense, embracing public libraries, museums and art galleries, public concerts and lectures.[23] Access to secondary and higher education, whether in local institutes or universities, should be free to those likely to profit from it. Local libraries should be free and funded by the exchequer, with stocks of books replenished from time to time by additional volumes loaned by the larger central libraries. By the same token, the smaller provincial museums and galleries should act as hosts to travelling exhibitions from what we now term the national museums. He was not by any means alone in advocating such an ambitious programme, and while over the next two decades of his life significant advances were made both in Ireland and Britain, Davitt, drawn to other issues, was not always able to devote the time and thought necessary to exercise any significant influence. When he did, he invariably came into conflict with others who disagreed with him. In the last few years of his life, for instance, he was in dispute with a formidable trio of prelates – Cardinal Vaughan of Westminster, Archbishop Walsh of Dublin and Bishop O'Dwyer of Limerick – on the question of public control of popular education. He was also at variance with many of his former associates in the Home Rule Party, who chose to accept the principle of the 1903 land settlement. He did not live long enough to see Ireland gain her freedom, but his faith in the power of education as a force that would make freedom a reality is best seen in words uttered in Chicago in 1880:

> If Ireland was ever to become independent ... she must socially emancipate her people by striking off the social fetters that bound their brains and muscles. When that was done, Irish brain and muscle would carve out a pathway to Irish freedom.[24]

NOTES

1. TCD, DP, MS 9346/478, George Poskitt to Davitt, 2 July 1889; John Macdonald, *Diary of the Parnell Commission (Revised from the Daily News)* (London, 1890).
2. Macdonald, *Diary of the Parnell Commission*.
3. Michael Davitt, *The Fall of Feudalism in Ireland, or, the Story of the Land League Revolution* (London & New York, 1904).
4. Theodore W. Moody, *Davitt and Irish Revolution 1846–82* (Oxford, 1981), pp. 478–9; 501–2; 505–12; Michael Davitt, *Jottings in Solitary* (Dublin, 2003).
5. Census of Great Britain, 1851 (Schools); *Parliamentary Papers*, 1852–3, XC, p. 175; John Dunleavy, *Haslingden Catholics, 1815–1965* (Preston, 1987), Chs 1 and 2. Not a great deal is

known of Bourke, the first head at St Mary's. Davitt refers to him as Daniel, while the local press accounts call him Michael: kinsfolk insist he was actually named William. Later in life, when compiling notes for his life story, Davitt explained he disliked St Mary's school since most of the scholars were little more than infants. TCD, DP, MS 9640 f. 29, 'Autobiographical notes. III: Factory life'; Moody, *Davitt and Irish Revolution*, p. 15.

6. George H. Tupling, *The Economic History of Rossendale* (London, 1927); Christopher Aspin, *Haslingden 1800–1900: A History* (Haslingden, 1962).

7. *Weekly Register*, 27 October 1855.

8. William O. Henderson, *The Lancashire Cotton Famine, 1861–1865* (Manchester, 1934).

9. Rev. Thomas Martin, a Meathman, trained for the priesthood at All Hallows College, Drumcondra, where he was ordained in 1854. Haslingden was his first mission, where he built the church, presbytery and school. Liberal minded, he raised no objection to Davitt and others attending the Wesleyan school. He died at Ribchester, Lancashire, in 1889. *Weekly Register*, 27 October 1855, 12 March 1864.

10. *Haslingden Chronicle*, 28 May, 11 June, 1870; *Accrington Times*, 5 October 1872, 20 January 1883, 11 June 1885; *Haslingden Guardian*, 1 June 1906; *Haslingden Gazette*, 2 June 1906.

11. *Accrington Observer and Times*, 18 July 1925. John Stelfox appeared to be a paternalistic kind of employer, according to reports appearing in the local press. In the space of one year he provided treats for his workers and served as president of the Baxenden Mechanics' Institute. *Accrington Free Press*, 22 January, 29 February, 17 December 1859. Like so many other businesses, his company became bankrupt during the cotton famine. Michael Rothwell, *Industrial Heritage: A Guide to the Archaeology of Accrington* (Accrington, 1979).

12. George Poskitt was a native of Howden, east Yorkshire. After a religious experience in his teens he left the Anglican faith and became a Methodist. Clearly an effective teacher, a gifted musician and writer, he had a lifelong devotion to his religion, serving as a Methodist local preacher for seventy-one years. He died in 1907, aged eighty-eight. David Stow, *The Training System* (London, 1840); *Accrington Times*, 20 January 1883; PRO, ED7/57 f. 2478, Preliminary Statement; Haslingden Wesleyan Day School, 16 March 1857. According to this document the so-called 'school pence' ranged from 2d to 8d per week, depending on the level of instruction received. The cost of Davitt's four years' schooling must have been expensive. It was assumed locally his fees were paid by his old employer, John Stelfox. After Davitt's death it was revealed that John Dean, a Methodist mill owner and keen supporter of the Mechanics' Institute, who died in 1873, was his benefactor. Moody, *Davitt and Irish Revolution*, p. 19.

13. Moody, *Davitt and Irish Revolution*, p. 18; *Bacup and Rossendale News*, 16 February, 9 March 1867; *Accrington Times*, 2 June 1868; *Haslingden Guardian*, 15 April 1893; Colin Cockroft, 'Michael Davitt's Haslingden', *Irish Post*, 30 June 1984.

14. *Hansard*, 125 (14 April 1853), c. 1158.

15. PRO, ED70/15566, Preliminary Statement; Haslingden Mechanics' Institute School, 16 September 1870; John Dunleavy, 'The mechanics' institute movement in Haslingden', PGCE dissertation, University of Leicester, 1968; *A reprint from the local papers of the proceedings connected with the presentation to Mr J Binns, of Haslingden, 16 May 1872.* (Durham, 1872); *Accrington Times*, 11 September 1875.

16. John Dunleavy, 'The provision of education for working people in evening institutes in east Lancashire, 1854–72', PhD thesis, University of Leeds, 1983.

17. David Newsome, *The Victorian World Picture* (London, 1997), p. 116. Prince Albert, in addressing the British Association for the Advancement of Science in 1859, deplored the neglect of the claims of science and technology by governments, educationists and the public at large.

18. Haslingden Institute, members' subscription book, 1846–67 [Haslingden Library local collection; currently missing from stock].

19. Michael Davitt, *Reasons Why Home Rule Should be Granted to Ireland: An Appeal to the Common Sense of the British Democracy* (London, 1886); Bernard O'Hara, *Davitt* (Castlebar, 2006), pp. 98–100.

20. Moody, *Davitt and Irish Revolution*, Ch. 3.

21. TCD, DP, MS, 9639, ff. 121–26.

22. Michael Davitt, *Leaves from a Prison Diary* (London, 1885), pp. 189 et seq; Michael Argles, *South Kensington to Robbins: An account of English Technical and Scientific Education Since*

1851 (London, 1964), pp. 16–18, 72–5, 101–2.

23. Michael Davitt, *Leaves from a prison diary; or, lectures to a 'solitary' audience* (1855), pp. 189–213.

24. The New Departure is the term usually applied to the policy of co-operation between the fenians, land reformers and parliamentarians in the late 1870s. D.B. Cashman, *Life of Michael Davitt, Founder of the National Land League* (London, 1882), p. 255. Among the aims of the National Land and Industrial Union of Ireland, section eight called for an improvement in the scientific and practical education of the people by the establishment of people's institutes, while section nine urged the need for the encouragement of national literature and the cultivation of the Irish language. *Special Commission Act 1888: Report of Proceedings before the Commissioners appointed by the Act. Reprinted from The Times* (London, 1890), vol. iii, p. 88.

CHAPTER FOUR

Political Economy and Nationality: Isaac Butt, Charles Stewart Parnell and Michael Davitt Reassessed

ALAN O'DAY

INTRODUCTION

Isaac Butt, Charles Stewart Parnell and Michael Davitt were key – probably the most significant – players in later Victorian Ireland.[1] They meet the demanding criteria of Professor Patrick O'Brien who suggests that 'unless the outcomes of a policy or set of policies are recognised by historians as significant and until those policies can be attributed in large measure to the ideas and leadership exercised by prominent politicians, then their lives, however deeply researched and readable, contribute very little to an understanding of the history of government and politics.'[2] Butt, rightly, is credited with reviving the idea of home rule; Parnell with turning it into so popular and durable a cause that Gladstone was persuaded to advocate Irish self-government for his remaining years; and Davitt, in conjunction with Parnell, created the movement that led the march towards the land for the people. Curiously, neither Butt nor Davitt has attracted a succession of biographers, though the volume of published material from both greatly exceeds the sources for dissection produced by Parnell, who suffers no parallel neglect.[3] With the partial exception of Butt, there has not been a great deal of interest in their respective ideas on political economy and even less in the linkage of economics and nationalism.

That the three men were in no way intellectual companions is well known; the differences are underlined in their approaches to the juncture of political economy and nationalism. For simplicity, these can be termed as a full-employment strategy (Butt), economic growth for

Ireland (Parnell) and redistribution and free trade (Davitt). All, of course, shared the aspiration to advance Ireland's prosperity, even though their strategies differed. In recent years, there has been a growing academic enthusiasm for political economy and economic development generally, but in the former case the discussion has centred on the ideas of key thinkers with less attention being paid to the actual adoption and application of these concepts.[4] A four-volume collection of Irish writings on political economy has made the subject more accessible.[5] Butt, partly, but Parnell, and even more Davitt, feature only marginally in this literature on political economy.

BUTT AND POLITICAL ECONOMY

Born in Donegal in 1813, Isaac Butt was successively a leading Irish Tory, a Conservative Party MP and, ultimately, the founder of the home rule movement. His writings range over the classics, Bishop George Berkeley, political economy, the land question, education, amnesty of political prisoners and federal home rule. Additionally, he turned his hand to writing histories of Italy and novels.

Butt's short spell between 1836 and 1841 as the second Whately Professor of Political Economy at Trinity College Dublin reveals a largely ignored path via economics to home rule.[6] This is to contest Mark Blaug's contention that 'Butt wrote no economics after his five-year appointment to the Whately chair', a judgement that stems from a tradition of separating theory and practice.[7] In contrast, it is suggested here that the greater portion of his considerable output of writing and speeches was rooted in a particular vision of political economy; it was the unitary nature of the Union of Great Britain and Ireland, Butt believed, which pressed doctrines upon Ireland that jeopardised prospects for prosperity and effective employment of human resources. 'Irish dissenters' – to employ R.D. Collison Black's designation – took exception to the pre-eminent *laissez-faire* doctrine.[8] Butt condemned the economic evil of landlord absenteeism and exalted the virtues of protectionism for Ireland. He defended the latter not on the usual basis that it would aid 'infant industries', but as a form of redistribution of taxation and a boost to employment, which was identified as a more valuable end than consumer satisfaction. No doubt Butt's denigration of consumer satisfaction will raise some eyebrows in view of his lifestyle, but, of course, he was commenting from an abstract position, not making a personal declaration, for, as the obituarist in *The Times* put it, 'when the choice was between the pleasure of the moment and the fulfilment of a duty, we will not say to others but to the higher gifts of his own nature, pleasure was sure to gain the day.'[9] In the 1870s, he argued for autonomy in domestic affairs, mainly from the vantage point of his ideas concerning Ireland's economic needs. He defended the necessity for home rule on the basis that Ireland required locally based economic policies.

In recent years, Butt's lectures while Whately professor have been recognised as significant contributions to the debate about Ireland's economy.[10] In 1837, in his first Whately lecture, 'The Poor-Law Bill for Ireland Examined', Butt bemoaned the poor law as a scheme alien to Irish circumstances, describing it as 'a plan utterly and miserably inefficient as a measure of relief, and just as foreign to the real character and causes of destitution in Ireland, as it is possible for any measure to be'.[11] Moreover, he believed that 'what we want in Ireland is not a shelter in a workhouse from the pressure of temporary penury: we want something that will raise the condition of an entire class ... We want, in a word, not relief for occasional want, but a remedy for general and permanent destitution.'[12] In 1846, Butt published two lectures delivered in the autumn of 1840 on the development of Irish industry and also that same year he considered the impact of the famine. Butt argued that he did not intend a general defence of protective duties but asserted that these might answer one or both of two great ends.

> First – They may bring into action and play sources and powers of production, in a country, which but for their existence, would lie utterly wasted and unproductive.
> Second – They may act the part of the most wise and wholesome poor law, setting the poor to work at a cost of some little self-denial to the rich; and by compelling a particular distribution of the wealth of the country, they may insure a certain amount of comforts to the condition of its labouring classes.[13]

The crux was 'to secure to all within the country the means of earning, by their labour, a comfortable independence, is an object to which, if it be attainable, all other objects should be subordinate'. To that end, he maintained that those who had only their labour should enjoy some portion of the country's riches. He found

> ... no difficulty in arriving at the conclusion that in a country like Ireland exporting articles of food, while many of her own people have not enough to eat, every importation from other

countries must tend to increase that exportation; and if it be produced by withdrawal of employment and wages from our
labourers at home, is a direct withdrawal from them of the support of human life.

From this, he argued, 'the effect of our using Irish instead of imported
manufacture would be, to leave all the present ability of paying for
labour undisturbed – to leave, therefore, the amount of our produce
the same, but to turn that produce from exportation to feeding our
own people'. For Butt, 'the true test of the prosperity of a country is
not what is sent out of it, but what is used in it. I mean by the prosperity of a country, the comforts which the great mass of its inhabitants enjoy. That nation deserts its duty, in which there are people
willing to work, who cannot, by any exertion, earn their bread.'

In linking the problem of landlord absenteeism to free trade he
maintained, 'it is impossible to distinguish the question of absenteeism
from that of the use of foreign commodities ...' While certainly not a
social revolutionary, Butt nonetheless believed that the wealthy had a
fundamental obligation to the poor. For him, 'inequalities of property
we must have; but it is open to us to control the effects of these
inequalities, so far as they affect the means of existence of any portion of our people.' The connection between economics and politics
was punctuated by his reflection: 'how deeply does the condition of
too many of our peasantry reprove the unprofitableness of our politics; and how bitterly, although silently, does it rebuke the rancour of
our disunion and the littleness of our feuds!' Butt's goal of securing
harmony between classes and creeds is emphasised in *'The Rate in
Aid': A Letter to the Right Hon. The Earl of Roden, KP*, published in
1849. The Rate in Aid 'teaches that the interests of all creeds, and
classes, and districts of Ireland, are inseparable'.[14] The object of policy
he urged should be to find profitable employment for the multitudes
willing to work, to bring into production under-utilised resources to
make use of Ireland's most precious resource – its people. 'Our first
step,' he wrote, 'must be to raise the condition of the mass of her people; until they are made comfortable, all hope of building up the
superstructure of society is vain.'[15]

Between 1852 and 1865, Butt was less active as a pamphleteer –
merely four appeared during the 1850s (1853, 1854, two in 1857)
and only one more (1863) until 1865. Although not entirely a lone
voice, his failure to support Manchester School doctrine made him an
outsider in the intellectual currents of the time. He never asked, for

example, to give a paper to the Dublin Statistical Society. His main political thrust during the next thirteen years was the forum of the House of Commons where he was one of the most consistently active Irish members. Much of his labour there affirmed the positions he had enunciated earlier in speeches, pamphlets and in the *Dublin University Magazine*. After his electoral defeat in 1865, Butt struggled to find a fresh foothold in politics. However, his essential motif remained the same. In 1869, he pronounced: 'I mean a self-government which gives us the entire right to manage our own affairs.'[16]

After the founding of the Home Government Association, Butt in 1870 penned *Irish Federalism: Its Meaning, its Objects and its Hope*, the most quoted of his later writings. He envisaged self-government as the means of reconciling creeds: 'It is from the joint deliberations of all classes of Irishmen that we may most confidently hope to present a plan of a national legislature, in which the just influence of property and education, and rank may be harmoniously combined with popular privileges and power, so as to make the legislature the real representative of the nation.'[17] Butt's vision set him apart from the bulk of Catholics who took up home rule in the 1870s; the majority of Catholics saw in the home rule campaign an opportunity to reverse the conquest and make pragmatic gains for themselves. Few of these were attracted to home government for the reasons that animated Butt. He and his fellow Protestants who supported self-government looked upon it as a way to reconcile the divisions between peoples in Ireland.

The fusion of economic and political ideas became more evident in the final phase of Butt's career, but the essential ingredients had been present from the 1830s. In essence, home rule alone offered the prospect of his panacea – full employment. Although he did not rule out the goal of economic growth, Butt's main thrust lay elsewhere. Many of the concerns he articulated were part of the debate of his day – the drive by European empires to harmonise and centralise, the impact of post-mercantilist economics, and the particular vulnerabilities of agricultural regions and late-starting industrialisation. Indeed, what Butt witnessed was the considerable de-industrialisation of much of Ireland in the face of the widening impact of British competition.

PARNELL, LAND AND INDUSTRIALISATION

Parnell and Davitt were born in the same year – 1846 – though into wildly differing circumstances. They worked together in the Land

League, but the two men held very different views about the ways to develop Ireland's economic potential. Yet, as Líam Kennedy notes, Parnell's agenda was primarily political, though, nevertheless, he gave political economy more serious attention than most nationalists.[18] For Parnell, the failure of economic development in Ireland could be attributed to the colonial relationship with Great Britain. There is no evidence that he read Butt's pamphlets, although it seems likely that he knew the essence of Butt's ideas. The two shared views on political economy that set them apart from the vast majority of home rulers.

Parnell's approach had two major prongs – the land question and industrialisation. At first sight, it is surprising that as a landowning member of the ascendancy, and with his identification with the 'land war', he appeared often to take more interest in the industrialisation of the country, though, somewhat oddly, he seldom took much notice of that part of the island that was already industrialised, the north-east. On closer examination his interest makes more sense. The Avondale estate he inherited was upland, with a quarry and timber reserves. East Wicklow then was still a mining region. Parnell took a keen interest in the mining and timbering on his estate. While an undergraduate at Magdalene College, Cambridge, he took leave of absence several times to deal with the complicated finances of Avondale. In one of his few speeches linking industry and agriculture, delivered in Ulster in October 1879, Parnell insisted that the depression in trade would not have been so severe were the countryside less impoverished.[19] His attitude to the land question can be distinguished in significant ways from both Butt and Davitt, and characterised as a resource analysis. Even before the 'land war', he advocated that the tenants should have 'the right and liberty of living on their own farms as owners'.[20] During his tour of North America in 1880, he urged the creation of a tenant-proprietorship, which then was only partly the policy of the Land League or in line with the attitude of the agrarian radicals who spearheaded the 'land war'. In a vital respect, he shared Butt's desire to foster rural harmony as a means to preserve his own order; he saw in land purchase the means to this wider end. A second part of his approach revolved around the question of congestion and rural poverty. Like Butt, he wanted to see uncultivated land put into economic use and he urged schemes of internal migration from the congested to unoccupied districts. He shared with Butt a belief that the core of the rural poverty trap was the misdistribution of physical resources, though their respective means of relieving the problem were not identical.

Above all, he seems to have believed that the colonial relationship had inhibited the growth of industry for, as he said in 1881, a resource base, surplus labour and capital were available, but the country was missing incentive and a market.[21] He contended that self-government could remedy the deficits and, like Butt, he favoured protection, though from the more traditional standpoint of aiding infant industries. In 1881, Parnell regretted that 'we cannot yet have our own Parliament to protect Irish manufactures.'[22] Without this, 'it is impossible for us to revive our native industries.' He remained quiet on the question of protection until 1885, though he urged the use of Irish-made clothing and other goods. Then at Cork on 21 January 1885, he said:

> We shall struggle, as we have been struggling, for the great and important interests of the Irish tenant farmer. We shall ask that his industry shall not be fettered by rent. We shall ask also from the farmer in return that he shall do what in him lies to encourage the struggling manufacturers of Ireland, and that he shall not think it too great a sacrifice to be called upon when he wants anything, when he has to purchase anything, to consider how he may get it of Irish material and manufacture, even suppose he has to pay a little more for it.[23]

To a no doubt incredulous audience, he went on:

> I am sorry if the agricultural population has shown itself somewhat deficient in its sense of duty in this respect up to the present time; but I feel convinced that the matter has only to be put before them to secure the opening up of the most important markets in the country for those manufactures which have always existed, and for those which have been reopened anew ...

When he met the Conservative lord lieutenant, Carnarvon, secretly in London on 1 August 1885, he emphasised the need to develop the country's industrial resources and said that this would necessitate some protection for a time.[24]

At the beginning of the general election campaign, he again professed, when speaking at the first National League convention held in Wicklow on 5 October, that the country must have 'a parliament that shall have power to protect Irish manufactures ...'[25] Indeed, he believed

> ... that it would be wise to protect certain Irish industries at all

events for a time; that it is impossible for us to make up for the loss of the start in the manufacturing race which we have experienced owing to adverse legislation in time past against Irish industries by England, unless we do protect these industries, not many in number, which are capable of thriving in Ireland.

Parnell declaimed:

Tell English Radicals and English Liberals that it is useless for them to talk of their desire to do justice to Ireland when, with motives of selfishness, they refuse to repair that most manifest injustice of all – namely, the destruction of our manufactures by England in times past.

Almost immediately afterwards, Davitt informed Henry Labouchere that he believed that 'Parnell's attitude on protection is absurd.'[26] Yet, as Kennedy observes, Parnell envisaged a specialised industrial structure and not the sort of closed economic system visualised by Butt or the Irish self-sufficiency model adopted in the 1920s.

Parnell's thinking on political economy, agricultural and urban, was joined to his general concerns about poverty and emigration. Rightly or wrongly, he subscribed to the notion that the country could support a much increased population, possibly numbering 10 to 12 million. For him, the problem lay in the bad distribution of resources, coupled with low levels of interest in an alternative, that is, industrialisation. Although Ireland was developing a services sector, Parnell, unlike many around him, did not look to this as a fundamental solution. In that respect, he was wedded to traditional concepts of production. Parnell believed that the rich agricultural lands of the east were under-utilised; poor areas of the west, on the other hand, were trying to support too many people. He deplored the vast tracts of land exploited for cattle ranching, which he termed a 'vicious system of farming'.[27] As he put it in the autumn of 1880:

Everywhere you go to you see all the rich lands without any inhabitants, and on the poorer lands and on the bogs you see people crowded together in small holdings. Well, then, before we talk of emigration to some other country, wouldn't it be better for us to develop the field of migration which exists in our own country.[28]

In this context, he also advocated measures to raise the quality of life of the agricultural labourers. At Cork in January 1885, he chided the farmers for their collective indifference, if not hostility, to the claims of the labourers. Parnell declared:

> We still also endeavour to secure for the labourer some recognition and some right in the land of his country. We do not care whether it be the prejudices of the farmer or of the landlord that stand in his way. We consider that whatever class tries to obstruct the labourers in the possession of those fair and just rights to which he is entitled, that class should be put down and coerced, if you will, into doing justice to the labourer.[29]

Parnell was not a backward-looking nationalist but one who, similarly to Butt, viewed the fate of the country and of his order through the lens of political economy. If both men in a sense advocated self-government and protection as a means to foster economic growth, Parnell assigned a higher priority to economic growth.

DAVITT, FREE TRADE AND REDISTRIBUTION

Michael Davitt's thoughts on political economy had the potential of originality and, in important respects, differed from his nationalist contemporaries. His assimilation of free trade, belief in the use of state power to redistribute wealth and nationalism does not fit neatly into any of the dominant ideologies.[30] From the Manchester School, Davitt adopted the concept that interdependence in the exchange of goods would lead to peaceful relations between peoples. This early version of globalisation flies in the face of Davitt's nationalism and is at odds with many aspects of his own career, especially the early portions. His concern to redistribute wealth owes its origin to radical and socialist ideas of his age. Moreover, his commitment to an often insular Irish nationalism adds an important ingredient to this unusual cocktail. Davitt's outlook was shaped by unconventional intellectual origins. As Carla King observes:

> Largely self-taught but widely read, Davitt was perhaps the most original thinker among Irish nationalists of his day. His ideas show a clear evolution from the Fenianism of his early years to the internationalism and social radicalism of his later career, while his commitment to Irish nationalism never wavered.[31]

His formative influences were distinctive – an upbringing in industrial Lancashire infused with family nostalgia for its origins in rural Mayo, involvement in fenianism in England and a long stretch in an English prison. The cotton districts of Lancashire understood the plight of urban poverty, exploitation of labour, of the international exchange of goods, and chronic flux of trade cycles. Again as King emphasises, 'Davitt's development shares some of the formative features of a British working-class radical, and one might look for the source of some of his later attitudes to this period of his life.'[32] Certainly his education in a Wesleyan school and frequent visit to the local Mechanics' Institute seem decisive to his intellectual outlook. It did give his conception of political economy some less typical characteristics, notably the linkage of rural and urban development and of British, Irish and, ultimately, world trade. Butt, specifically, had denied that there ought to be Irish concern for the fate of workers overseas; Parnell's concept of internationalism extended no further than keeping the impoverished rural labourers at home rather than shovelling them out to the New World.

Davitt's conception of political economy centred on land nationalisation. In his later career, he dropped the issue publicly, but the idea underpinning it remained central to his thinking. His intention, as with Butt and Parnell, was to relieve poverty and misery, through the elimination of the economic parasite of landlordism, the redistribution of income, and growth led by the international exchange of goods. In his first and most famous phase – the Land League period – Davitt, like most radical nationalists, believed that the landlord class received payment for which it did not render worthwhile service; their ownership of the land, therefore, should be surrendered. He told an audience in mid-1879 that 'the soil of Ireland should be returned to the people of Ireland.'[33] Yet, as King observes, this was neither simply an economic claim nor the by-product of a culture of grievance, but one that envisaged self-government.[34] Unlike Parnell, he did not believe that a Westminster parliament, composed of landlords, would concede real reform to Irish peasants and that home rule MPs would be obliged to withdraw from the London assembly and form themselves into a government in Ireland. No doubt Gladstone's concessions influenced Davitt's political outlook in the longer term, though in the immediate context he was deeply disappointed by what he believed was the premature cessation of the land struggle. This he attributed to Parnell. Davitt's perspective had a slightly different edge than the Irish leader and most of his Land League colleagues. They saw the end of landlordism in terms of reversing the conquest, as an attack on ascendancy, and returning control – part or complete ownership – to the tenants, the rightful inheritors of the soil. Davitt was not bereft of such feelings, but both his speeches on land nationalisation and *The Fall of Feudalism in Ireland* (1904) suggest that he wished to appropriate the unearned increment enjoyed by landlords and redistribute it to both those who worked the land, the farmer, who had first right to the proceeds, and the urban worker. With that object in mind, he promoted land nationalisation in the aftermath of the 'land war'. Under it, 'the land would be handed over to the people of Ireland, to be administered on their behalf in the interest not of one class, but of the entire Irish population ...'[35] Urban workers would share in the redistribution through the shift of taxation from them to the land, relieving the industrial classes of poor rates, county rates, police tax and breakfast table tax (protection). Free trade, then, was integral to this conception, for it would make goods cheaper for consumers and generate demand for labourers' output, thereby raising living standards. This was anti-landlordism for sure, but anti-landlordism with a difference.

Understandably, Davitt's association with Henry George and land nationalisation has received wide attention. His writings while imprisoned in 1881–2 considered many contemporary social problems but, as King describes, central to Davitt's thinking was state ownership of land. For him, peasant proprietorship would not cure Ireland's land question but might make it worse because it would tend to extend and consolidate the absolute ownership of land and lead to the re-establishment of large estates, albeit under so-called native landlords. Moreover, he wondered why the state should favour tenants at the expense of other interests, giving to them alone the resource that belonged to the whole community. 'By what right,' he queried, 'are the public funds or the public credit to be utilised for the benefit of a section of the community merely?'[36] Although subsequently he would abandon land nationalisation, in public at least he remained an implacable opponent of state-supported land purchase and was committed to ideas centred on communal rights. Following the first of the Conservative-sponsored legislative initiatives to foster tenant land purchase in 1885, Davitt voiced his disapproval of what he cited as a 'landlord relief bill'.[37] After the Wyndham Act of 1903, John Dillon mobilised Davitt against legislation for which William O'Brien had worked so diligently.[38] According to Davitt, 'the immediate effect of the publication of this agreement was to inflate the value of landlord property over thirty per cent.'[39] It made no provision for popular control, did not benefit the labourers and threw any bad debts onto the shoulders of the Irish people. There undoubtedly were important personal and political differences between Davitt and Parnell – Davitt's ideas were criticised by mainstream home rulers as 'a chaotic socialist experiment'[40] – but these dissimilarities were underpinned by a genuine chasm in their respective notions of political economy.

The emphasis on Davitt's adoption of land nationalisation tends to obscure recognition of the underlying motivation for his position. He subscribed to the common ascription of poverty and deficient economic growth to colonial dominance, a position held by Parnell and, indeed, by most conventional nationalists. His magnum opus, *The Fall of Feudalism*, summarised his position on the links between political economy and nationalism. In it, he argued 'the present condition and prospects of a depopulated country ... is alone a full condemnation of the system of government which has reduced it to the level of the poorest country in Europe ...'[41] He measured relative economic success by the level of growth in population. 'As a direct result of this fatal weakening of Ireland's vital energies,' he wrote, 'both the birth-rate and the marriage-rate of the country are now near the lowest of any nation in Europe.'[42] This was a different yardstick from Butt's and, though closer to some of Parnell's views, it had important distinctions. Thus, self-government was essential to revitalisation. However, he did not portend a purely internal approach, for

> ... what English, Welsh, and Scotch workers, traders, and tax-payers need in competition with the producers of other countries, is, not less, but more, free trade – free trade in the growing of food, in a legal protection against a private tax called rent upon its industry; free trade in the building of houses for the people, by protection against ground-rents levied upon the progress of industrial centres by landlordism; free trade in the production of coal and iron ore, by the application to public purposes of the private taxes called mineral royalties now imposed by landlords upon every workshop, manufacturer, artisan, trader, and domestic fireplace in the three countries by the class who are in legislative possession of the House of Lords and largely of the House of Commons.[43]

Moreover, his moral purpose was 'to point out to the thinkers and leaders of the industrial millions of Great Britain how the poorest of the workers – the tillers of the soil in Ireland – succeeded by the combination in overthrowing an all-important territorial aristocracy ...'[44]

Davitt, uniquely, found a means to harness nationalism, agrarianism, liberalism and radicalism into a fresh synthesis, but one that would fail to capture the imagination of the post-1900 generation of nationalists. His fundamental ideas came from an English rather than an Irish pool of thought. Davitt remained a product of his time and place. In his own age, he was hampered by both the origin of his concepts and his untutored approaches, which, predictably, his more schooled associates found naïve.

CONCLUSION

If Butt, Parnell and Davitt were, and will continue to be thought of as, political creatures, it is worth recalling that they did not see home rule or the land question as purely political or even solely national questions. Some nationalists had no wider ambition than self-government for its own sake, reversal of the conquest or an ethnic-religious society encased by a political state. However, the three giants of the age wanted something grander. Butt and Parnell wanted to preserve the place of their order in Ireland. To do so, they sought forms of self-government that could induce prosperity, seen largely through the lens of full employment in the first instance and internally generated industrialisation in the second. They failed in their prime mission, but the ideas of both appealed to the post-1916 generation of nationalists who, in common with the founders of new states across Europe, adopted restrictive and protective economic policies. Davitt had little time for these prescriptions and, consequently, his concepts found less of a place in the new state, only to resurface in the contemporary Ireland of the Celtic Tiger.

NOTES

1. I wish to thank the editors, especially Fintan Lane, along with Frank Bouchier-Hayes, D. George Boyce, N.C. Fleming, Liam Kennedy, Carla King and my aunt, Col. Helen O'Day, for assistance with this article.
2. Patrick O'Brien, 'Is political biography a good thing?' *Contemporary British History*, vol. 5 (winter, 1996), pp. 60–6.
3. See Neil C. Fleming and Alan O'Day (eds), *Bibliography of Charles Stewart Parnell, 1846–1891* (Westport, CT, forthcoming).
4. See Peter Gray, 'The making of mid-Victorian Ireland: Political economy and the memory of the Great Famine', in Peter Gray (ed.), *Victoria's Ireland: Irishness and Britishness, 1837–1901* (Dublin, 2004), pp. 151–66; Alan O'Day, 'Nationalism and political economy in Ireland: Isaac Butt's analysis', in Christine Kinealy and Roger Swift (eds), *Politics and Power in Victorian Ireland* (Dublin, 2006), pp. 119–32.
5. Tim Boylan and Tadhg Foley (eds), *Irish Political Economy*, 4 vols (London & New York, 2003).
6. O'Day, 'Nationalism and political economy in Ireland'.
7. Marc Blaug, *James Wilson (1805–1860), Isaac Butt (1813–1879), T.E. Cliffe Leslie (1827–1882)* (Aldershot, 1991), p. ix.
8. R.D. Collison Black, 'The Irish dissenters and nineteenth-century political economy', in

Antoin E. Murphy (ed.), *Economists and the Irish Economy from the Eighteenth Century to the Present Day* (Dublin, 1983), pp. 120–37.

9. *The Times*, 6 May 1879.
10. Laurence S. Moss, *Mountifort Longfield: Ireland's Professor of Political Economy* (Ottawa, IL, 1976).
11. See Butt's lecture in Boylan and Foley, *Irish Political Economy*, vol. 1, p. 6.
12. Boylan and Foley, *Irish Political Economy*, vol. 1, p. 6.
13. This and the following quotations are drawn from the original pamphlets, but also can be found in Boylan and Foley, *Irish Political Economy*, vol. 3.
14. Isaac Butt, *The Rate in Aid: A Letter to the Right Hon. The Earl of Roden, KP* (Dublin, 1849), p. 7.
15. Ibid., p. 32.
16. *Nation*, 20 November 1869 (speech at Dundalk, 11 November).
17. Isaac Butt, *Irish Federalism! Its Meaning, its Objects and its Hope* (Dublin, 1870), p. viii.
18. Liam Kennedy, 'The economic thought of the nation's lost leader: Charles Stewart Parnell', in D. George Boyce and Alan O'Day (eds), *Parnell in Perspective* (London, 1991), pp. 171–200.
19. *Ulster Examiner*, 16 October 1879.
20. *Hansard*, 234 (1 May 1877), c. 178.
21. Kennedy, 'The economic thought of the nation's lost leader', p. 172.
22. *Freeman's Journal*, 3 October 1881.
23. *The Times*, 22 January 1885.
24. BL, Carnarvon Papers, MS 60829.
25. *The Times*, 6 October 1885.
26. Cited in Algar L. Thorold, *Life of Henry Labouchere* (London, 1913), p. 234.
27. *Freeman's Journal*, 6 December 1880.
28. Ibid.
29. *The Times*, 22 January 1885.
30. An indispensable collection of his writings are found in Carla King (ed.), *Michael Davitt: Collected Writings, 1868–1906* (Bristol, 2001), 8 vols.
31. Carla King, *Michael Davitt* (Dundalk, 1999), p. 9.
32. Ibid., p. 11.
33. Cited in D.B. Cashman, *The Life of Michael Davitt* (London, 1882), p. 99.
34. King, *Davitt*, p. 23.
35. Ibid., p. 40.
36. Ibid., p. 41.
37. *Freeman's Journal*, 17 August 1885.
38. See Michael Davitt, *The Fall of Feudalism in Ireland, or, the Story of the Land League Revolution* (London & New York, 1904), pp. 702–12.
39. Ibid., pp. 707–9.
40. Cited in Fintan Lane, *The Origins of Modern Irish Socialism, 1881–1896* (Cork, 1997), p. 88.
41. Davitt, *Fall of Feudalism*, p. 717.
42. Ibid., p. 723.
43. Ibid., p. 725.
44. Ibid.

CHAPTER FIVE

Michael Davitt and the Personality of the Irish Agrarian Revolution

PAUL BEW AND PATRICK MAUME

The Cardiff-based home rule activist and ex-fenian James Mullin, who raised himself from a labouring background to become a successful doctor, recorded in his memoirs that he regarded Michael Davitt as having the most magnetic personality he ever knew.

> Its power to attract the love of friends and respect of enemies was irresistible ... He nurtured no conceit about his own powers, nor jealousy about his colleagues; and never, I am sure, uttered a mean insinuation against friend or enemy. He had the rare judicial capacity of viewing a controversial question from the opposite side, and giving his opponents credit for being actuated by motives as good as his own, however mistaken they might be ... It was this broadminded and generous tolerance that won him so high a place in the esteem of his opponents, so that even some of those from Ulster informed me that if all Home Rulers were like Michael Davitt they too would be like Home Rulers, for it was impossible to conceive him harbouring any sinister designs against them.[1]

Mullin is not the only memoirist who bears testimony to this side of Davitt's character; yet Davitt was also capable, during the heat of the Parnell split, of informing a public meeting that Parnell was trying to win the support of the working classes by offering them 'Eight hours at work/ Eight hours at play/ Eight hours in bed with Kitty O'Shea.'[2]

In 1894 Davitt visited Achill Island in order to deliver charitable aid. The boat swayed dramatically in heavy seas. This presented a particular problem for a man with one arm: Davitt found the trip both unpleasant and disturbing. In a charming indication of Davitt's popularity, however, the boatman proclaimed reassuringly that 'there's not a wave on this coast that would take you, Mr Davitt.' But on the island itself, another side of Davitt's relationship with the Irish people was revealed. As he moved among them distributing cash, he overheard the islanders muttering in Irish – which they assumed the elegantly dressed mainlander did not understand – about how much of the relief fund he had pocketed for himself.[3] This anecdote, which appeared in the *Leader*, tells us much about Davitt's relationship with the broader Irish populace. On the one hand, a true son of the people, the evicted Mayo cottier's son who had suffered long and harsh years in imprisonment on account of his devotion to the Irish cause. But, on the other hand, by the mid-1880s Davitt had made himself into something else: a man of letters, a hero of international progressive opinion, and by the mid-1890s a director of a substantial Dublin milling firm. An aficionado of white suits, he must have appeared to the western islanders as a *rara avis*: clearly not one to be entirely trusted. In many respects Davitt was a rather typical, uncomplicated Irish nationalist. This essay explores the duality at the heart of Davitt's career; intensely representative of mainstream nationalism and yet somehow slightly disconnected. Anyone of a number might have written his nationalist credo.

> The Irish race have a place in the world's affairs of today that is incompatible with the position which Ireland occupies as a kind of vegetable patch for selfish imperial purposes. We are fully 20 millions of the world's population, and though four fifths of those reside out of Ireland, they are potential factors, nevertheless, in the political faith and fortunes of the country from which a rule of stupidity and race-hatred drove their progenitors away. Moreover, Ireland and its race have a mission in the world, have national characteristics, a distinctive individuality and ideas, greatly differing from Anglo-Saxonism, with its purely materialistic spirit and aims. These alone entitle our country to a recognised and separate place in the ranks of civilised states.[4]

And yet, in the end, Davitt was not a conventional nationalist. His support for the theory of land nationalisation from early 1882 is one obvious proof of his willingness to go against the grain of a political culture devoted to peasant proprietorship. So how did his thought evolve? Any reader of his *Fall of Feudalism in Ireland* can see that it has two great Irish sources – James Fintan Lalor and John Mitchel – and time and again, Davitt underscores the value of their writings.

Mitchel infected Davitt with a particular toughness, some might say hardness of tone.

Consider, for example, his late contacts with the volatile anti-clerical journalist P.D. Kenny, whose Mayo small-farm background resembled Davitt's own, and who like Davitt presented himself in metropolitan circles as deriving privileged insights from his background, while his relatives and neighbours in Claremorris regarded him as a bizarre exotic. Like Davitt, Kenny had achieved a degree of educational opportunity unusual for his class – in Davitt's case, a factory owner paid for him to remain at school after he lost his arm as a child labourer in a machine accident (whereas of his siblings only one sister achieved literacy); Kenny had been a teenage migratory labourer in Lancashire when a farmer took an interest in him and enabled him to obtain further education. Both men were haunted by awareness of the difficulty with which they had achieved what more favoured youths took for granted, and it was this shared anger which drew them together in planning a campaign for non-denominational education, which they saw as likely to be more efficient and give greater opportunities to future Davitts and Kennys than the existing Church-controlled system; yet Davitt (with such awkward aspects of his legacy overlooked or treated as personal eccentricities) was remembered as a hero of Irish nationalism, while Kenny's campaign to develop the productivity of Irish agriculture developed into an ever-deepening contempt for the people around him, which led him from praising the *Playboy of the Western World* to openly embracing unionism and finally to an embittered and impoverished old age on a Mayo smallholding, constantly recalling Davitt's remark to him that the land campaign had turned out less satisfactorily than he had expected.[5]

It was not surprising that in describing what had made him what he was, Davitt stressed the horrors of the famine. Listen to the voice of his most reliable clerical ally, Bishop Thomas Nulty of Meath. Nulty's career was characterised by a mixture of social concern and intellectual vanity. The latter, expressed in his arbitrary and whimsical interventions over plans for a Mullingar waterworks in the 1880s and culminating in the savage intimidation exercised against Meath Parnellites in the 1890s, was to cost Davitt dearly both financially and in political terms (his 1892 election for Meath North was set aside because of this clerical intimidation and he was bankrupted by the legal costs). This has obscured the reason for Davitt's alliance with Nulty in the first place. Not only was Nulty the only Irish bishop who openly supported Davitt on land nationalisation (incidentally safeguarding Davitt from any possibility that the Irish bishops might mount an attack on land nationalisers such as that undertaken by the archbishop of New York against Fr Edward McGlynn for his support of Henry George) but he had a long record as an advocate of tenants' rights.[6] On 10 February 1881, Nulty recalled publicly how as a young curate he had witnessed famine clearances in Co. Cavan:

> He had seen 700 persons turned adrift in the wide world in one day; or rather in two, for it took two days to do. He had seen their houses levelled to the ground and demolished, while not a single person but one inside those houses owed a farthing rent ... He saw them to one place where there were in two houses fever stricken victims; and the crowbar refused to take them down. Death was very busy there and they were afraid of catching the disease.[7]

Davitt's condemnation of the 'crowbar brigades' is well known; after all, they bore down directly on his own family. But there is an aspect of Davitt's discussion of the famine which has escaped attention. Unlike his friend, Boyle O'Reilly, he was prepared to follow John Mitchel in blaming the Irish priesthood for encouraging passivity: 'Mitchel blames the priests, primarily, for persuading the people not to fight. Begging alms and making paupers of men they had already taught to be slaves was more in their line.'[8] Davitt went further: 'As the peasants had chosen to die like sheep rather than retain that food in a fight for life, to live or die like men, their loss to the Irish nation need not occasion many pangs of regret.'[9] The endless mantra of 'virility and manliness' in late nineteenth-century Irish nationalism had a harsher conceptual edge than many realised. There may have been a darker personal element in these denunciations; during the Parnell split, when Davitt described the family of the Parnellite journalist John Wyse Power as Waterford shebeen-keepers, Wyse Power referred to Mayo rumours that some of Davitt's relatives had been bailiffs during the famine.[10] Davitt declared:

> What are the doctrines of the Irish revolution? I will quote what they are from the columns of a paper which bore a very sugges-tive title, the *Irish Felon*. In the *Felon* of 24 June 1848, Lalor not only laid down the doctrine of the 'Land for the People', but also indicated the means by which a movement on these lines would ultimately achieve Irish national independence.[11]

Davitt loved to repeat Lalor's words: 'It is a mere question between a people and a class, between a people of eight millions and a class of

8,000. They or we must quit this island. It is a people to be saved or
lost, it is the island to be kept or surrendered.' The full significance of
Lalor is often obscured by seeing him simply as the origin of the view
that land agitation could be used as the engine to drive political
nationalism. Lalor did not merely put this forward as a tactic, he had
very definite views about its likely outcome. Like his mentor, William
Conner, Lalor had begun with the belief that land reform could be
achieved by intellectual demonstration, backed up by a petition to
parliament and if necessary by a rent strike modelled on that which
his father Pat Lalor had organised against tithes.[12] The Irish
Conservative who became founder of the Home Rule Party, Isaac
Butt, was to take up Conner's approach of seeking fixity of tenure
and fair rent by convincing the British parliament. Butt – primarily a
parliamentarian, unlike the agitator Conner – did not follow Conner
in moving from petitioning parliament to advocating a rent strike.

The famine, however, led Lalor to develop the view that the land
system could only be reformed through a change in sovereignty
whereby the Irish nation would replace the crown as source of land
title. He thus originated the 'neo-fenian' view that the British government was so dominated by the landed classes that it would never
pass any Irish land reforms that could serve as a precedent for
Britain, and therefore any land agitation must inevitably lead to a
challenge to British rule in Ireland.

But how quickly did Davitt become a Lalorite? There is no doubt
as to the agrarian radicalism of the fenian movement, which Davitt
joined as a young man. Its organ, the *Irish People*, declared that in the
Irish Republic, 'landlord tyranny would vanish when the land became
the possession of the people; it urged that every man has but one
object, to rid the land of robbers and render every cultivator of the
soil his own landlord; the proprietor in fee simple of the house and
land of his father; that the territorial magnates of the British Empire
are the grand obstacles in the path of Irish prosperity … Ireland for
the Irish and the land for the people. This is the grand idea now.'
Given such a rhetoric, 'it is somewhat singular', as the American academic D.B. King pointed out in 1882, that 'it did not appeal more
strongly to the tenant farmers.' In fact, there is a simple answer to the
question posed by Professor King. The fenians certainly supported the
destruction of landlordism, but this was to be achieved after the
accomplishment of a successful national insurrection. Many could not
believe in the likelihood of such a success. Fenian radicalism on the
land issue thus appeared to lack any real content.

In the aftermath of the defeat of the 1867 rising, some began to push for a more pragmatic political style for fenianism. The key figure here was John Devoy, the most capable and serious of the Irish-American militants. He had been the director of a great tactical success, the *Catalpa* rescue of fenian prisoners in Australia in 1876: a real achievement, which soon assumed mythic proportions.[13] He now became involved with Parnell by sending a public telegram on 25 October 1878, when he offered Parnell the New Departure package. Parnell had just been re-elected president of the Home Rule Confederation of Great Britain with fenian support, and Devoy felt – wrongly, as it turned out – that this was a moment of crucial significance. However, the important thing to note is that he offered Parnell the support of American militants on certain conditions: abandonment of Butt's federal demand and substitution of a general – that is, undefined – demand in favour of self-government; vigorous agitation of the land question on the basis of a peasant proprietary, while accepting concessions tending to abolish arbitrary eviction; exclusion of all sectarian issues from the platform; collective voting by party members on all imperial and home questions; the adoption of an aggressive policy; energetic resistance to coercive legislation; and advocacy of all struggling nationalities in the British empire or elsewhere.

Devoy's thinking was brilliantly expressed in a long letter (dated 11 December 1878) from New York to the *Freeman's Journal*. Devoy denounced the republican insistence that no alliance could be made with parliamentary nationalists unless the latter first adopted abstentionism:

> The result is that the advanced Nationalist party exerts less influence over the current of public events in Ireland, less influence in determining the opinion of the world, as to Ireland's want and wishes, than its numbers would entitle it to, if it took its proper share in public life and was organised for public action. No party or combination of parties in Ireland can ever hope to earn the support of the majority of the people except if it honestly proposes a radical reform of the land system. No matter what may be said of individual landlords, the whole system was founded on robbery and fraud.[14]

The New Departure package was a dagger to the heart of Buttism. Federalism was Butt's core principle, his deepest belief, and part of the point was that it could be precisely defined and did not deny a supreme authority to Westminster. Furthermore, Butt's land reform politics were focussed on security of tenure and franchise rather than peasant proprietorship.

This is the vital context to the Land League revolution. As Davitt insisted, the old cries of 'fixity of tenure' and 'fair rents' would do no longer: 'Ireland had had enough of futile agitations and semi-insurrections. They were going to fight it out this time.'[15] In 1884, Davitt explained the plan of the original Land League:

> The principle upon which the Land League is founded is, as a matter of course, subject for dispute and difference of opinion, and the programme which was drawn up by the persons named, and embodied in resolutions of the Conference on the 21st of October, 1879 (inasmuch as it did not comprise any demand for self-government) cannot be credited with containing the whole 'principle' upon which the Land League was founded. The organisers of the Conference had to consider the advisability of framing such a programme as would not 'scare' any timid land reformer away from the projected movement, and it was further considered necessary to render it eminently constitutional for the double purpose of legal protection against the Castle, and to enable members of Parliament to defend it within the House of Commons. What, then, was the principle upon which the Land League was founded? I maintain that it was the complete destruction of Irish landlordism: first, as the system which was responsible for the poverty and periodical famines which have decimated Ireland; and, secondly, because landlordism was a British garrison, which barred the way to national independence.[16]

What could Parnell do but make the best of it? In December 1879, Parnell told an audience at Liverpool: 'There are men in this land movement who consider that the free rights of Ireland must be won by the bloody battlefield and by the sword. But these men do not take part in this movement for the purpose of carrying out these ideas; they take part and to help to win peaceably the solution of the land question'.[17] In the end, however, the revolutionaries lost the battle for control of the Land League revolution.

Davitt always insisted that Parnell was a profoundly conservative politician. In this, he was perfectly correct, but he failed to see that Parnell also had a superior grasp of the workings of the British political system. Davitt and his neo-fenian colleagues in the Land League leadership did not believe that the British state would offer a substantial measure of land reform, and thus defuse their agitation. In this respect they remained the victims of John Mitchel's polemics. In fairness, it must be said that this perception was shared on the other end of the Irish political spectrum: the splenetically pro-landlord *Dublin Evening Mail* declared in tones of increasing rage and anxiety that any British government that infringed the property rights of Irish land-lords would be opening the way for a wider assault on property throughout Britain, so that everyone in Britain who had anything to lose should join in resisting the Land League. In January 1880, the *Mail* commented on a speech by Davitt at Rathdrum, Co. Wicklow, denouncing a case in which after an eviction 'three small children were left out – or kept out – in an open field for nights, when the snow lay nine inches deep upon the ground, the unfortunate children being without any protection from the weather but an old sheet':

> Mr Davitt proceeded to characterise the legal rights of a landlord to the resumption of his property. 'It was,' said this speaker, 'simply infamous, damnable, and diabolical, that any man should have such power of life and death vested in him under this infamous landlord system, and the Irish people would be cowards and false to their nature if they did not work unceasingly to put an end to it' ... We quite go along with Mr Davitt in his horror at this cruelty, which in the too probable case of the death of any of the children from exposure would have differed in no material respect from deliberate and wilful murder. And we also think that the perpetration of such cruelty ought to be strictly forbidden by the law, and rendered impossible so far as any changes in the existing law can have that effect. But we part company from Mr Davitt in his view as to the person who was guilty of the cruelty, and also as to the change that should be made in our existing legal system in order to prevent such acts of cruelty being repeated. It was not the landlord but the children's own unnatural mother that exposed the little ones to the horrid sufferings of exposure to the winter's cold. There was nothing to hinder her taking them to the warmth and food of the poorhouse, which the ratepayers and chief among them, the landlord, maintain at a heavy cost, precisely in order to avert such horrible sufferings. We can only guess at the motives of the female devil, real or suppositious, who submitted her helpless offspring to these sufferings ... The changes in the law which appear to us necessary to prevent such cruelty would be to abridge the parental power which can be so abused, and make the

removal of the children to the poorhouse compulsory on the parent. If the parent neglects this duty the police should take the children to the shelter provided for them, and the unnatural parent [be] indicted for cruelty.[18]

This provocatively blasé approach was hardly likely to reduce the demand for tenant rights among those already receptive to it (whether from conscience or fear of the impact of agitation). The *Evening Mail* combined with its taunts, however, a perceptive comment on the tensions within the Land League project which shaped Davitt's post-1882 career:

> Mr Davitt will have some trouble, we think, for all his eloquent denunciations of what he is pleased to call landlordism, in persuading the people of this country that owners of land must not hire the use of it to others. Even if his present protégés, the tenants, were by his efforts to be put in possession of their landlords' estates, they would at once proceed to exercise all those rights which property, whether in land or in anything else, involves. Among those rights is that of lending the use of it to another person for a money consideration, called rent; and if this right were denied to them a new agrarian agitation would spring up which would have much more reason, and therefore more force, on its side than the present one.[19]

That career, of course, was also to be heavily influenced by the fallout from the Phoenix Park murders of May 1882.

Davitt seems to have shared the neo-fenian assessment that it would be a mistake to invite British repression, and it was essential to sustain the agitation and its existing leadership for as long as possible. It is important to notice that he certainly did not go out of his way to court arrest. In January 1881, the government introduced the Protection of Person and Property Bill as a weapon against the Land League. It was designed to legalise the arrest and imprisonment without trial of anyone suspected of promoting illegal activities. His militant speech at Borris, Co. Carlow was the immediate cause of Davitt's arrest, his arrest in Dublin and his return to Portland prison where he was detained for the next sixteen months. However, he does not seem to have invited this martyrdom. He went out of his way to distribute to the press a much milder written version of his oration – unfortunately for Davitt, one journalist, Andrew Dunlop, refused to go along with this charade and printed his account of the speech as actually given.[20]

Sir Robert Anderson, the spymaster, later concluded: 'The Park murders were the work of the officials of the Land League, of which Parnell was the President and Davitt the founder. But their hands were clean. For while these plots were hatching, Parnell was under lock and key in Kilmainham, and Davitt was buried in a convict prison.'[21] In fact, Davitt's hands were cleaner than Parnell's; as Parnell later explained to Davitt when talking about the Kilmainham experience and Gladstone's role in putting him there: 'You know he put us in prison and we were obliged to strike back so as to deter others from returning to like methods again.'[22] Parnell's contacts with the world of fenian violence in this period are a matter of controversy, but they were certainly closer than those of Davitt.[23] In consequence, his break with the agitational aspects of Irish nationalism had to be all the more complete. From this point onwards, a new reserve on both sides enters into the Parnell–Davitt relationship. Parnell did try to persuade Davitt of the merits of his projected alliance with the Conservatives in 1885 but failed absolutely. On the contrary, Davitt became bitter about the way in which young nationalists, especially in the North, who had expressed any sympathy for Davitt-style radicalism, were ruthlessly marginalised and excluded.[24] The *Evening Mail*, having initially hoped that Davitt's espousal of land nationalisation marked the eclipse of Parnell by 'communist' forces which would drive the British political establishment into firmer alliance with Irish Conservatism, commented morosely that they expected Parnell to prevail over Davitt, for while measures of public plunder such as those espoused by the former had frequently been secured by demagogues throughout history, such a scheme as Davitt's land nationalisation had never been implemented anywhere.

In 1886, Davitt gloated over the discomfiture of Parnell's loyal lieutenants when Captain O'Shea was imposed on Galway. In the same year, meeting Parnell in Cardiff, James Mullin was permanently alienated when Parnell referred to Davitt as 'that fellow Davitt'. 'I felt a revulsion of feeling against him which lasted many a long day afterwards ... It was ... the utterance of an arrogant aristocrat against a democratic leader.'[25] In 1888 British intelligence reported that Parnell and Davitt were on terms of 'mock friendship only', while the pro-Unionist American journalist W.H. Hurlbert noted:

It is a curious illustration of the autocratic or bureaucratic system under which the Irish movement is now conducted, that Mr Davitt, who does not pretend to be a parliamentarian and owes, indeed, much of his authority to his refusal to enter parliament and take oaths of allegiance, does not hesitate for a moment to discipline any Irish member of Parliament who incurs his disapprobation.[26]

In 1890, the *Evening Mail* took comfort in Davitt's appearance at the head of the Irish Democratic Labour Federation as a sign of continued strain within the Parnellite support coalition. It may be seen that the estrangement of Parnell and Davitt at the time of the divorce crisis had many roots – not just Davitt's discomfiture with what he called Parnell's 'sensuous nature'.

During the Parnell split Davitt gave and received many hard blows. Attacking Davitt's view that only men of humble origins could be trusted, the Parnellite *Irish Daily Independent* accused him of jealousy towards Parnell and described him as 'this baseborn peasant'.[27] While Bishop Nulty defended his intervention in the Meath elections on the grounds that he was entitled to warn his flock against the evils of 'secret societies' (ironically, both Davitt and the other unseated Meath anti-Parnellite, Patrick Fullam, had been prominent IRB activists), many of Parnell's IRB supporters came to regard Parnell as an honorary separatist whose political shortcomings could be excused by his background, while Davitt was denounced as an apostate. This view occurs in many of Arthur Griffith's comments on Davitt and can still be found in a milder form in the 1949 writings of the hardline republican Brian O'Higgins (who came from a Meath Parnellite background).[28] Perhaps the most terrible impact of the split on Davitt was caused by an Achill Island servant whom the Davitts hired to look after their household in Ballybrack. This woman, whom they believed in retrospect to have been demented, first signalled her opinion of Davitt by decorating the dining room table with ivy leaves to mark Parnell's birthday. The Davitts displayed forbearance by continuing to employ her; but soon afterwards, when Davitt had gone on a lecture tour of Australia, she allowed Davitt's eldest daughter to play in puddles and catch a chill from which she died; she then accused Mrs Davitt of having killed the child.[29]

After the divorce crisis, Davitt remained an influential figure in Irish nationalism – supporting the United Irish League, for example, and opposing William O'Brien's rapprochement with the landlords in 1903. Yet, as always, his behaviour was not entirely predictable. O'Brien was furious about the way in which Davitt protected a Mayo grazier friend, Bernard Daly, just as he had been furious in 1888 when

Davitt supported the parliamentary ambitions of J.F. Taylor (the eloquent barrister and journalist now chiefly remembered for his appearance in Joyce's *Ulysses*).[30] Radical separatists and conservative clericalists and agrarians joined in denouncing the faith in an alliance between the 'British Democracy' and the Irish people that led Davitt to advocate a state-controlled system of secular education and to oppose any suggestion that the Irish Party should use its political influence to limit free trade, which might benefit Irish farmers in the short term but meant higher food prices for the poor in Britain and Ireland. In his last major statement, at the end of March 1906, Davitt acknowledged formally that the Irish agrarian revolution was not working out as planned and that the farmers who were benefiting from the process were only too willing to invest in cattle rather than tillage, thus undermining the social vision of popular agrarian nationalism.

Davitt's role both as a representative of the Irish radical republican tradition and, at the same time, as a somewhat estranged independent intellectual is the defining feature of his career. In the 1880s, he seemed to many to be the most impressive and confident voice of Irish nationalism. Given the ambiguities of his own early involvement in fenianism, it is remarkable how willing English commentators were to acknowledge a certain nobility of character. It is arguable that of all the Irish nationalists of this period, Davitt was the one who found his personal motivations questioned the least. Yet for all the purism of his public image, Davitt was a complex figure: tough-minded, at times unforgiving, but willing in the end to face up to unpalatable realities – unlike P.D. Kenny, who was destroyed by all-consuming anger and contempt.

NOTES

1. James Mullin, *The Story of a Toiler's Life*, edited by Patrick Maume (Dublin, 2000), pp. 181–3.
2. Frank Callanan, *T. M. Healy* (Cork, 1996), p. 309.
3. NLI, MS 4214, Sophie O'Brien's manuscript transcript (with commentary of her husband's letters) 1894 section p.8.
4. Michael Davitt, *The Fall of Feudalism in Ireland* (London and New York, 1904), p.724.
5. Patrick Maume, 'Between Fleet Street and Mayo: P.D. Kenny and the culture wars of Edwardian Ireland', *Bullán*, 6, 2 (2002), pp. 21–41; for his dealings with Davitt see p. 25.
6. McGlynn was reconciled to the Church in 1892 after Roman intervention; many of his followers (such as the parents of the future radical Elizabeth Gurley Flynn) were permanently alienated from Catholicism. Davitt's views on the McGlynn case are not known, though some of his American associates backed McGlynn; Patrick Ford initially supported McGlynn but changed sides after the priest's excommunication, while the American Georgist and prominent Land League publicist James Redpath served as vice-president of McGlynn's Anti-Poverty Society. For a brief account of the McGlynn case, see Hugh

McLeod, 'Edward McGlynn: A rebel against the archbishop of New York', in Stuart Mews (ed.), *Modern Religious Rebels* (London, 1993), pp. 166–84.

7. Quoted in Lord Robert Montagu, *Recent Events and a Clue to their Solution* (London, 1886), p. 423.
8. Michael Davitt, *The Fall of Feudalism in Ireland, or, the Story of the Land League Revolution* (London & New York, 1904), p. 64.
9. Ibid., p. 66.
10. *Irish Daily Independent*, 14 November 1892. In *Here and There Memories* (London, 1896, published as by H-R-N), John Joseph Dunne, an associate of Isaac Butt who supported Parnell in the split, explicitly claims Davitt's father had been a process-server (i.e. a bailiff). Neither Dunne nor Wyse Power claims any direct knowledge, and the story may be no more than an example of the bitter rumours which proliferated during the Parnell split.
11. An Irish Liberal, *The Speaker's Handbook on the Irish Question* (London, n.d.) p. 115.
12. Indeed, Lalor's twentieth-century nationalist admirers were surprised in 1962 when T.P. O'Neill revealed that in 1843 Lalor had written to Peel advising the Conservative government to take up land reform as a means of killing the Repeal movement.
13. Philip. A. Fennell, 'History into myth: The *Catalpa*'s long voyage', *New Hibernia Review*, 9, 1 (2005), pp. 770–4.
14. Quoted in Montagu, *Recent Events*, p. 383.
15. Montagu, *Recent Events*, p. 636.
16. *The Work of the Irish Leagues: The Speech of the Right Hon. Sir Henry James, Q.C., M.P., replying in the Parnell Commission Inquiry* (London: n.d. [1890]), pp. 128–9.
17. Montagu, *Recent Events*, p. 397.
18. *Warder and Weekly Evening Mail*, 10 January 1880.
19. *Warder and Weekly Evening Mail*, 10 January 1880.
20. Andrew Dunlop, *Fifty Years of Irish Journalism* (Dublin, 1911), p.123.
21. Robert Anderson, *Sidelights on the Home Rule Movement* (London, 1906), pp. 110–11.
22. Davitt, *Fall of Feudalism*, p. 481.
23. Patrick Maume, 'Parnell and the IRB oath', *Irish Historical Studies*, 29, 115 (1995), pp. 363–70; Patrick Maume, 'Rebel on the run: T.J. Quinn and the IRB / Land League diaspora in America', *Working Papers in Irish Studies*, vol. 1 (2000), pp. 1–12.
24. PRONI, John Pinkerton mss, D1078 P/13, S.J. Dempsey to Pinkerton, 7 February 1885.
25. Mullin, *Story of a Toiler's Life*, p.188.
26. William H. Hurlbert, *Ireland under Coercion: The Diary of an American* (Edinburgh, 1889, 2nd edn), p. 391.
27. *Independent*, 1, 6, 9, September 1892.
28. Brian O'Higgins, *Wolfe Tone Annual 1952: Parnell and the Fenians*, pp. 31–34, 38–40, 44–45, 47, 49, 94 (Davitt 'sneers' at 'hillsiders'), 100 (Davitt accused of renouncing separatism, unlike Parnell) 112, 124. For O'Higgins' background see Brian O'Higgins, *Wolfe Tone Annual 1949: My Songs and Myself* (Dublin, 1949).
29. NLI, MS 8507(3), recollections of the Davitts by Sophie O'Brien; Laurence Marley, *Michael Davitt: Freelance Radical and Frondeur* (Dublin, 2007) provides independent confirmation of the servant's role but does not give details.
30. Hurlbert, *Ireland under Coercion*, p. 469.

CHAPTER SIX

Michael Davitt and the Irish Working Class

FINTAN LANE

In the subtitle to his classic biography *Michael Davitt: Revolutionary, Agitator and Labour Leader* (1908), Francis Sheehy-Skeffington, a self-described disciple, sought to define the contours of his subject's life by stressing his social radicalism, his preference for extra-parliamentary agitation and his connections to the labour movement. Sheehy-Skeffington, a pacifist and social radical, constructed a Davitt where the accent was firmly on his desire for social change, rather than on his militant nationalism; Davitt was revealed as a democratic hero, who boldly confronted imperial Britain, an iniquitous land system and the conservative opportunism of Parnell, and was simultaneously an 'Irish rebel' and a 'cosmopolitan labour advocate'.[1] In many senses, it is a beguiling image of Davitt, but the book did not go unchallenged.

Reviewing Sheehy-Skeffington's book, shortly after its appearance, the trade unionist and socialist James Connolly took issue with the positive depiction of Davitt's labour advocacy, particularly in Ireland, and suggested that in reality he was profoundly distrusted, and even disliked, by Irish labour activists. Connolly's critical assessment of Davitt is worth quoting at some length:

> We conceive of him as an unselfish idealist, who in his enthusiasm for a cause gave his name and his services freely at the beck and call of men who despised his ideals and would willingly, but for their need of him, have hung himself as high as Haman ... He fought and campaigned for the Labor Cause in England, yet for the sake of harmony in the ranks he also supported and campaigned for a party – the Home Rule party – whose leaders were

the bitterest enemies of the newly enfranchised workers of the
Irish cities.

Again and again have the industrial proletariat of Ireland
closed in grapples with the representatives of Irish capitalism,
but never was the voice of Davitt raised in such a fight on behalf
of labor. We are convinced that he was quite as sympathetic to
the cause of Labor in Ireland as in England, but he had surrendered himself into the control of men who were quite willing to
play upon Labor sentiments in England where such sentiments
might be made a menace to British aristocracy, but were determined to scotch and oppose such sentiments in Ireland where
they might become a menace to themselves. Thus, in his later
days, Davitt became the idol of the revolutionary English democracy, and disliked and distrusted by the revolutionary working-
class democracy of Ireland. A poor ending for such a career, and
solely due to the fact that he did not possess that knowledge of
men of which his biographer gives him credit. Honest himself,
he believed implicitly in the honesty of others, and became the
tool of political crooks and social reactionaries.[2]

Of course, excoriation by what Connolly termed 'the revolutionary
working-class democracy of Ireland' is unlikely to have greatly troubled
Davitt, as Irish revolutionary socialists were relatively exotic creatures in
the first decade of the twentieth century. However, Connolly and Davitt
were not strangers; they had worked together on the Irish Transvaal
Committee in 1899, when both were active in opposing the Boer War.[3]
Moreover, Connolly had first-hand and wide knowledge of the political
views of socialists and other labour activists in Dublin, and it is sensible
to assume that his remarks reflected a real and significant hostility
towards Davitt in those circles. It is likely that a great deal of this antipathy was fuelled, if not engendered, by the role that Davitt played in the
Parnell split of 1890–1, but it is clear also that the general character of
his interaction with the Irish working class was a factor. This chapter
intends to explore that relationship and, concurrently, will examine
Davitt's views on class politics, nationalism and the organised labour
movement.

SOCIAL RADICALISM AND NATIONALIST UNITY

When Michael Davitt and three other (now almost forgotten) recently
released fenian prisoners arrived in Ireland on 13 January 1878, they

were greeted on the quayside by the young fenian and social radical Thomas Brennan, who read an address of welcome from the 'people of Dublin', signed by Charles Stewart Parnell, Joseph Biggar, John Dillon, Thomas Brennan, Patrick Egan and James Carey, all men who would play prominent roles in the agrarian and nationalist agitation over the next few years.[4] In a sense, this reception committee, bringing together as it did separatists and home rulers, exemplifies the nationalist unity that Davitt believed to be essential if home rule was to be won. Such an alliance had been in the making since the early 1870s, but the 'land war' of 1879–82 made it a reality, though elements of the Irish Republican Brotherhood (IRB) chose to remain outside the tent.

The consolidation and protection of this strategic alliance between radical and moderate nationalists became a central theme of Davitt's political thought from 1879 and hugely influenced his public actions. In fact, the depth of his commitment to an inclusive home rule movement meant that he was wary of sectional and even class interests that threatened to cause division and strife within the nationalist camp. Those who suggested alternative strategies – such as the tactical use of dynamite, for example – were soundly condemned.[5] In his acceptance of the need for unity, discipline and a centralised leadership rooted in the Irish Parliamentary Party, Davitt was not unusual among those who embraced the New Departure of the late 1870s. In certain important respects, however, the boundaries imposed by the new movement weighed more heavily on him than most. The social policy of the Land League, and later mainstream nationalist organisations, almost entirely reflected the concerns and aspirations of the middle class, who dominated the infrastructure of the movement. This acted to constrain individuals such as Davitt and Thomas Brennan, whose social agenda placed them to the left of the national leadership. Indeed, arguably, it constrained their political thought and ambitions with regard to Ireland as much as it restricted their actions.

Davitt claimed in evidence to the Special Commission on Parnellism and Crime that his time in Dartmoor prison was spent planning the construction of the Land League movement.[6] That claim almost certainly contained a large element of hyperbole, but it does remind us of Davitt's proclivity for long-term and strategic thinking.[7] It was as a result of such reflection that he concluded that the best route towards Irish independence lay in the home rule movement striking up an alliance with Liberalism and with the British working class (and, more specifically, with Radical and labour organisations on the left fringes of the Liberal Party). He believed this, not necessarily because he saw it as the quickest route, but because he viewed the Irish demand for home rule as part of a wider struggle for democracy that embraced British working-class aspirations for enhanced labour rights and democratic reform. The Irish Parliamentary Party, and the majority feeling within the home rule movement, was against such an approach and Parnell felt free to play both sides in British parliamentary politics – Liberals and Conservatives – against each other, with little attention paid to their wider social agendas. In British politics, Davitt of the 1880s and 1890s was very much associated with left-wing Radicalism, which pursued its objectives largely through the Liberal Party, and this shaped his attitude not just to conservatism but to the emerging demand for independent labour representation, which he effectively resisted until the beginning of the twentieth century, despite appearing to call at times for an independent labour party.[8]

The influence of the British Radical tradition on Davitt was significant. His political thought was an admixture of British Radicalism and Irish nationalism, though the direct influence of US-based radicals such as Henry George and Irish-born Patrick Ford was also considerable. Although not a socialist himself, like many left-wing Radicals, he was sympathetic to the small socialist movement that emerged in Britain during the 1880s; he was, for example, on friendly terms with H.M. Hyndman of the Social Democratic Federation and was a subscriber to *Commonweal*, the monthly newspaper of William Morris's Socialist League. More importantly, Davitt was an advocate of land nationalisation, a policy promoted by left-wing Radicals from the mid-nineteenth century and popularised among a wider audience by Henry George's book *Progress and Poverty*, published in 1879.

It is not clear when Davitt became a supporter of land nationalisation, but his interest in this policy seems to have predated the 'land war' of 1879–82. Henry George, who is sometimes assumed to have convinced him on the issue, claimed in November 1881 that Davitt was a believer in land nationalisation before they met for the first time in 1880 in Patrick Ford's house in New York: 'His idea of the ultimate solution of the question went as far as mine does – he wished to secure the land of Ireland, not for a class, but for the whole people.'[9] In 1882, George repeated this claim in even stronger terms.[10] Indeed, despite their public pronouncements in favour of peasant proprietorship, there is some evidence to suggest that both Davitt and his close ally Thomas Brennan were believers in land nationalisation at the outset of the Land League movement. Henry George later wrote that Davitt, Brennan and John Ferguson of Glasgow wanted to make land nationalisation a part of the Land League platform at its formation, but this was apparently rejected by the more pragmatic Parnell and his lieutenants.[11] Davitt himself, while arguing for land nationalisation in May 1882, commented that 'those who believed *with myself* that peasant proprietary ... would not meet to the full the final solution of the Irish social problem were two short years ago put down as utopian dreamers.'[12] In 1891, he stated that he had been 'an advocate of land nationalisation from the foundation of the Land League'.[13] It is likely that Davitt and Brennan realised that there would be little support for this policy in 1879–80 and quietly shelved it; certainly, key figures in the west of Ireland – where the Land League agitation began – such as James Daly and Matthew Harris, were utterly opposed to land nationalisation.[14]

Nonetheless, Brennan's social radicalism, in particular, did occasionally come to the surface during the 'land war'. For example, speaking at a land rally in Carlow in March 1881, he declared:

> I think there is fast growing up a feeling among workingmen of all countries that they should join in a grand movement for the redemption of labour from the coercion of moneyed power. We have no fight with the English workingman; they have been betrayed, as you have often been betrayed, by men who are anxious only for their own interests ... We need to commence by uniting the workingmen in Ireland, no matter how they work or at what altar they kneel.[15]

However, in the interests of nationalist unity, neither Davitt nor Brennan made any serious attempt to push land nationalisation as a policy until after the 'Kilmainham treaty' of May 1882 and the effective end of the Land League as an organisational entity. Following Davitt's release from prison, also in May 1882, he briefly and vigorously campaigned openly for land nationalisation, but did so while vehemently denying any desire to cause divisions in nationalist Ireland.[16] He rejected, for example, the idea that he was a 'leader' of the national movement; instead, he positioned himself as a 'freelance' activist (presumably in an effort to disentangle himself from Parnell).[17] It is clear that Davitt anticipated some resistance to his policy of land nationalisation, but, as events transpired, it seems that he may have greatly underestimated the opposition that he was to face from Irish nationalists as he travelled through Britain, Ireland and the United

States promoting his New Departure; the Irish community in Liverpool was perhaps more prescient: at the conclusion of a major speech on the issue by Davitt in early June, the Irish women of the city presented him with a 'travelling rig' while the young men gave him a revolver.[18] The following weeks certainly involved much travel and considerable conflict, and, ultimately, Davitt was to admit defeat with a promise to let the matter drop.

Thomas Brennan, when freed from Kilkenny jail at the beginning of June, immediately backed Davitt's land nationalisation demand and spoke strongly in favour of prioritising the concerns of the working class. Addressing a large crowd in Kilkenny following his release, he asked:

> Of what benefit to the labourers are the recent Acts and schemes? The rich farmers refuse to build habitable houses for the labourers, refuse to pay an honest day's wages for an honest day's work, and as long as such a state of things remains there can be no settlement of the Land Question. Artisans of Kilkenny, what have you gained by the recent Acts of Parliament? Are you not part of the people who have a right to the soil of Ireland – you who alone remained faithful to the principles of the Land League ... and kept alive the embers of patriotism, whose strong hands wield the banner of industry and power? You surely have some right to the land of your birth, and until the equal right of every citizen of Ireland to share in the benefits the land of his country confers is recognised, there can be, aye, there shall be no settlement of this great social question. (*Great cheering.*)[19]

In an interview with Patrick Ford's *Irish World*, Brennan repeated his belief that rural labourers and urban artisans had a 'right' to 'their native soil equally with the farmers', and he linked the struggles for social and national liberation: 'When we win the social independence of the people, we shall also win the political independence of the nation.'[20] Henry George had said much the same thing with regard to the agrarian agitation when speaking alongside Davitt in Manchester a few weeks earlier: 'There is to my mind a very close connection between the Land Question and the Labour Question ... Questions of work and wages – what opportunities a man shall have, what he shall get for his toil.'[21] However, both Brennan and George were to the left of Davitt on this issue. In fact, Brennan had clearly highlighted what Davitt needed to do but would not seriously contemplate – look to the rural labourers, artisans and urban radicals to form the basis of a new movement for land nationalisation and social progress. Instead, it seems that Davitt's ambition was to convert the existing petit bourgeois land movement, or a sizeable portion of it, to his new social policy; this was never a likely prospect, despite the high regard in which he was held by many Land Leaguers. Perhaps Davitt overestimated his standing in nationalist Ireland, but, when he challenged peasant proprietorship, his reputation could not protect him and James Daly's *Connaught Telegraph* was soon publishing hostile commentary, including an editorial titled 'Michael Davitt on the Rampage' in which the 'father' of the Land League was blasted unmercifully for his 'wild and impracticable theories'.[22] As far as the rural middle class was concerned, land was immensely more important than any national 'hero'.

In retrospect, it seems clear that if Davitt had moved to build a new social *movement* – though it is not clear that he wanted to – rather than a propaganda-based agitation through public meetings, then he would have had to adopt class politics, split from mainstream nationalism and accept a less central role in political life. Most importantly, he would have had to look to different social forces than those that he worked with during the Land League period. In fact, possibilities did exist at the time for the creation of a viable labour-nationalist movement: the rural labourers had begun to organise seriously in 1881 and by June 1882 their leagues had spread across Munster and Leinster; this emergent rural labour movement was small in comparison with the banned Land League, but it was vibrant and had potential.[23] It was this labour agitation that Brennan probably had in mind when he spoke of embracing rural labour and the artisans; Davitt, however, was not interested in helping to build a labour-nationalist movement to the left of Parnell and the Irish Parliamentary Party. This unwillingness to break clearly from Parnellism, on the basis of a distinct social platform, meant that his agitation was doomed from the outset; there were no significant social forces behind him as he faced the wrath of conservative nationalism. When Davitt visited the United States in late June, he was publicly criticised by Parnell and by several other advocates of the New Departure, including Matthew Harris of Galway and James J. O'Kelly, the widely respected advanced nationalist MP.[24] The primary accusation, of course, was that Davitt was seeking to divide the nationalist movement, in pursuit of a utopian social agenda.

His response to the onslaught was to go on the defensive. He denied a rift with Parnell, claiming that his position was misunderstood: peasant proprietorship, he insisted, would naturally lead to land nationalisation.[25] At Antwerp, on his way back to Ireland in late

July, he went even further, declaring in an interview with the *Freeman's Journal* that he could 'afford to wait for the adoption of my views by an Irish people that will be ruled over by an Irish parliament ... I will not fight the question of Nationalisation if there is the slightest chance of creating dissension in the Land League.'[26] This retreat in the wake of a public chiding from Parnell was not a singular event. In April 1884, as Henry George was visiting Ireland, Parnell, speaking in Drogheda, again rebuked Davitt and warned against disunion – and again Davitt backed down, resentful in private but loyal in public.[27] Davitt's behaviour irked his friend Henry George, who, writing to Patrick Ford in early August 1882, for example, expressed his surprise and dismay at Davitt's timidity:

> Even their talk affected him so much that he was oft afraid to be seen with me or to have me go where he went. And they made him morbidly afraid of the *Irish World*. It seems to me pitiable weakness when a man's enemies can thus make him afraid of and unjust to his friends.[28]

There was a limit – a political boundary drawn in the late 1870s – beyond which Davitt would not go.

Indeed, a discernible boundary always seemed to exist with regard to the constituency that he reached out to. Urban workers and rural labourers would have comprised Davitt's natural audience for a policy of land nationalisation; nonetheless, he made little attempt to interest the working class, appearing instead to speak to the remnants of the Land League movement. Farmers and the urban middle class, however, were never likely to be impressed by such a policy and it is no surprise that he made little progress. He made no serious effort to engage with radical urban workers, such as those who frequented the well-attended debates of the Saturday Club in Dublin in the mid 1880s, many of whom supported land nationalisation.[29] Indeed, there was significant support for land nationalisation among Dublin radicals in the 1880s, but Davitt made no attempt to harness this energy.

In August 1882, he did suggest to Parnell that a 'National Land and Industrial Union of Ireland' be formed, largely to replace the banned Land League, but also to embrace the concerns of urban and rural workers.[30] Parnell dismissed Davitt's proposal. However, in the same month, Parnell endorsed and accepted the presidency of an organisation called the 'Irish Labour and Industrial Union', a body formed principally to bring local rural labourers' groups under Parnellite discipline.[31] Davitt's suggested 'National Land and Industrial Union' was an abstract proposal for a pan-class organisation that would include labour demands as part of a wide platform, whereas the formation of the Irish Labour and Industrial Union (ILIU) was the result of an organic process and the coming together of scores of local labour leagues that had emerged over the preceding twelve months. Indeed, within a few weeks of its founding, the ILIU was claiming roughly 120 branches, most of which were pre-existing local labour leagues that had affiliated.[32] Davitt had no tangible links to this grassroots social movement and did not attend the founding conference of the ILIU in Dublin on 21 August, though Henry George was among those present.[33]

In fact, Davitt continued to put his energy elsewhere. Despite accepting a place on the executive of the ILIU, he was soon focused on the establishment of a new pan-class, nationalist organisation. Following negotiations with Parnell, he was instrumental in the formation of the National League in October 1882. (Davitt decided not to raise the issue of land nationalisation at the founding conference, fearing that it would be divisive and lead to attacks on him by Parnell's lieutenants.[34]) One would have expected the ILIU to continue regardless, but it is clear that the Parnellites distrusted nationalist organisations that pursued what they considered to be 'sectional interests'. Davitt held much the same view and on 16 December, at an executive meeting of the ILIU, he successfully proposed a motion, seconded by Joseph Biggar, that the organisation dissolve into the new Parnellite body and 'that secretaries of branches of the union throughout the country be requested to communicate henceforth with the honorary secretaries of the Irish National League'.[35] In effect, Davitt pushed through the disbanding of a significant labour–nationalist organisation in the interests of pan-class unity, a unity arguably of considerably more benefit to the middle class than rural labourers.

DAVITT AND THE IRISH DEMOCRATIC LABOUR FEDERATION

Despite his important role in the formation of the National League, Davitt found himself relatively isolated within the new organisation, which he soon left; his closest allies in the Land League – Thomas Brennan and Patrick Egan – both emigrated to the United States in 1882 and he did not manage to cultivate equivalent collaborators in Ireland afterwards. Likewise, despite his social radicalism, he had little interaction with Irish working-class organisations during the remainder of the 1880s; that changed with the emergence of 'new unionism' in Britain and Ireland in the late 1880s. The new general trade unions, unlike the craft unions, recruited from among unskilled workers, deployed militant tactics and were often led by socialists or social radicals. An upsurge in labour activism was apparent at the close of the 1880s and the general unions, mostly British-based, began to recruit unskilled workers in large numbers in the major Irish cities.[36]

In rural Ireland, also, where labourers had remained largely disorganised since the formation of the National League, there were renewed efforts to construct a coherent labour movement. In the Kanturk area of north-west Cork – a district long associated with rural labour agitation[37] – a Democratic Trade and Labour Association was established in 1889, led by the journalist Patrick Joseph Neilan; this group soon spread to other parts of the Barony of Duhallow and, at a meeting on 22 September, a series of resolutions was passed calling for the establishment of a national labour organisation, local government reform (in particular, an extension of the franchise) and asking the Irish parliamentary party to 'introduce a measure next session to make all local bodies elective on the parliamentary franchise'.[38] Copies of the resolutions were sent to Davitt and Parnell, eliciting a response from the former expressing his solidarity with the Kanturk labour organisation, though he declared himself against calling on 'the Irish representatives to ask these reforms from the existing Parliament'.[39] One of the rural labour activists, having read the letter to a meeting in the village of Cullen, addressed Davitt's curious remark sympathetically though not uncritically:

> With reference to the last paragraph of Mr Davitt's letter, I would point out that the writer is opposed to seeking any concession short of Home Rule from the present Parliament. But as long as the Irish members continue to propose any measures of reform to that assembly, we shall insist that our grievances, as the heaviest, most indefensible and intolerable, shall obtain a leading place in their proposals. But if the Irish representatives should adopt Mr Davitt's policy of asking no concession, then we will support that policy and rather bear with the bitter injustice than for one moment press our claim to the endangering or delaying of the National deliverance of our country.[40]

By the end of 1889, the north-west Cork activists had linked up with organised labour in Cork city. Despite Davitt's reservations, he was invited to endorse the formation of a new national organisation aimed at bringing together the urban and rural labour movements, although in practice it was to concentrate on rural and small-town workers. Davitt agreed and he travelled to Cork city, where on 21 January 1890 he was the main speaker at the founding conference – chaired by Eugene Crean, president of the local trades council – of the Irish Democratic Labour Federation (IDLF), sometimes called the Irish Democratic Trade and Labour Federation. Although several historians, such as T.W. Moody and Emmet O'Connor, have assumed that Davitt was the prime mover behind the IDLF, it is clear that this was not the case.[41] One Kanturk participant, D.D. Sheehan (later a home rule MP), described the formation of the IDLF in the following terms:

> The founder of that movement was the late Mr P.J. Neilan, of Kanturk, a man of eminent talent and of a great heart that throbbed with sympathy for the sufferings of the workers. I was then a schoolboy, with a youthful yearning of my own towards the poor and the needy, and I joined the new movement. Two others – the one John D. O'Shea, a local painter, and the other John L. O'Shea, a carman (the similarity of their names often led to amusing mistakes) – with some humble town workers, formed the working vanguard of the new movement, what I might term a sort of apostolate of rural democracy. Our organisation was first known as the Kanturk Trade and Labour Association. As we carried our flag, audaciously enough, as it seemed in those days, to neighbouring villages and towns, we enlarged our title, and now came to be known as 'the Duhallow Trade and Labour Association' ... In time we interested Michael Davitt in our movement, and we achieved the glorious summit of our ambitions when we got him to preside at a Convention of our Labour branches in Cork, where we formally launched the movement on a national basis under the title of the Irish Democratic Trade and Labour Federation. The credit of this achievement was altogether and entirely due to Mr Neilan, who had founded the movement, watched over its progress, addressed its meetings, framed its programme and carried it triumphantly to this stage of success.[42]

P.J. Neilan became joint secretary of the IDLF, along with Michael Austin, a Cork city trade unionist and nationalist. The labour organisation was explicit in its support for the home rule movement, and its programme, as well defending the 'rights of the working classes of Ireland', claimed that they were seeking 'to aid the rest of our fellow countrymen, under the leadership of Mr Parnell, to obtain for Ireland the right to manage her own affairs through a Home Rule parliament

for the better development of the trade and industries of our country
and the general advancement of all its interests'.[43]

From the outset, because of his public stature, this new
labour–nationalist organisation – which was more a political body than
a trade union – was seen widely as Davitt's initiative. Although this was
not quite the truth, he did accept the position of 'president' of the IDLF
and he spent the following months actively promoting the organisation;
he also clashed privately with Parnell, who had reservations about such
labour activism, despite the explicit pledge in the IDLF programme to
support the Parnellite cause. On the day of the labour conference,
Davitt stressed that he had no intention of straying outside the param-
eters of the home rule movement and, while accepting that differences
might exist on particular policies, he argued that all could be accom-
modated within the movement in the same way that the Liberal Party
in Britain acted as an umbrella for differing political factions. Speaking
at the Assembly Rooms on the South Mall in Cork after the conference
had concluded, he responded sharply to a letter from a prominent Cork
home ruler who had accused him of coming to the city to divide the
nationalist movement; Davitt's emphasis on the importance of nationalist unity was striking, as was his endorsement of Parnell's leadership,
though he also insisted on the toleration of diversity:

> I have not always agreed with Mr Parnell, as you know…but I
> have always found Mr Parnell a tolerant leader (*hear, hear*) and
> a man of broad and generous mind, who knows that he is lead-
> ing a nation, who knows, as all the world knows, that he is lead-
> ing a nation made up of men not all of one way of thinking. It
> would be humanly impossible to find a movement in the civilised
> world, embracing so many people as our movement, where there
> is absolute unanimity of opinion upon all questions, social, polit-
> ical and educational. Mr Parnell recognises that, as Mr
> Gladstone recognises a similar state of affairs in the Liberal party.
> We know that in the following of Mr Gladstone in Great Britain
> you have six divisions to one that you find in Mr Parnell's move-
> ment, and yet Mr Gladstone wisely allows this divergence of
> opinion to exist because he knows that it is inevitable in his
> movement, and he is sure that, notwithstanding this diversity of
> opinion, his followers all trust in him as their political leader.
> The same with us. There never was a leader in any country at the
> head of any movement that had been so implicitly trusted as Mr
> Parnell has been by the Irish people (*applause*).[44]

Moreover, referring to the charge in the letter that he was attempting to establish a rival organisation, Davitt countered:

> Let him write to Mr Parnell and repeat what he says in this letter and, if Mr Parnell agrees with his charges, I would not be only willing to leave all Irish politics but leave Ireland (*loud cries of 'No, no'*) because I will not be a factor, and I have never been a factor, of disunion in the Irish National movement (*applause*). I contend ... that I have striven to unite Irishmen, not only in Ireland but the world over (*hear, hear, and applause*), and what I propose here now is to strengthen the Irish cause by additional organisation – not by antagonistic organisation (*hear, hear*).[45]

In fact, according to later claims by Davitt, Parnell was anything but tolerant towards the new labour organisation when they discussed it in London a few days later. Moreover, during the Parnell split of 1890–1, Davitt used Parnell's hostility towards the Cork initiative as evidence of his indifference to working-class concerns; he also recounted the conversation in some detail in *The Fall of Feudalism in Ireland* (1904). 'What is trades unionism,' Parnell allegedly remarked, 'but a landlordism of labour? I would not tolerate, if I were at the head of a government, such bodies as trades unions.' Parnell, according to Davitt, went on to say:

> Any agitation in Ireland, except one making directly for Home Rule, increases the obstacles he [Gladstone] has to contend against over here. It diverts attention from the main issue of our movement, and your new labour organisation in Cork will frighten the Liberal capitalists and lead them to believe that a Parliament in Dublin might be used for the purpose of furthering some kind of Irish socialism. You ought to know that neither the Irish priests nor the farmers would support such principles. In any case, your labourers and artisans who have waited so long for special legislation can put up with their present conditions until we get Home Rule.[46]

However, Parnell, in March 1891, rejected Davitt's account of this conversation, claiming that, when they met, Davitt had convinced him that 'nothing was further from his thoughts than to use the organisation as an element of disunion'.

> He [Davitt] expressed himself perfectly willing, if I desired it, to write to his friends in the South of Ireland and to say that he did

not intend to take any further part in the movement. I was perfectly satisfied with Mr Davitt's explanation. I did not ask him
to withdraw from the movement. He did not withdraw from the
movement. That movement has progressed from that day to this,
and is still in existence, and there is no truth whatever in his recollection that I asked him to stop the organisation or to interfere
with the movement in any way whatever.[47]

During the heat of the Parnell split, Davitt insisted that Parnell had
requested him to abandon the IDLF; however, bearing in mind
Davitt's previous public promise to withdraw if asked, it seems more
plausible to assume that the truth lies somewhere between Parnell's
and Davitt's accounts. It is likely that Parnell criticised severely the
emergence of the IDLF but, having received assurances of loyalty
from Davitt, did not press him to withdraw from the labour agitation.

CONFLICT AND CONCILIATION

Davitt's involvement with the Irish Democratic Labour Federation
was limited by the fact that he was living in London in early 1890, but
this connection was indicative of an increased engagement with
labour issues, especially in Britain.[48] He espoused a variant of Lib-Lab
politics, continuing to believe that working-class concerns were most
effectively addressed through the Home Rule and Liberal parties.
Writing in 1893, for example, he remarked that 'The trend of the
Home Rule movement is all in the direction of social reform and popular administration, and in this respect it is ... the Irish phase of the
great and all but universal Labour movement of our time.'[49] In British
politics, he supported Liberals rather than independent labour candidates during Westminster elections, except where the Liberal candidate was an avowed opponent of Irish home rule; his advocacy of a
genuinely independent labour party was essentially rhetorical and
remained so until the end of the century.[50]

He was an advocate of trade unionism, but he favoured conciliation and arbitration rather than industrial conflict, and he tended to
frown upon strike action. In early 1891, for example, while politely
declining to embroil himself in a labour dispute in Sligo, he commented to the trade unionist Michael McKeown:

> I would be glad if I could help in any way the men on strike in
> Sligo as I am sure from what you say they are entitled to full
> sympathy and support, though I cannot but say that in my belief

that the strike policy has been carried too far in the three countries [in] the last six months. I [believe it would] be a wiser and
ultimately more beneficial course to pursue in the interests of the
labour cause, to suspend strikes for a year to develop in the
interval ... the work of organisation and strengthening the financial resources of the movement.[51]

On the surface, this reads like the advice of a cautious and thoughtful
strategist, but, as John Cunningham has pointed out, it was entirely
impractical in the light of how disputes developed and in terms of the
expectations that workers had of their trade unions. As Cunningham
argues, the 'union members did not always have control over when
they went on strike; it could also be determined by the provocative
action of employers', and a trade union that ordered a twelve-month
moratorium on industrial action would soon 'have found itself bereft
of members'.[52] Davitt's suggestion showed little insight into the realities of industrial relations, but it was consistent with his general dis-
taste for strike action. In short, he was never a trade union militant,
preferring a moderate approach and a speedy resolution to disputes.
In Britain, his interest in labour conciliation saw him called upon to
act as a mediator during the Liverpool and Birkenhead dock strike of
February/March 1890. He successfully negotiated an end to the dispute, earning the praise of the National Union of Dock Labourers,
which had decided that the strike simply was not winnable in terms
of a comprehensive victory and was looking for a way out. The agreement mostly favoured the employers.[53] In the short term, the negotiated settlement did secure some better conditions for the dock labourers, but it appears that within a year the old conditions were re-intro-
duced and a greatly weakened union was unable to resist.
Nonetheless, Davitt successfully avoided a full-scale defeat for the
workers and allowed the union to retreat with some honour. Davitt's
skills at mediation were deployed in Ireland in the same month –
March 1890 – when Archbishop William Walsh of Dublin asked him
to intervene in two Irish labour disputes. The first was between the
Amalgamated Society of Railway Servants (ASRS) and the Great
Southern and Western Railway (GSWR) company. This intervention
by Davitt was less than successful and a resolution, which was
unfavourable to the workers, was not reached until May.[54] The second
dispute was one involving the Dublin Builders' Labourers' Trade
Union, which was trying to win a general pay increase for its members. On 19 March, the union called a strike and 2,000 Dublin

labourers came out for an increase of 4 pence an hour. They received substantial support from other trade unions and Archbishop Walsh's interference was resented by the union leadership from the outset. However, Walsh's public call on the union to accept conciliation meant that they were forced to accept Davitt as a mediator. In the event, the men returned to work on 24 March and a deal was worked out that Davitt claimed favoured the workers, but the union activists and Dublin radicals were less pleased. Indeed, Davitt's mediation was attacked as an utter failure by *The Commonweal*, the organ of Britain's Socialist League, which had a few members in Dublin at that time.[55] In addition, Davitt came into direct conflict with a group of Dublin radicals organised in the Irish Socialist Union.

The Irish Socialist Union was a small Dublin-based organisation, but its membership included several prominent 'new unionists', such as the printer Adolphus Shields, who was connected to both the Dublin Builders' Labourers' Trade Union (of which he seems to have been president) and the militant National Union of Gasworkers and General Labourers of Great Britain and Ireland, of which he was Dublin district secretary. In March 1890, Shields was in communication with Davitt on labour issues and he invited him to preside at a labour demonstration to be held in the Phoenix Park on the 30th of that month. Davitt refused, claiming that he would be out of the country at the time, but Shields and the Dublin Gasworkers discovered that, in fact, Davitt would be in Dublin on the day of the rally. The outcome was a public conflict between Davitt and Shields – conducted through the press – in which Davitt implausibly claimed ignorance of the Gasworkers' Union and its principles.[56] More pointedly, he demanded to know what the 'union proposes to do for the labour interests in Ireland which Irish labour organisations are unable to accomplish?'[57] Davitt argued for co-operation between British and Irish workers, but against the presence of British trade unions in Ireland. In a letter to the *Freeman's Journal* in early April 1890, he wrote:

> All I ask for as a humble advocate of the cause of Irish labour ... is that we are not deprived of the principle of home rule in our Irish labour organisations which is conceded to us by our friends in Great Britain in the matter of the future government or our country.[58]

Shields and the Dublin socialists, not surprisingly, saw this as an attempt to undermine 'new unionism', which was beginning to make some progress in Ireland. Before a crowd of 10,000 workers in the Phoenix Park, Shields blasted Davitt and accused him of showing little interest in the Irish working class; Irish workers, he claimed, had 'as much claim upon Mr Davitt as the labourers of England, Scotland and Wales' and, though he 'did not object to his helping the labourers of other countries … they should remember that charity began at home.'[59] Although Shields indicated support for Davitt's work with the British labour movement, it is clear that some Dublin radicals were resentful; Fred Allan, for example, who was a close collaborator with Shields in 1890–1 in spreading 'new unionism' in Dublin, had attacked Davitt's emphasis on the British working class as far back as November 1883. Allan, a leading IRB member, in a letter to the *Freeman's Journal* had written scornfully of Davitt's call for an alliance with organised labour in Britain: 'The English Radical or Democrat or working man has always been an Englishman before he is a Democrat' and one had to look back as far as Chartist times for genuine solidarity from the British working class.[60]

Another issue that rankled revolved around the weekly labour paper, the *Labour World*, that Davitt launched in London in September 1890; Dublin socialists and trade union activists had previously pleaded with him to found a newspaper in Dublin in order to strengthen the Irish labour movement.[61] In February 1891, as the Parnell split was at its height, John Coleman, secretary of the Athy branch of the United Labourers of Ireland Trade Union,[62] reminded a labour meeting of Davitt's decision:

> Mr Michael Davitt speaks of home trade; but when the workingmen of Dublin introduced the starting of the *Labour World*, he would not consent to start that paper until he saw it was a matter of £ s. d [pounds, shillings and pence]. He was requested to start that paper in Dublin; but this great apostle of labour and home trade started in London to be worked by a staff of English workmen, and printed on English-made paper, so that not one farthing has Ireland gained by this enterprise. Was this the man that expected the labour platform to be at his disposal to use it as he might, and asks the working classes of Ireland to follow his teaching?[63]

His choice of London was seen as indicative of an unwillingness to engage fully with the Irish labour movement, an accusation that might hold more than a grain of truth. Laurence Marley is surely correct when he states that Davitt's primary concerns in launching the *Labour*

World were 'his fundamental commitment to land nationalisation and labour, and his view that home rule for Ireland was in the interests of the British working class';[64] he did not conceive the paper as a mobilising agent for the working class in Ireland.

THE PARNELL SPLIT AND IRISH LABOUR

Relations between Davitt and militant trade unionists in Ireland worsened considerably following the Parnell split in early December 1890 that resulted from the O'Shea divorce case; Davitt was morally outraged by Parnell's relationship with Katherine O'Shea.[65] Adolphus Shields, and many other radical labour activists, supported Parnell and believed that Davitt, in his trenchant opposition to Parnell, had succumbed to Catholic conservatism and clerical dictation. The Parnell split also sundered the Irish Democratic Labour Federation, with P.J. Neilan taking the Parnellite side and damning Davitt as no friend of Irish labour.[66]

Davitt reacted to the fall of Parnell with gusto. Indeed, in an editorial in the *Labour World* he was one of the first to call on him to stand down as leader of the Irish Parliamentary Party.[67] When Parnell, in his increasing isolation, turned to the Dublin labour movement, Davitt reacted with vehemence. In March 1891, Parnell attended a labour conference, organised by Shields among others, and declared his support for a range of left-wing policies such as land nationalisation and the eight-hour day. Davitt was caustic in response. At a rally in Sligo town hall shortly after Parnell's declaration of support for the eight-hour day, Davitt mocked Parnell's new-found interest in the demand for a shorter working day with a direct sexual reference to Katherine O'Shea:

> I wish in my heart that Mr Parnell was in earnest in advocating it. (*Cries of 'He is not.'*) An addition has been placed to this programme by some of your local wags ... and it reads 'Eight hours work, and eight hours play: and eight hours in the company of —— .' (*Loud cheers and laughter.*) I didn't repeat these words. Mr Parnell would tomorrow call it hitting below the belt. (*Laughter.*)[68]

During the course of 1891, Davitt was one of the most energetic campaigners for the anti-Parnellite cause and he played a direct role in undermining Parnell's attempts to appeal to the Irish people. Parnell, a consummate opportunist, sought support from fenians, socialists and radical labour activists – and received it – despite his inattention to these constituencies in the past.

Organised labour in Ireland was severely affected by the Parnell split. The old craft unions and many of the trades councils attempted to steer clear of the controversy, though they were not always successful. In Cork city, for example, the local trades council was badly divided; the Parnellites, who dominated by a slight margin, were able to depose Davitt's allies Michael Austin and Eugene Crean as secretary and president respectively and replace them with Parnell loyalists.[69] Dublin Trades Council managed to avoid a similar purge and eschewed embroilment in the crisis, despite the fact that most Dublin workers seemed to strongly support Parnell.[70] In Waterford, another bastion of the Parnell camp, the trades council endorsed Richard Power, the local pro-Parnell MP.[71] While the craft unions struggled to ignore the controversy, the 'new unions', which were composed mostly of unskilled and semi-skilled workers, were more decisive in taking sides. Working-class communities were also divided by the Parnell split, though this is an area that, unfortunately, has yet to be seriously researched; it seems that workers in the larger urban cities and towns were more likely to support Parnell but this is a hypothesis that needs to be tested by micro-studies of political allegiances in localities before and after the split.[72]

In Dublin, Davitt's reputation was badly damaged among radical labour activists because of his anti-Parnellism. He had already incurred the wrath of the 'new unions' in March 1890 because of his failure to attend the Phoenix Park labour rally and by his decision to base the *Labour World* in Britain; in early November, these labour activists – who included Adolphus Shields, John Coleman and Fred Allan – established their own one-penny weekly labour newspaper in Dublin: the *Irish Labour Advocate*. When the Irish party deposed Parnell as leader, this new labour paper took a strongly Parnellite line and by the beginning of 1891 its directors included two Parnellite MPs – Alexander Blane and W.A. McDonald – as well as several well-known labour activists, such as P.J. Neilan, James A. Poole and Michael Canty.[73] Likewise, the Gasworkers' Union, which now had as many as fifty-nine branches in Ireland, was strongly associated with Parnell; certainly, the Dublin district organisation was actively Parnellite. Similarly, the Central Executive of the United Labourers of Ireland Trade Union, which had fourteen sections in and around Dublin, declared in favour of Parnell, causing their Mountrath, Co. Laois branch to dissolve in protest.[74] The Irish Democratic Labour

Federation was also affected and the 'parent branch' in Kanturk split when P.J. Neilan and the Cork city fenian and trade unionist Cornelius P. O'Sullivan pledged the loyalty of the IDLF to Parnell rather than Davitt; in fact, Neilan's action was quickly repudiated by John L. O'Shea, Michael Austin and Eugene Crean, and much of the organisation appears to have remained loyal to Davitt, though it went into terminal decline.[75]

With the collapse of the Irish Democratic Labour Federation, Davitt's interaction with the Irish working class diminished; both the *Labour World* and the *Irish Labour Advocate* folded as the internecine feuding continued through 1891. In fact, Davitt focused primarily on the anti-Parnellite cause in this period, even taking the position of secretary in the National Federation when it was founded in March and the *Labour World* became a vociferously anti-Parnellite paper. For many labour activists, Davitt's role in the downfall of Parnell, who died in October 1891, irreparably damaged his credibility. Parnell's conversion to labour radicalism was taken seriously by Irish socialists and other social radicals. In the mid 1890s, for example, when branches of the Independent Labour Party (ILP) were formed in Dublin and Waterford, the three leading organisers – Adolphus Shields, Robert Dorman and Laurence Strange – were all promoters of the myth of Parnell as a 'lost leader' of the left; all three, incidentally, were also Protestants and wary of the political influence of the Catholic Church. It is within this context that one should read the remarks by Connolly on Davitt that were quoted at the outset of this chapter. Likewise, IRB labour activists, such as Fred Allan and C.P. O'Sullivan, remained nostalgic for Parnell and hostile to Davitt; their admiration of Parnell was a curious position for separatist revolutionaries that would hardly have survived long if Parnell had not died in 1891. Imagine, for example, Parnell's reaction to the following espousal of Parnellism by Allan in 1894: 'I am a Parnellite on the two broad questions of clerical and English dictation, but I need scarcely say that I nor those who think like me ever take the remotest interest in the parliamentary work of the party, for we regard it as so much waste of time.'[76]

During the general election of 1892, Davitt promoted a number of moderate anti-Parnellite labour-nationalist candidates and two were elected – Michael Austin and Eugene Crean (both of whom had been associated with the IDLF) – but neither set the world on fire as labour advocates. When the Irish Land and Labour Association was formed in 1894, he spoke on its behalf from a number of platforms, despite hostility from some Parnellite elements. He also attended trade union conferences in Ireland, but he tended to act more as an observer than a labour advocate and never took on a position of leadership in the Irish labour movement.

CONCLUSION

After 1900, Davitt supported the emerging Labour Party in Britain, but he continued to give his backing to the Home Rule Party in Ireland; he was a dissident voice – arguably a labour nationalist – but he remained unflinchingly aligned to constitutional nationalism. The ambiguous nature of his place in Irish working-class history was underlined by the three general studies of the Irish labour movement that were published in the two decades following his death. James Connolly, unsurprisingly, scarcely mentioned Davitt in *Labour in Irish History* (1910), while W.P. Ryan, in *The Irish Labour Movement from the Twenties to Our Own Day* (1919), concurred with an element of Connolly's earlier assessment, when he wrote that Davitt 'felt compelled or was content to come nearer the level of his time', a pragmatism that Ryan excused limply by explaining that Davitt was 'before his time as great spirits often appear to be'.[77] The American academic Jessie Dunsmore Clarkson, in his *Labour and Nationalism in Ireland*, published by Columbia University in 1925, referred to Davitt only in passing.

Davitt's relationship with the Irish working class was troubled, complex and greatly informed by his prioritisation of the campaign for home rule. Until the end of the nineteenth century, he defined nationalist unity as the subservience of 'sectional interests' within the mainstream home rule movement; he was never an advocate of class politics in Ireland. Certainly, he could be described, in his Irish context, as a social radical and a moderate labour advocate, but Sheehy-Skeffington's description of him as a 'labour leader' is misleading and exaggerates his role in the Irish labour movement.

NOTES

1. Francis Sheehy-Skeffington, *Michael Davitt: Revolutionary, Agitator and Labour Leader* (London, 1967 edn), pp. 144, 148–9.
2. *The Harp*, August 1908.
3. Donal P. McCracken, *Forgotten Protest: Ireland and the Anglo-Boer War* (Belfast, 2003), p. 43.

4. D.B. Cashman, *The Life of Michael Davitt, Founder of the National Land League* (London, 1882), pp. 45–6; *The Irishman*, 19 January 1878.
5. Michael Davitt, *The 'Times'–Parnell Commission: Speech Delivered by Michael Davitt in Defence of the Land League* (London, 1890), pp. 60–1, 407–8.
6. Ibid., p. 2.
7. Davitt was severely restricted during his time as a fenian prisoner in the 1870s, but his writings from his time in Portland convict prison (February 1881 to May 1882) are clear evidence of his capacity for constructive reflection while imprisoned; see Michael Davitt, *Leaves from a Prison Diary*, 2 vols (London, 1885), and Michael Davitt, *Jottings in Solitary* (Dublin, 2003).
8. See, for example, his remarks in 1885 in Davitt, *Leaves from a Prison Diary*, vol. 2, pp. 160–1.
9. *The Radical*, 26 November 1881. F.S.L. Lyons, in his biography of Parnell, suggests that Davitt's time in prison in 1881–2 led to 'a profound rethinking of his position', and a Pauline-like conversion to land nationalisation, as a result of his reading of Henry George's *Progress and Poverty*; this is an improbable contention that is directly contradicted by George's claims before and after Davitt's release (see F. S. L. Lyons, *Charles Stewart Parnell* [London, 1977], pp. 230–1). However, it is likely nonetheless that Davitt's reading of George's book at this time did influence the depth of his commitment to land nationalisation and impelled him to campaign on the issue when released; moreover, the physical presence of George in Ireland and Britain in 1881–2 was almost certainly a crucial motivating factor.
10. *The Nation*, 1 July 1882.
11. Ibid.
12. *Manchester Examiner and Times*, 22 May 1882. My emphasis added.
13. *Labour World*, 3 January 1891.
14. For the views of Daly and Harris on land nationalisation, see Fintan Lane, *The Origins of Modern Irish Socialism, 1881–1896* (Cork, 1997), pp. 82–3, 84.
15. *Freeman's Journal*, 21 March 1881.
16. On Davitt and land nationalisation in the 1880s, see Lane, *Origins of Modern Irish Socialism*, pp. 77–90.
17. *Manchester Examiner and Times*, 22 May 1882; *Irish World*, 17 June 1882.
18. *Irish World*, 17 June 1882.
19. Ibid.
20. Ibid.
21. Ibid.
22. *Connaught Telegraph*, 1 July 1882.
23. Fintan Lane, 'Rural labourers, social change and politics in late nineteenth-century Ireland', in Fintan Lane and Donal Ó Drisceoil (eds), *Politics and the Irish Working Class, 1830–1945* (Basingstoke, 2005), pp. 124–34.
24. Lane, *Origins of Modern Irish Socialism*, pp. 81–2.
25. *Freeman's Journal*, 5 July 1882.
26. Ibid., 29 July 1882.
27. Ibid., 16 April 1884.
28. NYPL, Henry George Papers, Henry George to Patrick Ford, 4 August 1882.
29. On the Saturday Club and land nationalisation, see Lane, *Origins of Modern Irish Socialism*, p. 89.
30. Carla King, *Michael Davitt* (Dundalk, 1999), pp. 42–3.
31. Lane, 'Rural labourers, social change and politics', p. 132.
32. *The Irishman*, 30 September 1882.
33. *United Ireland*, 26 August 1882.
34. Michael Davitt, *The Fall of Feudalism in Ireland, or, the Story of the Land League Revolution* (London & New York, 1904), p. 379.
35. Lane, 'Rural labourers, social change and politics', p. 133.
36. John W. Boyle, *The Irish Labor Movement in the Nineteenth Century* (Washington, DC, 1988), pp. 104–17.
37. On Kanturk and rural labour agitation, see, for example, Fintan Lane, 'P.F. Johnson, nationalism and Irish rural labourers, 1869–82', *Irish Historical Studies*, xxxiii, 130 (November 2002), pp. 191–208.

38. *Cork Examiner*, 24 September 1889.
39. Ibid., 1 October 1889.
40. Ibid.
41. Theodore W. Moody, *Davitt and Irish Revolution, 1846–82* (Oxford, 1982), p. 548; Emmet O'Connor, *A Labour History of Ireland, 1824–1960* (Dublin, 1992), pp. 52–3.
42. D.D. Sheehan, *Ireland Since Parnell* (London, 1921), pp. 172–3.
43. *Cork Examiner*, 22 January 1890.
44. *United Ireland*, 25 January 1890.
45. Ibid.
46. Davitt, *Fall of Feudalism*, p. 636.
47. *United Ireland*, 21 March 1891. On this disagreement, also see F.S.L. Lyons, *The Fall of Parnell, 1890–91* (London, 1960), pp. 258–9.
48. On his involvement with the labour movement in Britain, see T.W. Moody, 'Michael Davitt and the British labour movement, 1882–1906', *Transactions of the Royal Historical Society*, 5th series, vol. iii (1953), pp. 53–76.
49. Quoted in Laura A. McNeil, 'Land, Labor and Liberation: Michael Davitt and the Irish Question in the Age of British Democratic Reform, 1878–1906', PhD thesis, Boston College, 2002, p. 257.
50. Davitt supported Keir Hardie in the Mid-Lanark election of 1888, but adopted an unfriendly attitude to the Independent Labour Party throughout the 1890s, even referring to Hardie 'and his friends of the Tory Party' during an 1894 by-election, while deriding Hardie's parliamentary record. Davitt believed that, tactically, it generally made more sense for Irish voters in Britain to support Liberal Party candidates, in the interests of home rule. On Davitt and the ILP, see David Howell, *British Workers and the Independent Labour Party, 1888–1906* (Manchester, 1983), pp. 141–2, 147, 155, 187.
51. Quoted in John Cunningham, *Labour in the West of Ireland: Working Life and Struggle, 1890–1914* (Belfast, 1995), pp. 22–4.
52. Ibid., p. 24.
53. Laurence Marley, *Michael Davitt: Freelance Radical and Frondeur* (Dublin, 2007), pp. 184–5; Eric Taplin, *The Dockers' Union: A Study of the National Union of Dock Labourers, 1889–1922* (Leicester, 1985), pp. 37–8.
54. Boyle, *Irish Labor Movement*, pp. 101–2.
55. Lane, *Origins of Modern Irish Socialism*, pp. 166–7.
56. For further detail on this controversy, see Lane, *Origins of Modern Irish Socialism*, pp. 167–9.
57. *Evening Telegraph*, 29 March 1890.
58. *Freeman's Journal*, 2 April 1890.
59. Ibid., 31 March 1890.
60. Ibid., 27 November 1883.
61. For an interesting discussion of the *Labour World* and Davitt's pioneering labour journalism, see Marley, *Michael Davitt*, pp. 99–128.
62. This union was previously known as the Dublin Builders' Labourers Trade Union, which had some interaction with Davitt in March 1890.
63. *Irish Labour Advocate*, 21 February 1891.
64. Marley, *Michael Davitt*, p. 125.
65. On the Parnell split, see Lyons, *Fall of Parnell* and Frank Callanan, *The Parnell Split, 1890–91* (Cork, 1992).
66. *Labour World*, 3 January 1891.
67. Ibid., 22 November 1890.
68. *Sunday World*, 5 April 1891.
69. Maura Cronin, *Country, Class or Craft? The Politicisation of the Skilled Artisan in Nineteenth-Century Cork* (Cork, 1994), pp. 115–16.
70. Seamus Cody, John O'Dowd and Peter Rigney, *The Parliament of Labour: 100 Years of the Dublin Council of Trade Unions* (Dublin, 1986), p. 31.
71. Emmet O'Connor, *A Labour History of Waterford* (Waterford, 1989), p. 96.
72. On the urban working-class base of post-1890 Parnellism, see Matthew J. Kelly, *The Fenian Ideal and Irish Nationalism, 1882–1916* (Suffolk, 2006), pp. 44–5.
73. *Irish Labour Advocate*, 14 February 1891.
74. Ibid., 21 February 1891.

75. *Labour World*, 3 January 1891.
76. Quoted in Kelly, *Fenian Ideal*, p. 126.
77. William P. Ryan, *The Irish Labour Movement from the Twenties to Our Own Day* (Dublin, 1919), p. 135.

CHAPTER SEVEN

Michael Davitt and the Irish Revolutionary Movement

OWEN McGEE

Michael Davitt joined the Irish Republican Brotherhood (IRB) at a time of great turmoil in Irish revolutionary circles. Up until the spring of 1865, the IRB was focussed on running the *Irish People* newspaper and simply establishing its organisation, sometimes through popular-political networks initially put in place by the confederate clubs of 1848. All this changed, however, when members of the 'Fenian Brotherhood', an Irish pressure group in American politics, set sail for Ireland during the final stages of the American civil war and tried to force a totally unprepared IRB to organise an immediate uprising. Some British intelligence agents, intent only on sabotaging the IRB, were to be found among these Americans. Partly as a result of this, the entire leadership of the IRB was arrested before the year was out, habeas corpus was soon suspended, while many more arrests occurred in March 1867 after the Irish-American 'fenians' forced futile struggles to take place between the police and unarmed IRB followers in Dublin and Cork. Once these arrests had begun, the IRB became a victim of informers and factional disputes.[1]

DAVITT, FENIANISM AND ENGLISH RADICALISM

As the Irish-Americans had set up their headquarters in Manchester, these developments naturally affected the IRB in northern England, which Davitt joined sometime during 1865. In February 1867, John Corydon, a British spy within the Fenian Brotherhood, helped to organise and then foiled a raid upon Chester Castle, while an attempt to purchase a large quantity of firearms in Birmingham (then the arms capital of Europe) failed when the leader of this operation, Ricard

O'Sullivan Burke, was arrested in November 1867. It was only then that Davitt became an active figure in Irish revolutionary circles, when he was delegated to take on Burke's responsibility of acquiring firearms, a job he did efficiently. As the police had already established an effective intelligence network against Burke, however, not surprisingly it was able to clamp down on Davitt's activities as well. He was arrested in Paddington, London, on 14 May 1870 and, three months later, he was convicted of as grave an offence as treason-felony, being sentenced to fifteen years' imprisonment and hard labour for simply purchasing firearms and arranging their transportation to Ireland.[2] In this pre-democratic age, the right to bear arms was still considered a basic civil liberty in Britain and, indeed, across Europe, but this liberty was severely curtailed in Ireland as a security precaution.

During 1869, Davitt promoted branches of the 'Amnesty Association' of England. This was set up to petition for the release of IRB prisoners and was led by J.P. McDonnell, a former IRB man and journalist in London who became Ireland's representative on the council of the First International.[3] On visiting the English capital in 1870, Davitt may well have become aware that many London Irishmen were involved in a short-lived English republican movement. This favoured a radical alteration of the land ownership laws in Britain, which were the most illiberal in all Europe: in no country in Europe was more land owned by fewer people than in the United Kingdom.[4] Following his amnesty from prison in December 1877, Davitt again became involved in popular political activity as well as in the IRB, of which he was elected co-leader in northern England around March 1878. Having spent seven long years in prison, however, Davitt was by now contemplating working instead with a British radical movement.[5]

After 1878, the IRB was financed by its Irish-American supporters to launch an extensive arms importation scheme and promote a radical tenant-right agitation. Davitt supported this initiative and felt that the IRB and the Irish Catholic establishment would have a shared interest in destroying the power of the landed gentry with a view to launching a political revolution. When other IRB leaders disagreed with him, he accused them of irrationally 'drawing a single-line of distinction between the West Briton and the Irishman who accepted its program'.[6] The IRB leadership was well aware of its need to find prospective political allies in the public sphere. Unlike Davitt, however, it was also aware of the history of all past Irish land agitations. Ireland was a country where 43 per cent of the landed gentry were

Catholics (48 per cent, including the most wealthy, were Church of Ireland, while 7 per cent were Presbyterian),[7] and so an attack on the property rights of the gentry was not something that Catholic elites were likely to support. There was an extensive history in post-famine Ireland, however, of the new propertied Catholic middle class in rural Ireland seeking to establish a more equitable relationship for themselves with the great landowners. As Davitt had no prior experience of Irish politics, he was less alert to these realities. Furthermore, since he had grown up in a Lancashire Irish community that had no reason to question the role of the Church in politics, he was never inclined to share the anticlericalism of much of the IRB leadership.

THE LAND LEAGUE PERIOD

The greatest impact Davitt ever made on Irish public life was undoubtedly as a result of designing the organisational structure of the Land League during the winter of 1879. This allowed for the existence of a central branch consisting of conservative elements, but kept control of the executive in the hands of radicals and permitted all branches to elect their own leaders, a mechanism that made the Land League a potential source of great political radicalism. Indeed, initially, it called on the Irish public to rely totally upon itself, not Westminster politicians, to achieve its goals.[8] After the 1880 general election, however, C.S. Parnell worked to have the league's organisational structure modified so that MPs would be included. Parnell also persuaded Davitt (against the IRB's wishes) to leave for the United States to collect funds, a development that led to Davitt's demotion from the Supreme Council. During his time in the US, Davitt vented his rage to John Devoy, the well-known Irish revolutionary exile in New York, regarding what he considered to be a reactionary, or untrustworthy, stance by the IRB leadership.[9] That summer and autumn, however, while Davitt talked passionately about the 'abolition of landlordism' in New York, Boston or Philadelphia, Parnell's supporters in Ireland worked with the Catholic hierarchy in calling for an agitation in defence of *both* the landlords' and tenants' rights. They also attempted to subvert the influence of various democrats or revolutionaries within the Land League, whose views 'smacked too much of Belleville and Montmartre [Parisian republicanism] for Catholic feeling to approve'.[10]

The IRB withdrew its followers from the Land League during the autumn of 1880, not least to ensure that its firearms did not fall into the wrong hands after peasant secret societies began committing outrages.[11] On returning to Ireland in November 1880, Davitt was quite angry to find that the Land League agitation was declining in several parts of the country because of the IRB's withdrawal. He would have little opportunity, however, to find out why this was happening. Within a couple of months, his amnesty was revoked and he was imprisoned without trial, being sentenced to solitary confinement in an English jail after he made a public speech that was interpreted by Dublin Castle as expressing sympathy with Irish-American terrorists.[12]

Davitt's imprisonment from February 1881 until May 1882 played a major role in creating his reputation as 'the father of the Land League' because he was made an icon of the whole movement for the duration of his imprisonment, not only in Ireland but also in Britain, where a land agitation had just been launched.[13] This iconising of Davitt, however, belied the fact that he never had a real opportunity of directing the Land League, having spent well over half of its existence either in the US or in jail. From prison, however, he could feel proud that his opposition to Gladstone's legislation of August 1881 (which provided for the setting up of state courts to settle land disputes) was shared by the league itself. Indeed, the democratically governed branches of the Land League opposed this legislation against the wishes not only of Parnell's party but also some of the IRB leadership,[14] the latter evidently fearing, correctly as it turned out, that Dublin Castle would clamp down on all popular political activity in the country if the league did not cooperate with the government's initiative. Indeed, that winter the league was suppressed and over 300 officials were imprisoned without trial, while auxiliary police forces were established to track down the IRB and its arms depots. This intelligence work reached even greater heights after a splinter group carried out the Phoenix Park murders on 6 May 1882, which led to the establishment of a very well-financed 'Crime Special Branch', set up to crush the IRB.[15]

AFTER THE LAND LEAGUE

The Phoenix Park murders no doubt increased Davitt's resolve to cease any connection with the IRB after his release from prison, justifying this decision to John O'Leary by apparently announcing that he had now become a socialist rather than an Irish nationalist.[16] In practical terms, however, Davitt's career as an Irish social radical agitator had already come to an end. As Parnell had pledged himself under the

'Kilmainham treaty' to cooperate fully with the British government in the future, virtually all Davitt's suggested policies for the National League (the proposed successor to the Land League), most notably that it should be independent from the control of Westminster MPs and governed democratically, were ignored.[17] As a result, the only public movement that Davitt could now identify with was essentially the land movement in Britain. Indeed, from 1882 onwards he spoke at several meetings of an emerging 'Christian socialist' movement led by non-conformist liberals in Scotland and England.[18] This movement favoured a policy of 'land nationalisation' through the democratisation of local government and the subsequent imposition by local government bodies of new 'land taxes' on the great landowners, thereby effectively making the British landed aristocracy subject to urban civil authorities for the first time.[19] This policy became practicable after the democratisation of local government in England, Scotland and Wales in 1888, which led, in turn, to the establishment of the first-ever labour party as well as public debate on socialism in Britain. To Davitt's irritation, however, this legislation allowing for democratic local government was not extended to Ireland,[20] a fact that doomed to failure his 'Irish Democratic Labour Federation' in the late 1880s and inherently made the 'land nationalisation' idea a complete irrelevance in Ireland. Indeed, Irish supporters of this policy, such as the Ulster Protestant radicals Richard McGhee and Edward McHugh, had no option but to turn their attention instead to the Scottish labour movement, as did Davitt himself.[21] During early 1884, a Belfast IRB activist, John Duddy, had also attempted to promote the 'land nationalisation' policy after he became the leader of the National League in Ulster, but this initiative was suppressed by Parnell that summer.[22]

Despite its standing army of 20,000 men and a semi-military police force of over 10,000 men, Dublin Castle augmented its security department significantly after 1881 because it was genuinely anxious about its seeming incapacity to govern Ireland. Apart from the formation of the Crime Special Branch in 1882, auxiliary Royal Irish Constabulary (RIC) forces were created in 1881 to work for new 'Special' resident magistrates – an extension of the existing resident magistrate system of justice and policing, the personnel of which consisted invariably of retired army officers.[23] This system, created and perfected between 1881 and 1887, formed the basis of all Dublin Castle's security work up until 1922 (including, most notoriously, the employment of auxiliary police during the war of independence), but the British government was always hesitant in implementing this system fully because it knew that it could then be accused of despotism. Indeed, from its inception, this system was always rationalised by British officials as one that should be activated fully *only* in emergency circumstances, when there was a need to deal with extensive 'crime'.[24] Practically speaking, it was seen as a perpetual and necessary alternative to formally deploying the army itself in Ireland.[25] If the army was ever used, it could create intense reaction and, more importantly, would make it impossible for the British cabinet to maintain its claim that its purpose in introducing special coercive legislation for Ireland was only ever to deal with *non-political* crime. This claim was absolutely essential to uphold at all times because the Irish administration, together with that in Britain, formed the administrative kernel of the whole British empire and, therefore, the degree to which its moral authority in Ireland was seen as politically unimpeachable inherently cast reflections on the credibility of the British political system everywhere.[26]

During 1883, the first leader of this new administrative system at Dublin Castle, E.G. Jenkinson (a former governor in India), wrote to cabinet members that securing convictions in cases of agrarian disturbances, or in cases against IRB leaders, was 'just as important' as solving the Phoenix Park murders case had been, as 'the future condition of all the counties in the west depends upon the results of the trials ... there must be perfect cooperation between the lawyers and the crime investigation department.'[27] That year, £6,500 was spent in buying informers while a further £2,725 was granted as rewards to men who were enticed to give information in court,[28] actions that were beyond the normal operations of British law but were justified by Jenkinson on the grounds that 'we are passing through a very critical time':[29]

> Ireland is passing through a revolution, and what we have to try to do is to guide her through that revolution without the shedding of blood, and without injury to certain classes, and to find a settlement which will be final, and will at the same time satisfy the aspirations of the Irish people, and not interfere with the unity of the British Empire, or the supremacy of parliament [Westminster].[30]

Although rural disorder was its greatest concern, Dublin Castle was anxious that the IRB (which still had almost 40,000 members),[31] along with Davitt's political supporters, might be able to force the Irish Party into adopting a revolutionary political stance. In April 1884, after completing 'a tremendous hunt after P.N. Fitzgerald [the IRB's chief travelling organiser]' and other ex-comrades of Davitt's on the Supreme Council (who were imprisoned),[32] Jenkinson, a self-professed 'home ruler at heart', wrote to the lord lieutenant in praise of Parnell's recent denunciation of Davitt's ideas on the land question.[33] Simultaneously, he advised the government to accept the reasoning of a prominent Irish priest who had called for improved British diplomatic relations with the papacy and stressed how Catholic politicians in the Irish Party only desired that their interests (particularly with regards to denominational education) were listened to and treated with respect: they did *not* desire political independence.[34]

Noting that 'we cannot always go on ... keeping the people down by force',[35] Jenkinson advised Gladstone's cabinet during the autumn of 1884 (just prior to the passing of legislation that tripled the UK franchise) that the time would soon be right for the prime minister to '*avow the principle* of Home Rule', even though the government should 'not grant it' for the foreseeable future.[36] Simultaneously, Parnell began negotiating with the Catholic hierarchy, offering them potential powers of veto over the choice of Irish Party candidates and policies through having a right to be *ex-officio* members of the National League executive, while the hierarchy, in turn, recognised the Irish Party as being the Church's spokesmen in British politics in October 1884.[37] These developments not only negated the possibility of the IRB imposing the revolutionary, or nationalist, New Departure policy on the Irish Party (calling for all MPs to withdraw from Westminster and making a stand for independence in Ireland, which the IRB would then back up),[38] they also reinforced the marginalisation of Irish radical democrats that had occurred during 1882. This was something, however, of which Davitt does not appear to have become immediately aware.

During the spring of 1885, Davitt worked with the hierarchy in their efforts to find trustworthy Catholics (whether nominally 'nationalist', 'unionist' or neither in sympathies was essentially beside the point) as Irish Party candidates for the forthcoming general election, while Davitt also began acting as the lay intermediary between Dublin and Rome for Archbishop Walsh, the recently elected president of Maynooth College.[39] As a sincere Catholic, Davitt appreciated the fact that Ireland had the only predominantly Catholic population in the English-speaking world and so the Irish population was central to Rome's missionary work both in North America and the British territories,[40] a fact that made the greater integration of Irish society into the United Kingdom opportune for the sake of the Catholic religion generally. Having rejected the nationalist cause of the IRB and committed himself to the cause of labour across the United Kingdom, Davitt was quite comfortable with this political situation, although he may have developed reservations as the critical November/December 1885 general election grew near. Writing to Richard McGhee that November, he complained that the Irish Party clearly 'fear the democracy' and that 'priests, parsons, Parnellites and peers appear to be on the one platform now' with the sole purpose of keeping Irish parliamentary representation conservative, or 'keeping the democracy out of Westminster'.[41] He also spoke during November alongside IRB leaders at Manchester Martyr demonstrations in Dublin and Tralee.[42] Nevertheless, Davitt's political and religious sensibilities clearly prompted him not to protest against the new high political consensus being established.

HOME RULE, THE STATE AND THE IRB

During early 1886, Davitt spoke before several Liberal party meetings in Britain in defence of the Gladstone–Parnell pact.[43] At the request of Parnell and Archbishop Walsh, he also spoke at the Chicago convention of the Irish National League of America (INLA) that August in defence of the Irish Party's and the Church's support for Gladstone's recent Home Rule Bill, a measure that would have granted Ireland no legislative or fiscal autonomy whatsoever.[44] In February 1886, the Catholic hierarchy had formally declared their total support for the (then) undefined concept of 'home rule' after various British political figures (including Jenkinson)[45] held private meetings with Cardinal Manning in London. Meanwhile, it is probable that Parnell's concerted efforts to commit the INLA to this new political consensus motivated the decision of Patrick Egan (a long-term friend of Davitt's and formerly the Land League treasurer) to resign suddenly as INLA president in January 1886,[46] rather than risk controversy by expressing political reservations in public. This 'first home rule episode' in Irish history, which stemmed from secret negotiations of which the Irish public were completely unaware, arguably formed the precedent, or basis, for all future developments in Anglo-Irish relations: the American historian Emmet Larkin has described it as a concordat-like arrangement between Church and state that was never broken.[47]

Jenkinson, who was granted a CBE in January 1884 and a knighthood in 1886 in recognition of his important role in managing Irish affairs,[48] remained a political supporter of Parnell up until 1890 and, being proud of his role in initiating the home rule settlement, even considered running for parliament himself as a Gladstonian home ruler.[49] After his retirement from the Special Branch, Jenkinson, being a Liberal, also provided information secretly to Davitt to assist him in countering the Tory propaganda campaign against Parnell during 1888.[50] Notwithstanding Davitt's support of Parnell at this time, however, he clearly felt some reservations about how the Irish Party leader managed the political situation during the early to mid 1880s. Once his own political career was over, Davitt admitted publicly that the eclipse of the Land League by a caucus controlled by Parnell and the Catholic hierarchy marked 'the counter revolution', resulting in a total containment of democracy in Ireland, as well as the demise of Irish nationalism,[51] a revolutionary politics previously maintained almost singularly by the underground IRB. Indeed, the IRB never really recovered from the setbacks it received during the mid-1880s,[52] while British intelligence clearly never lost its upper hand over the Irish revolutionary underground, particularly in the US, from that time onwards.

Between 1884 and 1890, a British propaganda war was waged against the IRB, their Irish-American supporters and, ultimately, against all who had formerly been connected with the Land League of 1879–81. This particularly grieved Davitt since it discredited himself and very many other popular agitators in the Irish political world. Therefore, he devoted much space to this issue in the *Labour World* (London) and delivered a retrospective and lengthy 'speech in defence of the Land League' at the *Times* Commission during 1889.[53] Davitt first became interested in this British propaganda campaign after he met Eugene Davis, a Parisian Catholic journalist, while on his way to Rome during 1885. Reputedly, Davis was actually the author of a lot of this propaganda:[54] later, he provided Davitt with information about Richard Pigott. Be that as it may, Davitt's participation alongside various Irish Party figures at the Special Commission (1888–90) was clearly intended to demonstrate to various Tory and Liberal critics his unwillingness to reverse the post-1886 political consensus. Indeed, at this event, Davitt, Parnell and many others generally denounced all Irish revolutionaries in strident terms.[55]

Although Davitt's career as an Irish revolutionary had clearly come to an end by 1886, privately he continued to be uncomfortable about various Irish political developments. For example, he was not impressed with the 'exclusively Catholic'[56] 'Plan of Campaign' agitation launched by sections of the Irish Party in late 1886 with the support of some Catholic bishops. This agitation called for 20 per cent rent reductions on particular estates so that, thereafter, comfortable farmers could better avail of 1885 legislation that allowed farmers to purchase all rights to their land in return for paying a single lump sum equivalent to twenty years' rent. Davitt's dissatisfaction with this agitation (which was boycotted by the IRB leadership) stemmed from the fact that it did absolutely nothing to assist the poor and landless classes in Irish society, namely the rural and urban working class. Meanwhile, more radical efforts at land agitation (run adjacent to, but essentially separate from, the Plan), such as 'no-rent' campaigns launched by rural IRB circles in counties such as Galway, Clare or Kerry, continued to be outlawed and suppressed by Dublin Castle, much to Davitt's irritation.[57]

LATER INTERACTION WITH FENIANISM

Between 1885 and 1888, Davitt occasionally engaged in political discussions with John O'Leary, the IRB's respectable face and public spokesman, at Dublin debating societies. By 1885, O'Leary was preoccupied by the rise of a heated politico-religious controversy in Ireland after Parnell practically committed the Irish Party into serving Catholic, rather than nationalist, interests, a development that had led to a rival (and equally confessional) 'Ulster Party' being established.[58] That August, O'Leary complained that 'slavish or corrupt' Irish Party figures were presenting their 'Chief' (Parnell) as being as 'infallible' as the pope,[59] while O'Leary also maintained that Ulster Protestants were fully capable of becoming Irish nationalists, for 'it is not that these people love England or English rule over much, but that they hate the Pope', and, therefore, Catholic clericalism in Irish politics was at the root of the ever-deepening polarisation between north and south.[60] Similarly, in February 1886, when the Irish Party's press denounced all Ulster Protestants as 'Orange bigots' and argued that 'to deprive the clergy influence in the State necessary means to deny the Church supervision over the morals of the people',[61] O'Leary responded by reprinting Irish nationalist writings from 1848 which protested that, contrary to the perpetual claim of the Catholic press in Ireland, it was not the Protestant Orangemen (who 'do not govern this country, or themselves') but rather the Catholic hierarchy that the British government always relied on to uphold the union in Ireland.[62] As a Catholic, Davitt was not inclined to enter into these debates, which touched too many raw nerves in Irish society. He was very inclined, however, to counter O'Leary's arguments at this time that the resolution of Ireland's difficulties depended on social and political leadership rather than the extension of the franchise. Indeed, there can be little doubt that Davitt's remark years later that some IRB leaders held an absurd belief that the gentry could be won over to Irish nationalism 'by learning Davis's poems or reading Meagher's speeches' was written specifically with O'Leary in mind.[63]

Notwithstanding his dislike of O'Leary, Davitt agreed in June 1887 to join him in becoming a patron of the IRB's recently established National Club on Rutland (later Parnell) Square, formed as a home for the Young Ireland debating societies (YIS).[64] Later that year, however, a serious controversy broke out between the IRB and the Catholic Church over the issue of who should have supervision of the GAA flock, a recently established nationalist and social movement which, like the YIS, the IRB was attempting to use to bring Protestants and Catholics together. Davitt was called on to mediate in these arguments between P.N. Fitzgerald and Archbishop Croke, and he tried to avoid taking sides in the dispute. On one hand, he resigned as a patron of the National Club but, unlike the somewhat parsimonious Archbishop Croke, he remained a generous patron of the GAA during the late 1880s.[65]

After returning from the US in the autumn of 1886 (accompanied by an Irish-American wife, having just married at the relatively late age of forty), Davitt was provided with a free home by Archbishop Walsh and started a new career as a businessman, creating an 'Irish Woollen and Manufacturing Company', a bottle-making business, as well as a fishing company.[66] Recently, he also acquired several wealthy and influential friends in Irish-America. These included Alec Sullivan, the leading political spokesman for the American Catholic community between 1884 and 1888, his wife, Margaret Buchanan Sullivan (a Catholic convert and leading spokeswoman for the American Catholic community until the 1900s), Patrick Ford, the editor of the New York *Irish World* (a journal that also changed its politics during 1886),[67] and Patrick Egan, who served as US minister to Chile between 1889 and 1893 and was for many years a prominent figure in Republican Party circles in New York.[68] Having such contacts, Davitt was often relied on to collect funds in America for the Irish Party, which he joined on becoming an MP in 1892. This further alienated him from John Devoy, his one-time ally. It also led James Connolly to denounce him during 1899 as a sham socialist on the grounds that Davitt often spoke in favour of non-denominational education, democratic local government and humanitarian prison reform in Britain, specifically to maintain his labour party support in industrial England, but regarding all Irish affairs, he acted as an arch-conservative and tool of the Irish Party.[69] Certainly, it appears that Davitt had resigned himself in his later years to accepting the political status quo within Ireland itself, and, quite naturally, continued to focus on his business career: in 1904, Egan informed him that he had contacted President Roosevelt and the president of the Russian-Chinese Bank (a confidant of the Tsar) to financially support 'your proposed news agency'.[70]

If Davitt valued having friends in high places, it seems clear that, on a personal level, he remained an unaffected figure in later life and was not inclined to disown less fortunate old friends. For example, he was solely responsible for organising a large demonstration (as well as erecting a cenotaph in Glasnevin) in memory of an old IRB figure, John 'Amnesty' Nolan, who had died alone, forgotten and in great poverty in New York city, but whom Davitt remembered because Nolan played a large part in campaigning for his release from prison during 1870–7.[71] During the late 1890s and early 1900s, whenever he was in Ireland, Davitt appears to have remained on fairly good personal terms with some ex-comrades on the IRB Supreme Council of 1878–80, while in 1899, after resigning as MP, Davitt accepted honorary membership of a public IRB veterans' association and workers' benefit society, known as the 'Old Guard Union' (the IRB itself, together with all forms of radicalism in Ireland, had virtually fizzled out during the early to mid-1890s).[72] In this capacity, Davitt supported a few republican commemorative projects, arranged the granting of charity to James Stephens (the destitute IRB founder, who always refused to work for a living) during the final year of his life and also financed Stephens' small public funeral in March 1901.[73]

CONCLUSION

In his introduction to *The Fall of Feudalism* (1904), Davitt reversed some of his former viewpoints by celebrating the special land courts and land purchase schemes that Whitehall had introduced in Ireland between 1881 and 1903, claiming (as did the Irish Party and the British government itself) that these measures had 'solved' the land 'question'. In recent years, however, historians have begun to dismiss this view as grossly simplistic, noting how the country still experienced great emigration every year, while the peasantry's struggle for land continued to be a major issue during the 'ranch war' of the later 1900s, the 'Irish revolution' of 1916–23 and even de Valera's economic war of the 1930s.[74] It should not be forgotten that land reform during the later nineteenth century was a UK-wide phenomenon, never a specifically Irish development, and the pace and extent of these reforms, as in the case of all pieces of Westminster legislation, was not determined primarily by Irish circumstances or the efforts of Irish MPs but by the needs of the two principal British political parties as they attempted to meet the perceived needs of the greater majority of their English, Scottish and Welsh constituents.[75] Equally, however, it should be acknowledged that the Land League slogan 'the land for the people' was essentially only a rally cry, rather than an actual policy, during Davitt's lifetime. Property remained the basis of political power, while the idea of a society where no individual would ever have to pay rent, due to the abolition of landlords or property owners, was certainly utopian and clearly never seriously considered, even by Davitt himself. However, Davitt's original programme for the Land League does raise some interesting questions of 'virtual history'. What would have happened if Davitt's political desires prior to 1886 had *not* been frustrated, if the National League was governed in the same radical manner as the Land League had been, or if local government was democratised in Ireland at the same time as in the rest of the United Kingdom?

While the threat of an Irish nationalist revolution underpinned the 'first home rule episode' of 1884–6 and, thereafter, became the basis of Anglo-Irish relations, Irish political society was probably far too deeply divided, or in too many ways, to make any struggle for independence practicable at that time. By contrast, the creation of an Irish labour party might well have happened during the mid-1880s if local government was democratised. Indeed, it is not a coincidence that the holding of the first democratic local government elections in Ireland during 1899 (the same year as Davitt practically retired from public life) coincided with efforts by James Connolly, P.T. Daly (IRB) and others to form a labour party. Although these efforts met with little success, the containment of agrarian and working-class radicalism ever since the forcible suppression of the Land League in October 1881 certainly played a significant part in ensuring this would be the case. Indeed, this factor, combined with the concordat-like arrangement established during the mid-1880s, was probably responsible for creating the strange 'one party', yet non-totalitarian, mentality which has been the predominant feature of modern Irish political culture ever since the Irish Party's hegemony was first established in 1886.[76] Davitt, however, was clearly never wholly comfortable inhabiting this peculiar political culture. Indeed, perhaps more so than anything else, it was Michael Davitt's firm belief in individual liberty of conscience, on a political and not just a religious level, that marked him out as one of the most thoughtful Irish political commentators of his day. This admirable personal trait of Davitt's – evident in so many of his writings – may well ensure that he will always be regarded by historians as one of the most significant figures in the political history of post-famine Ireland.

NOTES

1. The best account of these developments is Shinichi Takagami, 'The Dublin Fenians, 1858–79', PhD thesis, Trinity College Dublin, 1990, especially pp. 64–72, 191–202.
2. Theodore W. Moody, *Davitt and Irish Revolution* (Oxford, 1984, 2nd edn), pp. 53–105.
3. McDonnell's career is the basis of Seán Daly's study, *Ireland and the First International* (Cork, 1984).
4. Roy Douglas, *Land, People and Politics: A History of the Land Question in the United Kingdom, 1878–1952* (London, 1976), pp. 18–19; Moody, *Davitt and Irish Revolution*, p. 29; Royden Harrison, *Before the Socialists* (London, 1965), Ch. 5.
5. Douglas, *Land, People and Politics*, p. 28.
6. Speech of Davitt in Boston, 5 December 1878, published in *Irish Nation* (New York), 17 December 1881.
7. William E. Vaughan, *Landlords and Tenants in Mid-Victorian Ireland* (Oxford, 1994), p. 11.
8. Land League manifesto, republished in *Irishman*, 20 March 1880.
9. William O'Brien and Desmond Ryan (eds), *Devoy's Post Bag*, vol. 1 (Dublin, 1948), p. 555; vol. 2 (Dublin, 1953), pp. 21–5.
10. Alexander M. Sullivan, *New Ireland* (London, 1882, 2nd edn), p. 440.
11. Owen McGee, *The IRB: The Irish Republican Brotherhood, from the Land League to Sinn Féin* (Dublin, 2005), pp. 79–80.
12. 'Introduction' by Carla King to Michael Davitt, *Jottings in Solitary* (Dublin, 2003), p. x.
13. Douglas, *Land, People and Politics*, pp. 45–6.
14. McGee, *IRB*, p. 97.
15. Richard Hawkins, 'Government versus secret societies in the Parnell era', in T.D. Williams (ed.) *Secret Societies in Ireland* (Dublin, 1973), pp. 113–25.
16. O'Brien and Ryan, *Devoy's Post Bag*, vol. 2, p. 125.
17. Moody, *Davitt and Irish Revolution*, pp. 543–5.
18. A selection of these speeches are reproduced in Carla King (ed.), *Michael Davitt: Collected Writings, 1868–1906* (Bristol, 2001), vol. 1.
19. Douglas, *Land, People and Politics*, pp. 113–15.
20. Michael Davitt, *Leaves from a Prison Diary* (London, 1885), pp. 252–3; C.C. O'Brien, *Parnell and his Party* (Oxford, 1957), pp. 96–7.
21. For the history of Irish involvement in the Scottish labour movement of this time, see Máirtín Ó Catháin, 'Michael Davitt and Scotland', *Saothar*, vol. 25 (2000), pp. 19–28; Elaine W. McFarland, *John Ferguson* (East Linton, 2003); Andrew G. Newby, *Ireland, Radicalism and the Scottish Highlands, 1870–1912* (Edinburgh, 2007).
22. NAI, Police reports, ref. 3/715 carton 1, packet (iii), reports of E.G. Jenkinson and Chief Inspector Townsend, 5 March, 9 August, 16 October 1884; Michael Davitt, *The Fall of Feudalism in Ireland, or, the Story of the Land League Revolution* (London & New York, 1904), p. 502.
23. Charles Townshend, *Political Violence in Ireland* (Oxford, 1983), Ch. 3.
24. Ibid., BL, Althorp Papers, Add. 77031–37 (Jenkinson–Spencer correspondence, 1882–93).
25. Townshend, *Political Violence*, Ch. 3; E.A. Muenger, *The British Military Dilemma in Ireland, 1886–1914* (St Louis, MO, 1991).

26. Townshend, *Political Violence*, Ch. 3. Also, see Margaret O'Callaghan, *British High Politics and a Nationalist Ireland* (Cork, 1994).

27. BL, Althorp Papers, Add. 77032, E.G. Jenkinson to Lord Spencer, 18 October 1883.

28. BL, Althorp Papers, Add. 77032, E.G. Jenkinson to Lord Spencer, 15 January 1884.

29. BL, Althorp Papers, Add. 77034, E.G. Jenkinson to Lord Spencer, 14 September 1884.

30. BL, Althorp Papers, Add. 77037, E.G. Jenkinson memorandum regarding events of 1884–6 (dated 5 August 1886).

31. *Special Commission Act, 1888: reprint of the shorthand notes of the speeches, proceedings and evidence taken before the commissioners appointed under the above-named act*, 12 vols (London, 1890), vol. 5, pp. 143–4.

32. BL, Althorp Papers, Add. 77033, E.G. Jenkinson to Lord Spencer, 12 April 1884. Constant efforts were made thereafter to acquire information to help to secure convictions. (Add. 77033–4). McGee, *IRB*, pp. 110–12, 119–31.

33. BL, Althorp Papers, Add. 77033, E.G. Jenkinson to Lord Spencer, 19 April 1884.

34. W. Maziere Brady, 'A plea for an Anglo-Roman alliance', *Fortnightly Review*, 35, CCVIII (1 April 1884), pp. 453–62. Fr Brady, a native of Dublin, was then private chaplain to the pope.

35. BL, Althorp Papers, Add. 77033, E.G. Jenkinson to Lord Spencer, 19 April 1884.

36. BL, Althorp Papers, Add. 77034, E.G. Jenkinson to Lord Spencer, 14 September 1884.

37. O'Brien, *Parnell and his Party*, pp. 89–90, 128–30; Emmet Larkin, *The Roman Catholic Church and the Creation of the Modern Irish State, 1878–86* (Dublin, 1975), passim.

38. O'Brien and Ryan, *Devoy's Post Bag*, vol. 1, pp. 162–5; John O'Leary to *Irishman*, 11 January 1879, 3 April 1880; A.M. Sullivan, *New Ireland* (London, 1877), p. 394.

39. Larkin, *Roman Catholic Church in Ireland*, pp. 257, 263–4, 272–3, 275, 280, 282, 284 fn.

40. Larkin, *Roman Catholic Church in Ireland*, p. 257.

41. Douglas, *Land, Politics and People*, p. 53.

42. NAI, CSORP 1885/21082.

43. King, *Collected Writings*, vol. 1.

44. Larkin, *Roman Catholic Church in Ireland*, pp. 384–5. An Irish exchequer, or economy, had already ceased to exist by 1831. R.B. O'Brien, *Dublin Castle and the Irish People* (London, 1909), pp. 336, 342.

45. BL, Althorp Papers, Add. 77037, E.G. Jenkinson to Lord Spencer, 24 January 1886. Shortly beforehand, Jenkinson advised the cabinet to work very closely with Archbishops Walsh and Croke, as 'we know that the Roman Catholic Church is in favour of the Union'. Althorp Papers, Add. 77036, Jenkinson to Spencer, 20 December 1885.

46. *New York Herald*, 20 January 1886. Thomas Brennan, the (other) closest former ally of Davitt in the Land League, seems to have resigned from the INLA in late 1884.

47. Larkin, *Roman Catholic Church in Ireland*, p. 396.

48. BL, Althorp Papers, Add. 77033, Jenkinson to Spencer, 4 January 1884; K.M. Short, *Dynamite War* (Dublin, 1979), pp. 230–1.

49. BL, Althorp Papers, Add. 77037, Jenkinson to Spencer, 14 October 1891.

50. Christy Campbell, *Fenian Fire* (London, 2002), pp. 309–11, 378; BL, Althorp Papers, Add. 77037, Jenkinson to Spencer, 1 October 1888.

51. Davitt, *The Fall of Feudalism*, pp. 377–8, 466–7.

52. Owen McGee, 'Who were the Fenian dead? The IRB and the background to the 1916 rising', in Gabriel Doherty and Dermot Keogh (eds), *1916: The Long Revolution* (Cork, 2007), pp. 102–20.

53. Michael Davitt, *Speech in Defence of the Land League* (London, 1890). A bound volume of the *Labour World* can be found in TCD, DP, MS 9632.

54. Davitt would later give some credence to these rumours through his comments on Davis in *The Fall of Feudalism*, pp. 434–38.

55. Parnell, for example, freely admitted at the Special Commission that he considered Irish 'nationalism' a gravely criminal offence ever since he first entered public life in 1875. *Special Commission Act, 1888*, 12 vols (London, 1890), vol. 7, pp. 217, 227–8 (evidence of Parnell).

56. Laurence M. Geary, *The Plan of Campaign* (Cork, 1986), p. 3.

57. Ibid., pp. 74–5.

58. Alvin Jackson, *The Ulster Party, 1884–1911* (Oxford, 1986).

59. *The Times*, 25 August 1885 (speech of John O'Leary at Mullinahone, Co. Tipperary).

60. NLI, John O'Leary Papers, MS 8002, unpublished paper, 'Unionist and Home Delusions'.
61. 'The Church in Politics', editorial in the *Nation*, 20 February 1886. The editorial board of the *Nation* at this time was T.D. Sullivan, MP, T.M. Healy, MP, J.J. Clancy, MP, Dan Crilly, MP, Thomas Sexton, MP, Donal Sullivan, MP, D.B. Sullivan, BL (supplement to the *Nation*, 16 January 1886). Anti-Orangeman propaganda was also a frequent feature of Parnellite political cartoons of the time. L.P. Curtis, *Images of Erin in the Age of Parnell* (Dublin, 2001).
62. Richard D'Alton Williams, 'Orangemen – Irishmen', reprinted in *Irish Fireside*, 6 February 1886. Williams (1810–61) was a free-thinking Catholic who helped T.F. Meagher, another free-thinking Catholic, design the green, white and orange tricolour of 1848.
63. Davitt, *The Fall of Feudalism*, p. 117; Dominick Daly, *The Young Douglas Hyde* (Dublin, 1974), pp. 72–3.
64. NAI, DMP files, carton 2, folder entitled 'Fenian doings in Dublin city, 16 May to 7 June 1887'.
65. W.F. Mandle, *The Gaelic Athletic Association and Irish Nationalist Politics* (Dublin, 1987), p. 71.
66. King, *Collected Writings*, vol. 1, p. xviii; TCD, DP, MS 9562, Account book for the Western Islands' Fishing Boat Company (1886–1906). The latter company was co-owned with James Rourke, an ex-Land Leaguer who also ran the North City Milling Company, one of the largest bakeries in the country, formerly owned by Patrick Egan.
67. Up until 1885, the *Irish World* was a radical newspaper that had supported the Land League and the 'populist party' cause in America. After 1886, however, it became a Catholic newspaper that denounced all forms of radicalism; see J.P. Rodechko, *Patrick Ford and his Search for America* (New York, 1976).
68. TCD, DP, MS 9432/2584–2606 (Sullivan correspondence, 1888–93); MS 9483/4735–48 (Ford correspondence, 1899–1900).
69. *Workers Republic*, 2 September, 7 October 1899.
70. TCD, DP, MS 6569f/13, Egan to Davitt, 7 July 1904.
71. NAI, CSORP 1887/20584.
72. McGee, *IRB*, pp. 224–9, 296, 303–4, 319. Particularly after the semi-collapse of the IRB during the mid-1890s, it was common for ex-IRB figures in the Irish Party to engage in these activities in an attempt to convince rebels to throw in their lot with the MPs.
73. Stephens was given £10 a month (from the former 'Parisian Funds' of the Land League) during the final six months of his life, while £43 was spent on his funeral. Davitt spent £45 on Stephens' private papers. TCD, DP, MS 6569d/462–78.
74. Terence Dooley, *The Land for the People: The Land Question in Independent Ireland* (Dublin, 2004), introduction; Terence Dooley, *The Greatest of the Fenians: John Devoy and Ireland* (Dublin, 2003), p. 104.
75. For the interrelation between Irish, English, Welsh and Scottish land acts, see Douglas, *Land, People and Politics*, and John P.D. Dunbabin, *Rural Discontent in Nineteenth-Century Britain* (London, 1974).
76. Tom Garvin, *The Evolution of Irish Nationalist Politics* (Dublin, 2005, 2nd edn), pp. 176-7 and *passim*.

CHAPTER EIGHT

Davitt and Education

PAURIC TRAVERS

> Make no mistake about it, my Lord Bishop of Limerick, democ-
> racy is about to rule in these countries ...
> Michael Davitt, January 1906[1]

The last great campaign of Michael Davitt's life was on the subject of
education and, in particular, what he termed 'Home Rule in education'.
This was appropriate: education was central to his vision for Ireland
and was inextricably linked to his social and political philosophy.
When, in his last will and testament, he left to Ireland 'the undying
prayer for the absolute freedom and independence which it was my
life's ambition to try to obtain for her', there is no doubt that Davitt
understood that education was crucial to both real freedom and real
independence.[2] Early in 1906, he became embroiled in a short and
occasionally ill-tempered controversy with Bishop O'Dwyer of
Limerick on the subject of education. While the specific context was the
1906 general election and control of schools in England, it developed
into a wider debate on denominational education, diversity and local
control. The controversy came at an important moment in the development of the home rule movement and at a time when the moulds for
the future were being set. Davitt had a clear view of what shape the
future should take; needless to say, so too did the bishop of Limerick.

In this paper, I will examine Davitt's views on education: I will
suggest that educational reform was close to the heart of his mission,
that his views are revealing about his outlook and identity and that
they have a continuing relevance for contemporary Ireland. Davitt's
educational philosophy was shaped by his own family background
and upbringing. He combined the fenian suspicion of clerical prescription and the English radical attachment to local control and the
commitment to self-improvement and societal transformation
through education. His outlook was further refined by his experience

in prison, his career as an activist and campaigner in Ireland and his observations on different societies and systems during his extensive travels.

Davitt's own education was unusual by any standards, and not least for an Irish nationalist, extending as it did beyond the familiar confines of his own faith community. Restricted in his opportunities because of the amputation of his arm, education was also more than usually important for Davitt personally and for his progress. His earliest educational influence was his own family and, particularly, his father's informal 'evening school' when Martin Davitt taught his neighbours to read and write English. He attended Dan Burke's infant school before going to work in the cotton mill at the age of nine and later, following his accident, a local Wesleyan school run by George Poskitt, a gifted teacher. Significantly, he was encouraged in this by his parish priest, Rev. Thomas Martin, who believed in different denominations mingling together in one brotherhood.[3] Davitt recalled his four years in the Wesleyan school as a largely positive experience which helped persuade him that, depending on the context and circumstances, Catholics had nothing to fear from integrated schooling. Clearly the circumstances of ethnically and religiously divided Haslingden were somewhat different to those of his Irish homeland but this experience certainly encouraged Davitt in his exploration of alternative models for the provision and control of schooling.

Davitt developed and retained many of the characteristics of the auto-didact, notably the avid interest in reading and the commitment to personal responsibility in a life-long quest for self-improvement. In the typical trajectory of the British working-class activist in the Chartist tradition, he joined the Mechanics Institute, attending classes and lectures and becoming inducted into a rapidly expanding radical tradition. He recalled that the Mechanics Institute, one of the great English social and educational institutions, was 'the regular meeting place of men from factories and workshops who had the ambition and the stamina to improve themselves'.[4] Throughout his life, he retained a firm belief in the importance of such institutions in facilitating personal and social improvement as well as promoting scientific and practical education. He sought to promote the Mechanics Institute in Ireland, for example in his proposals for a National Land Reform Industrial Union in 1882 to replace the Land League; he also encouraged the establishment of public libraries.[5] He argued that economic prosperity for Ireland was inextricably linked to reform of technical education in particular but that both were dependent on 'a groundwork of solid, elementary, secular education'. The aim of such a system would be 'to nourish a muscular and practical intellectual growth'.[6]

For Davitt, education had a key role in rectifying social problems as diverse as criminal recidivism, emigration, agricultural backwardness, industrial under-development, cultural impoverishment or intellectual dependency. Whether the cause was prison reform, of which he was an eloquent advocate, or agricultural underdevelopment, education was Davitt's prescription: it was a means to rise above or transcend the restrictions imposed by poverty and class and to ensure real freedom. In June 1885, he told a friend that he wanted to nationalise not only the land of Ireland but also its administration and its education.[7]

When Davitt, then aged nineteen, became a fenian in 1865 he joined an organisation which had a fixed outlook on education and a clear disposition in relation to clerical influence and control. The fenians believed that the long- and short-term aims of education were or should be 'national' – to promote and support Irish freedom. The hostility of the Catholic Church to the fenians and its perceived acquiescence in, if not outright comfort with, 'English' rule entrenched anti-clericalism in that movement. As John Devoy wrote in the 1878 article that was a forerunner to the New Departure:

> We don't propose to turn over the education of the rising generation to the Catholic hierarchy, many of whom are the bitterest enemies of an independent Irish nationality. We want a sound national education for all creeds and classes ... Our grievance with regard to the present so-called 'national' system of education is that while the teaching is really very good, it is not national in any sense of the word, but the bishops offer us nothing better. The Catholic university wastes the people's money on illuminations for the Prince of Wales and gives its best professorships to English Catholics.[8]

One of Davitt's own conditions for agreeing to participate in the New Departure was 'vigorous efforts' to improve education and to eliminate 'anti-national bias'.[9] He was even more critical of education in Ireland than Devoy. Irish education was, he declared, 'a disastrous and humiliating fake'.[10] In 1900, in an article entitled 'What I think of the English', he wrote:

> ... take our system of education. This is placed in the hands of the anti-National party in Ireland – that is, the pro-British section – almost exclusively. It is in more respects than one the most back-

ward system of education in Europe. Its books are antiquated in purpose and in spirit. There is little or no scientific teaching found in them or imparted. The instruction given is suited more to any other purpose of life than to the purpose which should direct and influence the elementary education of a country, 70 per cent of whose people live upon or in connection with land industry. There is neither popular, local, or national control exercised over this educational system. It is all in the hands of a board nominated by whatever Englishman may chance to be the Lord Lieutenant or Chief Secretary for Ireland for the time being. And one of the chief objects of this reactionary system of popular instruction so administered has been to kill the Irish language.[11]

Davitt could not easily be dismissed as an anti-cleric. He retained devout religious convictions throughout his life. In Haslingden, he had actively supported a campaign in favour of his local church. When he burst on the wider stage as leader of the land agitation, he attracted the suspicion of many senior Churchmen in Ireland and the grudging admiration of others. His status as hero of the Land League was eroded somewhat in their eyes by his outspoken dismissal of clerical interference in the 'Plan of Campaign' in the shape of the Papal Rescript and his espousal of radical causes including land nationalisation and the cause of labour. Yet he continued to tread a fine line during the 1880s, even seeking to influence the appointment of a new archbishop of Dublin in 1885. The following year, when Fr Edward McGlynn, a priest in New York, was suspended by Archbishop Corrigan for his support of Henry George and summoned to Rome, Davitt was reticent to become involved but urged him to fight his case. He recorded in his diary that Fr McGlynn 'believes public schools should be upheld & that religion should be taught in churches. So believe I.'[12]

The Parnellite split temporarily brought Davitt back into the clerical fold – he took a virulently anti-Parnell stand both on pragmatic political grounds and because of his own stern moral code. The moral indignation in his attacks on Parnell and his apparent ease in the ranks of the anti-Parnellite vanguard shocked many of his radical colleagues. Ironically, and much to his discomfort, when Davitt won a bitterly contested election in Meath in July 1892 with strong support from Bishop Nulty and his clergy, he found his election challenged and overturned on the grounds of improper clerical interference. He responded with an article on 'The Priest in Politics' which was a subtle explanation, if not defence, of the role of the clergy in Irish affairs.[13] He argued that clerical involvement in politics was a product of British misrule and the educated status of priests and that their influence was only in proportion to the extent to which they identified with the national cause. Moreover, Irish voters had proved their ability to ignore the counsel of their prelates:

> The Church, in a political sense, is a tower of strength to a popular cause when its ministers are heart and soul with the people's aspirations. Churches may be dangerous to liberty when they are rich and trammelled by State obligations or by class influences. If the Catholic church had been endowed by the English government in Ireland, it would have lost every vestige of political power with our people. As it is, it has preserved an influence commensurate with the fidelity of its priests to the people's cause. It is only in their absolute devotion to the people's interests wherein resides their political strength. Wherever and whenever they have taken sides against the popular movement of this generation they have been beaten.[14]

Davitt predicted that, in a home rule Ireland, politics would divide along other lines and Catholic opinion would do likewise. In the autumn of 1902, he became embroiled in a public controversy with Bishop Clancy of Elphin. Ostensibly the point at issue was the landlord–tenant dispute on the de Freyne estate but it quickly deteriorated in to a more personal exchange, with Clancy accusing Davitt of preaching doctrines inimical to Church teaching and Davitt counselling the prelate to confine himself to spiritual matters and to desist from siding with the class enemies of Irish tenants.[15]

Davitt's views on education were unusual for a committed Catholic, at least one living in Ireland, but he consistently denied the accusation that he was an 'enemy of Catholic education' or that his views posed any threat to Catholicism.[16] At the time of the 1906 controversy, the *Irish Times* described him as 'a sound Roman Catholic' and 'a leading Irish Roman Catholic layman' who combined religious conviction with secularist and socialist views and suggested that the sincerity of his views 'have never been held in an instant's doubt. He cannot be frowned or shouted down like critics of other creeds.' According to the *Irish Times*, Davitt belonged to a type which was 'very common in France, and not uncommon in England, but of which, in Ireland, he is perhaps the only prominent exemplar'.[17]

Davitt thought deeply about how best education should be organised in democratic societies, and during his frequent travels in Australia, New Zealand and the United States frequently inspected schools and wrote about education. He believed that these countries were social laboratories from which working people in Britain and Ireland could learn much and he eagerly reported on their successes and failures in education, prisoner reform, extension of the franchise and democratic reform generally. It is significant that he gave the title *Life and Progress in Australasia* to his account of his travels in the antipodes in the 1890s. Davitt had a fixed view of the progress of society and sought signposts for the future wherever he could find them. The Australian colonies were, he wrote, 'a study in social and political independence, with men and women of my own race as the fortunate exemplars of courage, industry, progress and wealth'.[18] Irish emigrants in these countries were arguably part of the secondary wave of immigration rather than a founding people. Certainly they constituted a minority who were conscious of their disadvantaged and vulnerable status. This contributed in part to a propensity to establish a separate denominational education system rather than participate within the public system of their new homeland, as Davitt would have preferred.

In Australia and New Zealand, Davitt was impressed by the progress in public education at all levels but he was impressed too by the denominational system. Catholics, he reported, would have nothing to do with the public system so they supported their own system, which entailed sacrifice and hardship. This contributed to a sense of grievance which Davitt acknowledged, as, unlike Britain, no assistance was provided by the state. He visited large numbers of Catholic schools in Victoria, Queensland, Tasmania, Western Australia and New Zealand and found them generally 'in the capable hands of teaching orders and more than holding their own in the educational race with the schools of the State'. He felt that the Catholic schools had a great advantage because nuns and brothers were teachers 'not for salaries, but for higher considerations. They bring self-denying zeal and the energy of enthusiasm to their work, and are stimulated in the noble task of instructing youth by the taunts of those who think, or seem to do so, that education and Catholicism are mutually antagonistic.' Davitt then proceeded to offer an even more glowing endorsement:

> I will offer no opinion on the question of higher education, but in the tuition and training of children the ideal teacher is the Catholic Nun; and familiar as I am with convent schools in many

parts of the world, I have never found better teachers or happi-
er-looking children at school than it was my privilege to find in
each of the Australian colonies.[19]

Davitt was intensely aware of the Irish diaspora, its ongoing relationship with the home country and its contribution to shaping an Irish
sense of identity. He knew that this relationship and identity was
actively nourished by Catholic schools. From the 'wildest districts of
New Zealand' to the 'remotest gold-mining camps of Queensland', he
was greeted by children singing 'The Wearing of the Green' or
Moore's melodies or 'Come Back to Erin' – and was inspired by the
experience and renewed in his commitment to the cause of Irish freedom.[20] However, this presented something of a dilemma: philosophi-
cally Davitt's preference was for public schools but these inevitably
would tend to erode particularism and difference.

As in the case of clerical involvement in politics, Davitt struggled
to reconcile his commitment to democratic society – a central feature
of which, he believed, should be free, state-controlled, public education – with his nationalism and his belief in religious freedom, particularly for minorities. He insisted that religion had nothing to fear
from popular control of schools 'unless it be from the unwisdom of
churchmen, Catholic or Protestant, who consider all progress to be a
fatal strife against faith and who look upon Democracy as a power to
be fought or curbed'.[21]

Davitt's often-expressed preference was for a public education system that provided for religious instruction for all who required it. He
rejected the notion of a 'common form of Christian instruction' as it
'solves no difficulty. The Catholic and the Episcopalian and the Jew
will not agree to this, neither will the agnostic and the atheist – all are
equal in the eye of the State in the matter of educational rights and
civil and religious liberties.' He also rejected the other alternative
which he dubbed the American remedy – i.e. no religious teaching of
any kind. He argued instead for what he saw as the emerging
Canadian model: 'free education, in the full meaning of the term –
freedom for the citizen to have his child educated by the State and
taught in the faith of his Church, be that church what it may'.[22] Davitt
advocated that purely secular education should be provided during
school hours and that religious instruction should be provided,
preferably in churches, chapels and Sunday schools but, if necessary,
in school but outside of normal hours.[23] He also insisted that, insofar
as possible, religious instruction should be provided by clergymen

rather than lay teachers whose competence and commitment, he considered, was open to question.

Davitt observed to his own discomfort that democracies everywhere were inclined to pit themselves against the teaching of religion in state schools. In France and America, despite the principles of equality and fraternity which were claimed to underlay their revolutions, in England, 'where democracy rules more or less', and in Australia, 'where democracy is omnipotent', the prevailing sentiment was to banish religious instruction from state schools. Davitt attributed this to the policies rather than the teaching of the Churches, which had allied themselves to the cause of classes and dynasties – the old regime – and against the advance of democracy. He conceded that the problem of 'how to reconcile the conflicting interests of secular and religious teaching with State rights in the education of the people is not a simple or a single one'. However, he believed that in the longer term, a failure to resolve the issue satisfactorily would do more damage to the state and its cohesion than to the Church.[24] If friction were to be avoided, a just recognition of two rights was required: the right of the state, which was expected to pay for primary education to direct and control its purely secular interests and determine what is best for the education of its citizens, and the right of individual parents to decide whether their children would have a religious education and of what sort.

In his later years, Davitt became increasingly preoccupied with education in Ireland, and particularly elementary education. He corresponded with the Irish National Teachers' Organisation about the state of schools and repeatedly called for root and branch reform.[25] As a first step, he called for a 'radical reform of the existing national school system' which would embrace 'every portion of the educational machine – books, teaching, teachers, school and [...] management'. He was critical of both the structure and content of the curriculum and the organisation of schools. Schools, he contended, should be managed by a board elected by parents and the patron system should be abolished. The school principal should be the 'director of the school' and should not teach a class but supervise the instruction of the pupils and the work of the teachers. All classes should have their own rooms, and class size should not exceed thirty – he initially said forty. On the basis of his own analysis, he concluded that the English readers in use in Irish schools were inappropriate, 'barbarous and antiquated' and 'all sentimentality'. He criticised the lack of 'national' content, history and practical and technical education, the absence of references to industry, discovery and natural resources and, notwithstanding his own interest in poetry, the predominance of verse – there were 190 quotations from poets in the second to sixth class readers. He was particularly critical of the negative impact of teaching children in Irish-speaking areas through English in their early years.[26]

The education of females as well as males attracted Davitt's attention. He was critical of the resistance to female education in some quarters but equally deplored what he perceived as a tendency among those who could afford it to ape polite middle-class mores and elevate 'accomplished uselessness and learned indolence' as the goals of education. Davitt's interest was the education of the poor and their social improvement. In the case of girls, he argued that schools should prepare them in a practical way for 'the sphere of duty which Society recognises as essentially belonging to women but also with a view to their being qualified for those clerical and other light occupations which are rapidly becoming an open field for female labour'.[27]

Davitt's observations on the religious issue in schooling were based on societies where there were dominant and minority religious denominations or a multiplicity of denominations. Catholics were a minority with a sense of grievance. In Ireland, however, the situation was somewhat different – Catholics were in the majority. The 1906 controversy gives a clear indication of the evolution of his thinking in relation to Ireland.[28] It should be noted, however, that his exchange with Bishop Edward O'Dwyer arose as much from the English political situation as the Irish. The return of the Liberals to power in December 1905 after a prolonged period in the wilderness and the likelihood of their victory in the subsequent general election made the revival of the Liberal alliance inevitable and progress for the Irish and the radical cause a real possibility. Better still for a re-invigorated Davitt, a political breakthrough for Labour, which he had worked so hard to achieve, offered the possibility of an unusually favourable configuration in the new parliament. In this context, a public call from Bishop O'Dwyer for Irish support for the Conservatives in the election as a means of averting a perceived threat to Catholic schools in England was doubly unwelcome – on educational and pragmatic political grounds.[29]

Davitt had been infuriated by the stance adopted by the Irish Party on the Education Bill of 1902 when they had been reluctantly persuaded to defend the interests of Catholic schools in England by allying with the Tories and the Established Church against the non-conformists who complained bitterly of discrimination. Insofar as the return of a

Liberal government pledged to popular control of education posed a threat to Catholic schools in England, Davitt placed the blame squarely on 'the weak and culpable compliance' of John Redmond and the Irish Party and the interference of the Catholic bishops.[30] In any case, he unreservedly supported the Liberal programme for school reform. In April 1906, he wrote to Augustine Birrell seeking to influence the shape of the Education Bill which was then imminent. He estimated that 1.9 of 2 million English Catholics were Irish by birth or descent and the majority of them supported Irish nationalism, labour and the radical cause. He explained that his concern was for the 'better secular education' of this 'preponderating Irish section' and not the minority of English Catholics who were 'hopelessly Tory in political faith' and who were supported by all of the bishops and seven out of ten of the priests. To this end he suggested a solution based on a scheme of Cardinal Manning, published in 1882, which provided for universal education which was 'coextensive with the needs of the whole population', with religious instruction being provided by teachers or clergy at the expense of the Churches.[31]

In Davitt's view, the intervention of Bishop O'Dwyer threatened to set back both educational and political reform. He responded quickly and forcefully in a long letter to the *Freeman's Journal*, published on 22 January 1906. In his view, the best defence of English Catholic schools was a strong Irish Party and that was not likely to be achieved by supporting the Tories. As ever, he did not confine himself to pragmatic politics but addressed the central issue of popular control, which the prelate had been unwise enough to raise; he also turned his attention to Ireland:

> ... are there no schools here in Ireland requiring reforms; no education problems demanding solution on lines of modern progress and for imperative Irish secular and national needs; no Irish children to be intellectually equipped for the battle of industrial life; no youths of both sexes to be induced or sympathetically 'coerced' by new projects of a more hopeful kind than now prevail, to live and work in Ireland, instead of being 'educated' in Catholic schools and seminaries, as at present, to leave Ireland and enrich other nations, with the mental vigour and robust hearts and hands of a hardy Celtic race. Wake up, my Lord Bishop of Limerick, and look around you in your own country.[32]

For Davitt, the most pressing question demanding reform was the organisation and control of Irish schools which he saw as the ground-work for other reforms.

More forcefully than before, he argued the case for a public education system organised and funded by the state that allowed religious instruction for those who wished it. He rejected the argument that this posed a threat to the religious faith of Catholic children, pointing out that the 'people rule their schools' in America and Australia, and yet Catholicism thrived. He lauded the American system of universal and free secular education as 'the best all-round plan yet devised' and accused the Catholic bishops of supporting 'Castle' rule and denying the Irish people home rule in education. He made a stark prediction:

> Make no mistake about it, my Lord Bishop of Limerick, democracy is about to rule in these countries; and if you are wise, you will cease to uphold the class dominance in State and in Universities, of the Dukes of Norfolk and Lords Dunraven, and try to find in government by the people, the best and surest safety, for the religious and educational rights of all faiths, in equality for all, and in supremacy for none.[33]

In the exchanges which followed, Davitt was roundly attacked in strong and personal terms by the defenders of Bishop O'Dwyer – he was condemned as a Martin Luther and a sympathiser with international socialism.[34] While Davitt received many private letters of support for his 'manly and outspoken' letter, publicly there was outright hostility or a 'chilly silence'. James Murphy thoughtfully sent Davitt a letter which the editor of the *Weekly Freeman* had refused to publish; and more of his supporters had a similar experience, despite protest from Davitt. If, as Terence O'Brien assured Davitt, there were 'thousands of good Catholics who think as you do', few were willing or able to enter the lists publicly on his behalf.[35]

Dr O'Dwyer avoided engaging directly with Davitt but called on the Irish Party to defend Catholic schools and strenuously resist the forthcoming Education Bill. Davitt for his part responded with three further published letters (30 January, 6 February and 12 February) restating his position, arguing that O'Dwyer's view was not shared by his fellow bishops in other countries and that it was precisely short-sighted political meddling of this sort which associated the Church with the old regime and ensured that it seemed to be threatened by the advance of democracy.

At the beginning of Lent, on 25 February, both O'Dwyer and Archbishop Walsh of Dublin issued Lenten pastorals that strongly attacked Davitt but not by name. O'Dwyer dismissed the 'uninformed assertions of Anglo-Irish socialists' and referred to the 'proposed robbery of Catholic schools in England by the bigots who have temporarily got the upper hand in England' while Walsh denounced the 'great and growing evil' of newspapers affording widespread publicity to 'persons lamentably uninformed in such matters ... much harm is done by such publications, for, especially among the less intelligent and less educated class of newspaper readers, the mischief done by them cannot be counteracted by even the most effective replies.'[36]

This shot across the bows of the editor of the *Freeman's Journal* had the desired effect. A detailed letter of reply by Davitt on 2 March was not published. The editor requested Davitt to make some changes and omissions, necessitated, he felt, by the personally offensive tone of some references to the bishops. Davitt refused and the letter remained unpublished until its inclusion in Carla King's invaluable collection of his writings.[37] Davitt's reply did contain strong words but no stronger than had been used before both in the *Freeman* and in the bishops' pastorals. He categorised O'Dwyer's policy as blundering and his comments as 'hopelessly stupid' and 'spitefully vindictive' in tone and temper while referring in Walsh's case to 'the amiable and fickle disposition of a prelate who is not always too consistent with himself and who, as Cardinal Manning once said of a French Archbishop, "has nothing to recommend him but his goodness"'.

Davitt took grave exception to the use of the medium of the pastoral letter to attack and silence him on what he saw as a political matter. Perhaps in retaliation, part of his reply is a withering attack on Maynooth in comparison to Louvain as a centre of higher education but in the main the letter is a restatement and elaboration on his earlier arguments. He defended the public school system in America and repeated his claim that the Church was prospering in countries with public control of education, again citing statements from Archbishop Croke expressing satisfaction with the New Zealand system where denominational instruction in state schools was facilitated. He advocated the teaching of religious instruction in schools but urged that it should be 'made a real and an effective, and not a sham, teaching'. He predicted that leaving religious instruction to lay teachers would ultimately prove a sham and reminded the clergy that they should bear the main burden in this area of:

> In every word I have written or spoken on this question, I have tried to discuss it, not as it affects Catholics alone but as it con-

cerns the civic and secular education of all citizens, irrespective of religious differences. I have been governed by the conviction that Catholic rights in educational matters are strengthened in similar justice and treatment at the hands of the State.[38]

Davitt concluded that, where there were divided creeds or convictions, as in England, America, Australia and Ireland, the best system was secular schooling with appropriate provision for those of different denominations.

There was a wider Irish as well as an English context for this controversy, which is important. Since the appointment of Antony MacDonnell as under-secretary for Ireland in 1902, education at all levels had become a significant policy issue for Dublin Castle and the Irish Executive. The Irish university question, described by one student in 1904 as 'the oldest of all living Irish movements ... a sort of political Pompeii',[39] was the subject of intense public discussion and private negotiation which culminated in the settlement of 1908. Davitt was critical of the tendency of Irish Churchmen to see the university question in purely religious terms:

There is another besides the religious view of this question of University Education, and it is about time its importance to the vital interests of the country was insisted upon. It is true man does not live by bread alone, but neither does he exist very long in Ireland or elsewhere, even spiritually, without this same bread. In other words, the secular side of Education is of supreme importance, even if we consider the question from the point of view of the religious and moral welfare of the nation.[40]

He took an active interest in the university question and a characteristically independent stance, arguing the case for a publicly funded national university. He was critical of the Catholic bishops for their attitude to the 'Godless' Queen's Colleges and to Trinity College which impacted more on the less well-off than those who could afford to circumvent the ban. 'Irish Catholics,' he declared, 'have been deprived of higher education through the combined efforts of two policies and influences, represented respectively by our political rulers in London and our spiritual guides in Rome.' (Davitt initially wrote 'rulers' but replaced it with 'guides'.) He predicted that the bishops would oppose any settlement that did not allow them direct or indirect control. The country had 'so far patiently tolerated this state of things, notwithstanding the serious injury that has been done to its highest educational interest ... but the time has come when the people must ask themselves how long more it is going to be put up with. What we want is a National University and neither London nor Rome will give us this unless we assert the paramount claims of the people as to what Ireland requires and what she must have."[41]

In 1906, following an inconclusive commission, James Bryce, the new Liberal chief secretary, announced the government's support for a 'federal' university to consist of TCD, a new college in Dublin – with 'a Roman Catholic atmosphere' – and the three Queen's Colleges of Cork, Galway and Belfast. In the event a vigorous 'Hands Off Trinity' campaign ensured this option was unlikely to pass the House of Lords so Bryce's successor, Augustine Birrell, abandoned it and substituted a proposal that preserved the independence of Trinity and Queens Belfast and established the new National University of Ireland comprised of University Colleges Cork, Galway and Dublin. Although this outcome was widely welcomed by nationalists, it would hardly have pleased Davitt, whose desire had been for a national university that was unambiguously national and non-denominational. It was also the outcome least favoured by liberal, non-conformist opinion in England, which was opposed to the creation of what would, in practice, be denominational universities.[42]

The solution of the university question served no purpose unless it was accompanied by the reform of primary and secondary education. When he was appointed, MacDonnell had quickly concluded that some coherence should be brought to the mishmash of boards and bodies that exercised responsibility for education and contemplated the establishment of a department along the lines of the Department of Agriculture and Technical Instruction. Crucially this would have some element of popular and local control. This idea was subsumed into his ill-fated devolution proposals of 1904–5 and re-emerged in 1906–7 as part of the Irish Council Bill, which would have transferred responsibility for much of the administration of Ireland to a popularly elected council. Having been initially accepted by the leadership of the Irish Party, the 1907 Irish Council Bill was unexpectedly rejected by a nationalist convention in Dublin. Crucial to that outcome was the outright hostility of the bishops to the creation of a Department of Education and the transfer of control to local education authorities.[43] While this outcome lay in the future, it does highlight how critical these years were for Irish education and for Irish society. As Paul Bew and others have argued, they were also important in the direction of the Irish Party and the nationalist movement generally.[44]

What Davitt would have made of these events and later developments one can only speculate. However, he did leave us some clues: in April 1905, he published 'The Irish National Assembly', a humorous and, in some respects, highly prescient prophecy of the shape of politics in the future parliament of a home rule Ireland. He predicted that one of the first serious measures to be taken by the new government would be to protect the right of Orangemen to hold a Twelfth of July celebration in a district of mixed religious population, where serious trouble was anticipated by Catholics. In the area of education, Davitt predicted that the new parliament would debate and divide on the question of a proposed Catholic rather than a national university. The newly emerged National Democrats and the Labour members who commanded a majority over the Conservative Nationalists led by 'Sir John Waterford' (a thinly disguised John Redmond) would unite to insist on a system of education that was efficient and not wasteful from primary to university level. All sides would support religious instruction in public schools and adequate safeguards in colleges and universities against both anti-religious and proselytising influences. But, he continued, it would be demanded that Irish education should be 'national rather than denominational, and that the people who paid for the secular training of their children should exercise complete financial and administrative control over the entire co-ordinated system of education in Ireland'.[45] Davitt's predictions proved to be seriously astray in the area of education, a fact that would certainly have disappointed him. Policy and practice in the new state ran in precisely the opposite direction. However, the fundamental issues he raised remain as relevant today as they were a hundred years ago, perhaps, in some ways, even more relevant.

NOTES

1. *Freeman's Journal*, 22 January 1906; TCD, DP, MS 9373/981–2. I am indebted to Dr Carla King for advice and assistance in relation to sources for this paper.
2. 'Michael Davitt's Will', 1 February 1904, published as the final entry in Carla King (ed.), *Michael Davitt: Collected Writings, 1868–1906* (Bristol, 2001), vol. 2.
3. Theodore W. Moody, *Davitt and Irish Revolution 1846–82* (Oxford, 1981), p. 19.
4. Ibid., p. 21.
5. Michael Davitt, *Jottings in Solitary* (Dublin, 2003), p. 253; Bernard O'Hara, *Davitt* (Castlebar, 2006), p. 117; TCD, DP, MS 9653/20, 'Rough Notes on Popular Education in Ireland', n.d. [1906].
6. TCD, DP, MS 9653/20, 'Rough Notes on Popular Education in Ireland', n.d. [1906].
7. TCD, DP, MS 9518/5819. Letter reprinted in *Irishman*, 15 September 1928.
8. Moody, *Davitt and Irish Revolution*, pp. 252–3.
9. Ibid., p. 263.
10. *Freeman's Journal*, 30 January 1906.
11. Michael Davitt, 'What I think of the English', *Universal Magazine*, vol. 1 (July 1900), pp.

425–6; reprinted in King, *Collected Writings*, vol. 2, p. 4.
12. TCD, DP, MS 9663b/22, Davitt's diary, 13 December 1886.
13. Carla King, *Michael Davitt* (Dundalk, 1999), p. 59; Michael Davitt, 'The priest in politics', *Nineteenth Century*, vol. 33 (January 1893), pp. 139–55; reproduced in King, *Collected Writings*, vol. 2.
14. King, *Collected Writings*, vol. 2, p. 15.
15. For the relevant news cuttings, see TCD, DP, MS 9498/5212–40.
16. *Freeman's Journal*, 3 February 1896; TCD, DP, MS 9620/7.
17. *Irish Times*, 23 January 1906; TCD, DP, MS 9616/5778.
18. Michael Davitt, *Life and Progress in Australasia* (London, 1898), p. 307.
19. Davitt, *Life and Progress*, pp. 125, 326, 372.
20. Ibid., p. 126.
21. *Freeman's Journal*, 30 January 1906.
22. Davitt, *Life and Progress*, pp. 127–9.
23. *Freeman's Journal*, 30 January 1906.
24. Davitt, *Life and Progress*, pp. 126–7.
25. See, for example, TCD, DP, MS 9653/37, Davitt to Terence Clarke, Central Executive Committee, INTO, 28 March 1906.
26. TCD, DP, MS 9653/20, 'Rough Notes on Popular Education in Ireland', n.d. [1906].
27. Ibid.
28. For a good if occasionally partisan account of this controversy, see Francis Sheehy-Skeffington, *Michael Davitt: Revolutionary, Agitator and Labour Leader* (repr. London, 1967), pp. 199–214.
29. *Freeman's Journal*, 15 January 1906.
30. *Freeman's Journal*, 22 January 1906; *Irish Times*, 23 January 1906.
31. Davitt to Birrell, 4 April 1906, TCD, DP, MS 9653/93; for Cardinal Manning's scheme see *Nineteenth Century*, December 1882.
32. *Freeman's Journal*, 22 January 1906.
33. Ibid.
34. For negative reaction, see letters from 'A Catholic Democrat', and 'A Christian Democrat', *Freeman's Journal*, 30 January, 3 February 1906. See also *The Leader*, 3 February 1906; TCD, DP, MS 9516/5783.
35. TCD, DP, MS 9653/61, 68, 70, 79 & 81; Charles Birmingham to Davitt, January 1906; Terence O'Brien to Davitt, 22 January 1906; James Murphy to Davitt, 17 February 1906; Dan Shine to Davitt, 4 February 1906; Joseph Dundon? to Davitt, 6 February 1906.
36. Quoted in Sheehy-Skeffington, *Michael Davitt*, p. 204.
37. Sheehy-Skeffington, *Michael Davitt*, p. 205; Michael Davitt, 'Education: Denominational and National', 2 March 1906, in King, *Collected Writings*, vol. 2, pp. 1–17. See also Sheehy-Skeffington's earlier account in *Independent Review*, September 1906. John Dillon considered some of the passages 'very strong' and advised Davitt against publication. TCD, DP, MS 9653/31, Dillon to Davitt, 10 March 1906.
38. Davitt, 'Education: Denominational and National', p. 3.
39. Chanel, 'What are we to do?', *Irish University Advocate*, 1 May 1904, p. 18; quoted in Senia Pašeta, 'Trinity College, Dublin, and the education of Irish Catholics, 1873–1908', *Studia Hibernica*, vol. 30 (1998–99).
40. TCD, DP, TCD MS 9653/96, ms notes on University Question, n.d. [1902–1906].
41. Ibid.
42. Pauric Travers, *Settlements and Divisions: Ireland 1870–1922* (Dublin, 1988), p. 80.
43. Ibid.
44. Paul Bew, *Conflict and Conciliation in Ireland, 1890–1910: Parnellites and Radical Agrarians* (Oxford, 1987).
45. Michael Davitt, 'The Irish National Assembly', in King, *Collected Writings*, vol. 2, pp. 16–17.

CHAPTER NINE

'Put Not Your Faith in Irish Parliamentary Politics': Michael Davitt, Scotland and 'Loyal Opposition', 1879–1890

ANDREW G. NEWBY

The twin issues of Irish and Scottish land agitations have been linked in the minds of observers ever since a 'Crofters' War' began in northern Scotland in the early months of the 1880s. More recently it has often been taken for granted that the Highland land agitation led directly from the parallel agitation in Ireland, either through direct Irish intervention or the 'inspirational' impact of the 'land war'.[1] Direct Irish action in the Highlands was the work of a handful of radical Irishmen, based in Glasgow, and was undertaken with the close cooperation of migrant Highland Gaels in the city. These Irishmen often had to face a great deal of opposition from within their own community, which generally failed to understand their social reform ideals and perceived them at best as an irrelevance, but at worst as a hindrance to the main political goal of home rule. It must further be stressed that any cooperation over the land question was unusual in the context of Scottish–Irish antagonism both before and after the Crofters' War.[2] Only fleeting references in the decades immediately prior to its outbreak hint that there was anything other than mutual apathy, even antipathy, between Scotland and Ireland.[3]

One of the results of the burgeoning historiography of the Scottish Highlands over the last three decades is that the huge demonstrations of support which met Michael Davitt throughout the region in 1887 have come to represent Davitt's involvement in Scotland more generally.[4] Moreover, the historiography of Davitt's career, dominated until recently by the work of T.W. Moody, has emphasised the 'land war' period, and therefore associated him strongly with rural agitation.[5] The Highlands and Islands, as a rural parallel to the west of Ireland, have thus taken precedence over Davitt's interest in the urban low-lands when seeking to explain his activity in Scotland. This is despite the fact that during many engagements in Scotland he only visited the Highlands on three occasions: in 1882 he spoke in Inverness Music Hall, and in 1887 he had a tour of Caithness, Sutherlandshire, Ross-shire and Skye, before returning later in the year to address an audi-ence in Oban. He never again visited the Highlands, even though the 1893 Highland Land League convention was put back by two weeks with the sole intention of allowing him to attend.[6]

Davitt's interest in Scotland was prompted by internationalist social reform ideology and the potential for Scotland as a base for his 'loyal opposition' to Parnell as much as his advocacy of the Highland croft-ing community. It is, therefore, important to guard against overly simplistic presumptions based on theories of a shared Celtic identity and an overwhelmingly rural support base.[7] In Davitt's own analysis during the 1880s, the Lanarkshire miner, or indeed English factory worker, was just as oppressed as the Highland crofter.

LAND AND AGITATION IN SCOTLAND

Early manifestations of a land agitation in Scotland brought with it nervous references to 'fenianism' from the British press and authorities. A small-scale skirmish on the Hebridean island of Bernera in 1874 pro-voked limited disquiet, with *The Scotsman* claiming that local crofters 'were stimulated by a sort of Fenian conclave in the country, who are ever hostile to the "powers that be"'.[8] Although the idea of 'fenianism' in cases such as this was rather amorphous, provoked by the national fenian scares of the later 1860s and often used as a by-word for a more general sense of anarchy, the land question in Scotland would become ever more closely linked with events in Ireland.[9]

The advent of John Murdoch's campaigning *Highlander* newspaper ensured that the land became a central plank in a wide-ranging pro-gramme of reform he envisaged for the Highlands, and beyond.[10] From the outset, Murdoch was determined that his journal would stimulate Highlanders into affirmative action to better their position.[11] Having been influenced during his stint as an excise man in Dublin in the 1850s by the writing of James Fintan Lalor, Murdoch also hoped to present an alternative to the standard portrayal of Ireland.[12] Furthermore, he had lived in Lancashire and attended Chartist meetings during the

1840s, adding to the affinity he would feel with Davitt and an urban dimension to his land reform agenda.[13] John Murdoch's voice was one of many which ridiculed the idea of Irish agitators directly fomenting crofter grievances, but it was also Murdoch who tirelessly promoted the idea of a united approach between Irish and Scottish smallholders, English rural labourers, and even the English and Scottish urban proletariat, in prompting social reform.[14] It was during Murdoch's fund-raising tour of the USA and Canada in 1879–80 that he first met Michael Davitt, but it is likely that Davitt had been kept abreast of events in Scotland by John Ferguson, with whom he had first corresponded during the Amnesty campaigns of the 1870s.[15] Ferguson, indeed, spoke for Davitt at the iconic Irishtown meeting of April 1879.[16]

While Davitt had been imprisoned in Dartmoor, Ferguson, along with allies such as Edward McHugh and Richard McGhee, had helped to develop a strong Irish political organisation in western Scotland.[17] From the mid-1870s, Scots had commenced a friendly infiltration of the Home Government Association, and subsequently the Land League, in Glasgow.[18] Some of these Scots were protégés of John Murdoch and were actively involved in politicising urban Celtic societies. Others, such as the proto-socialists J. Bruce Glasier and J. Shaw Maxwell, had Highland blood but had grown up in an urban context.[19] Alongside John Ferguson's developing social reform ideas, which often mirrored (and may have been influenced by) those of Henry George, the presence of Scots, and the urban issues which surrounded political discourse in Glasgow, meant that Glasgow-Irish politics took on a more 'socialist' aspect than Irish politics more generally.[20]

Frequent meetings were held by these branches, but more importance was placed on the public demonstrations and mass meetings.[21] At a well-attended lecture in Glasgow in December 1879, Davitt bracketed the pit-owning nobility of the central coalfields with rapacious Highland lairds.[22]

> They would have read that the intentions of [the Land League's] organisers were to confine themselves to the organisation of Ireland alone, but they also intended to carry on this open war against landlordism into Scotland, England and America ... The time might come when the tenant farmers and people in Scotland might question the Dukes of Sutherland and Buccleuch and other landlords whether their titles to such large tracts of ground rested on any better foundation than confiscation ...[23]

Evictions in Wester Ross at this time, however, emphasised that the

land question in rural Highland Scotland had greater publicity potential than urban issues, and the Glasgow Land Leaguers helped
Highland campaigners to keep the issue of Highland evictions in the
public eye throughout 1880.[24]

Shortly after Davitt's imprisonment in Portland, a meeting of Land
League leaders in February 1881 saw John Ferguson express fears for
the future of the movement, with suppression inevitable if lawlessness
in Ireland persisted. One way of countering this problem was to cultivate the support of the English and Scottish people on the Irish question, and Ferguson, with his practical experience in this matter,
deserves as much credit as Davitt for persuading Parnell to advocate –
albeit temporarily – a 'junction' between Irish nationalism and the
British democracy.[25] One of the notable results of this meeting was the
establishment of the National Land League of Great Britain, with similar objectives to the Irish league but with the special responsibility of
disseminating ideas about the Irish land question throughout the
working classes of England, Scotland and Wales.[26]

August 1881 saw John Ferguson begin to refine the principles, as
he saw them, of the 'Land for the People' doctrine.[27] He claimed that,
back in 1879, no-one believed that a measure of peasant proprietary
could be gained from the government, but by 1881 'everyone' was for
it, including Gladstone and the press. The fact that they had convinced the masses of the validity of their claims, however, should have
been a platform for further reforms, not for complacency. Ferguson
explained further why owner-occupation was inconsistent with the
idea of 'the land for the people', and demanded the rejection of
Gladstone's land act. 'The great object,' he said,

> was to make the land not for a class, but for the nation; they did
> not want 10,000 landlords of Ireland, no more than they wanted
> 30,000 owners of Great Britain ... Natural Agents should be
> free: the air, the sunshine, the land ...[28]

The relationship between Irish agitators, Glasgow Highlanders and
the Skye crofters was strengthened by the establishment of the 'Skye
Vigilance Committee', effectively a local offshoot of the Irish Land
League, which helped to fund and publicise rent strikes on the
island.[29] A dispute over grazing land near Portree, on Lord
MacDonald's estate, during the winter of 1881–2 led to the tenants
withholding rent, and violence ensued when bailiffs were sent in to
recover the arrears.[30] This event, the 'Battle of the Braes', gained the
crofters' struggle celebrity throughout Britain and struck fear into the

heart of the government, who suspected an Irish nationalist plot aimed at throwing the whole country into chaos.

Though Skye took the headlines for a few days, political attention soon re-focused on Ireland. Under the terms of the 'Kilmainham treaty', Gladstone pledged to free imprisoned Irish leaders and extend the benefits of the 1881 Land Act in return for Parnell calling off the 'land war' and supporting the Liberals' home rule scheme. For Parnell, the 'land war' was over, but for Davitt and other radicals the 'treaty' was unacceptable, with the terms of the 1881 act falling far short of the root and branch land reform they desired.

If Davitt had planned to confront Parnell openly after the betrayal, as he saw it, of the 'Kilmainham treaty', the Phoenix Park murders, and the shock waves they sent throughout the Irish nationalist movement, forced him into a position of 'loyal opposition'. May and June 1882 saw Davitt make clear his support for Henry George at speeches at Manchester and Liverpool, followed by a disheartening three-month tour of the United States, where there seemed to be little support for land nationalisation.[31]

It was among the Irish in Scotland, and the Scots themselves, that Davitt finally found a willing audience. A contemporary comment from Henry George claimed that 'two-thirds of the population of Scotland now live in towns. It is not until these begin to realise their own direct interest in the settlement of the land question that the movement will reach the strength of which it is capable.'[32] The land issue in Scotland thus had a strong urban resonance, in addition to its better-publicised and more emotionally-charged rural aspect.

DAVITT'S 'SCOTCH CAMPAIGN' OF 1882

In the opening speech of his 'Scotch Campaign', in Glasgow, Davitt declared 'irreconcilable war on landlordism in Ireland, England and Scotland'; he also referred to the crofting agitation and joked that landlordism would soon be blown 'Skye-high'.[33] The audiences for Davitt's initial speeches were predominantly made up of exiled Irishmen, although he was heartened by the presence of a 'large number of Scotchmen' at Glasgow City Hall.[34] In Inverness and Aberdeen, where his audiences were more mixed, Davitt felt less inclination to stress his continued loyalty to Parnell. Davitt's discontentment with the situation in Ireland served to heighten his enthusiasm for the increasing possibilities in Scotland – 'put not your faith in Irish parliamentary politics,' he warned himself in his diary.[35]

Negative press reaction in Scotland tended to focus on Davitt's fenian past and his potential for transmitting 'Irish-style' agrarian mayhem into Scotland. The Inverness Tory newspaper, the *Northern Chronicle*, perhaps recognising Davitt's wider ambitions, warned readers that:

> The land-resumption scheme of Mr Davitt is only the thin end of the wedge, or rather the stone, by which the formidable Trade Unionist confederation wish to test the strength of the ice to see whether it will bear the nationalisation of mills, workshops, warehouses, railways, canals, banks, and capital in every shape and form ... Mr Davitt, in a small way, and the English Trades Unionists, in a less observable but far more powerful manner, are now trying to plunge this country into the vortex of all-swallowing socialism.[36]

Despite press assaults, it was with a great deal of enthusiasm for the Scottish agitation that Davitt left Greenock for Dublin the following Thursday.[37] Conversely, upon his return to Ireland, he seemed somewhat depressed about the cult of Parnell: 'Arrived in this dead country once again,' he wrote. 'Oh that I could really rouse it into full throbbing life once more ... But I fear it is a man-worshipping, begging nation after all. Still, *nil desperandum.*'

Enthusiastically, he described 'the active mind of the Scotch people', which had spent months, or years, considering the land question from 'various angles'. Because the land question had not yet assumed the crisis proportions seen in Ireland, it allowed for greater reflection in Scotland, a process also assisted by the nature of the people. Davitt considered Scotland, like Ireland, to be a 'landlord-ridden country', but felt that a 'land movement of the most advanced and radical kind' was more likely to develop in Scotland:

> Peasant proprietary finds no acceptance here; neither is the question of compensation to landlords exercising the consciences of the people overmuch. They are a logical, hard-headed people, who reason out their position first, and then resolve upon working out the legitimate conclusions, *coûte que coûte*. The native impulsiveness of the Celt is kept strictly under control by the intermixture of Saxon coolness and calculation, from which union springs a people possessed of qualities that enable them to give a good account of themselves, either where physical courage is required or in the higher moral field of intellectual effort.[38]

Although there was a good deal of debate about the merits of land nationalisation in the local press, there was little evidence that the mass of crofters were interested in anything more than an extension of the 1881 Irish Land Act, adjusted to local circumstances. The crofting question nonetheless retained great publicity value. Between 1882 and 1886, images of gunboats and marines being sent to quell disturbances in the Hebrides were used by various radical and Irish groups as stark examples of state aggression. And yet, although the establishment of a Royal Commission to examine the crofters' conditions, and the extension of the male franchise, gave grounds for optimism, Davitt, like Ferguson and George, came to see urban Scotland as the area in which radical reform would receive the most enthusiastic support and prompt the most determined action. Soon after writing this optimistic account, Davitt was imprisoned once more for making seditious speeches, but during his spell in Richmond Bridewell he was confident that Scotland was in capable hands.[39] The link with John Ferguson, and several years of political agitation with Glasgow's early labour agitation and the nascent Highland land question, gave Davitt a platform which allowed for a greater degree of 'loyal opposition' than was ever likely to be possible in Ireland or Irish-America.

LAND, LABOUR AND 'LOYAL OPPOSITION'

The formation of the Irish National League (INL) in October 1882 had emphasised the primacy of home rule over further land reform, though Irish political organisation in Glasgow continued along well-established lines. Davitt's allies in the city had congregated in the 'Home Government Branch' (HGB) and continued to speak out on all manner of social issues, often to the annoyance, and embarrassment of other INL branches in Scotland. The radicals were buoyed by the possible extension of suffrage in Britain and Ireland which, in Henry George's words, they hoped would 'end the power of the Parnell combination and give the lead to men of Davitt's type'.[40]

After his release from Richmond in June 1883, Davitt continued to lecture in British towns and cities, both on Irish issues and more general social problems.[41] When he spoke at Glasgow City Hall in February 1884, Scots took prominent positions on the platform. The main point of this meeting was to stress loyalty to Parnell as the Irish leader, but, subtly, it was proclaimed that 'the real leaders of men were siding with them'.[42] Antipathy increased between the 'Parnellite' Irish nationalists and the radicals, resulting in frequent, and often unconvincing, assertions of unity from Davitt.[43] His private contempt for Parnellism remained undiminished, confiding in Henry George that 'Irish people are too prone to man worship to lead a movement of ideas', and opining in his diary that the Irish Parliamentary Party were 'idiots' for not only ignoring the British land and labour movement, 'but actually to obstruct me in my efforts to help it along'.[44]

The leadership's increasing concern that Davitt's agenda was interfering with nationalist aspirations led to rumours that *United Ireland* was being used to sabotage a joint Davitt–George lecture tour.[45] Davitt himself, however, was acutely aware of the pitfalls of linking George openly with Irish agitators, and he expressed concern about Edward McHugh being chosen to accompany George around Scotland in early 1884. Davitt not only believed that McHugh was needed in Glasgow to agitate against the supporters of Parnell; he queried whether it would be 'politic' for McHugh, an Irishman, to do the work, again showing the sensitivity to public opinion that had characterised the early work of the Land League in Glasgow.[46] By 1884, opponents of the reformers knew that the radicals and the Parnellites were at loggerheads, but continued to emphasise a unity of purpose between them, such was the adverse reaction which Ireland could still provoke among the British public. McHugh dismissed such worries, and Davitt stayed away while two of his closest allies toured Scotland.[47]

George's Highland speeches were well received, but it was 'to the men of the cities' that he looked to be the standard bearers for reform.[48] Two meetings in Glasgow had the strongest impact on the land movement in Scotland.[49] Though not a sell-out, the first lecture drew an enthusiastic response from those who attended, and five hundred people remained afterwards to instigate a Georgite organisation.[50] As a way of launching the new body, the Scottish Land Restoration League (SLRL), the second meeting was held, with George as the chief spokesman, assisted by John Murdoch and William Forsyth, a Glasgow hotel proprietor who became the organisation's president. Membership in Glasgow grew briskly, and branches soon appeared in other cities around Scotland.[51]

Soon after the formation of the SLRL, during a speech in Drogheda, Parnell condemned both Davitt's plans for land nationalisation and his courting of the British working classes in almost mocking terms.[52] Davitt's fears that the 'man worshipping' Irish would blindly follow Parnell seemed confirmed when George's Dublin address was unenthusiastically received.[53] It is clear, though, that Davitt had sound pragmatic reasons for at least paying lip service to Parnell. Responding to a concerned John Ferguson in 1884, Davitt argued that any attempt to speak out against the 'retrograde speeches' of the Parnellites would be crushed at once as an attack on the leader himself:

> ... in my opinion to allow the country to wake up of itself to the knowledge that men who have been masquerading as land lea-guers are now insidiously apologising for landlordism ... There is great strength in a well-regulated silence, particularly when ideas are ripening in the popular mind ... Do nothing to create division, let it come through a defection from principle over the other side ... to preach ideas and not men, or wait for the victory of the franchise. On these lines, the future is ours, that is, it will be won by a platform of truth and justice.[54]

He advised his friends in Glasgow to continue with the attack on dual ownership and peasant proprietary:

> It is only by some such programme of labour on our part as that which you outline that the land movement in Scotland can be kept on the right lines, and the People's Cause from being attacked by the teachings of landlords' ministers on the one hand and compromise-proposing parliamentarians on the other ...[55]

The divisions between Parnell and Davitt at this time were reflected within the Irish community in Glasgow, with the HGB passing a vote of censure on Owen Kiernan, the organiser of the INL in Scotland, for his attacks on Davitt.[56]

With the franchise being extended, 1885 saw large numbers of Highlanders voting for the first time, and also saw a large-scale effort on the part of Highland land reformers to harness the potential of this new electorate. By the same token, although the extension of the urban vote was not so dramatic, many of the reformers were well aware that the new franchise could be used to further the cause of labour in the Scottish towns. Davitt returned to Scotland in November 1884, which presented him with an excellent opportunity to chart the progress of the land agitation.[57] In Hamilton, before a large crowd of mineworkers, Davitt made an explicit link between the urban and rural aspects of the land question:

> Mr Davitt ... first dealt with the alleged injustices done to all miners in general throughout Great Britain in the exaction of royalties. The remainder of Mr Davitt's talk was taken up with his views on the land question ... A series of resolutions were passed agreeing to form a Labour Union, and to send a message

of sympathy and condolence to the Skye crofters in their struggle against the landlords and the iniquitous land laws. The resolutions further deprecated the employment of an armed force
against a peaceful and law abiding people.[58]

Soon afterwards, at a meeting of the English Land Restoration League
in London, Davitt admitted that, although Ireland had been in the
vanguard of the land reform movement, there were, at that time,
more possibilities for radical reform in Scotland.[59]

With the home rule question taking on a critical aspect, the policy
of 'loyal opposition' from Davitt and his followers continued throughout 1885. Scotland seemed an ideal platform to promote radicalism,
and at the same time avoid open conflict with Parnell and his devo-
tees.[60] Even those other men who made up the 'left wing' of the Irish
movement in Glasgow spoke out on home rule, especially after it
became the main political issue in the whole of Britain, as well as
Ireland, after 1885. Having met secretly with Lord Carnarvon earlier
in the year, Parnell came to believe not only that a solid Irish vote for
the Tories could hand the Parnellites the balance of power, but also
the Conservative Party might be more inclined to 'concede a statutory
legislature' for Ireland in the event of an election victory.[61]

John Ferguson and the HGB split the ranks on a local level, advocating support for the SLRL candidates and their avowedly Georgite
platform, even if it meant keeping Tories out and therefore depriving
the Irish MPs the balance of power in Westminster.[62] Although Davitt
believed that attempting to persuade Parnell to allow support for SLRL
candidates would be 'useless', he eventually gave in to the wishes of his
Glasgow friends and issued a plea to the local electorate:

> ... strongly recommending the Irishmen to vote for ... the Land
> Restoration candidates on the ground that they are true friends of
> Ireland, and that the Scottish Land Restoration Association has
> made a gallant fight in the interests of true land reform, and in
> preparing the ground for more determined action in the future.[63]

The results of the 1885 election demonstrated the power of Parnell's
opinion, with SLRL candidates, including John Murdoch, receiving
hardly any Irish votes.[64] The subsequent recriminations divided the
Irishmen in Glasgow into those who prioritised social issues and those
who continued to champion the national cause above all.[65] Davitt was
perceived by nationalists as having sacrificed his principles on the
bonfire of land nationalisation.[66]

HOME RULE AND DAVITT'S HIGHLAND TOUR

If the 1885 election had demonstrated the gulf between opposite wings of the Irish nationalist movement in Scotland, the early months of 1886 brought a plethora of other divisions – this time between different reform ideologies – to the surface. The rejection of home rule by some prominent members of the SLRL forced Davitt, Ferguson and their allies to assert their nationality as well as their concern for social and land reform.[67] Moody wrote that Gladstone's attempt to get a home rule bill through parliament in 1886 had convinced Davitt of his integrity, and that Davitt thereafter 'regarded the Liberal party as entitled to generous support'.[68]

The Home Rule Bill came before Gladstone's cabinet on 26 March 1886, precipitating the resignation of the two leading radicals, Joseph Chamberlain and G. O. Trevelyan, along with some other minor ministers.[69] On 8 April, in a long speech to the Commons, Gladstone introduced the plan to the public – to establish a parliament and executive in Dublin, having power to legislate over all subjects which were not 'reserved' by Westminster.[70] The Crofters' Holdings (Scotland) Act received parliamentary assent in June 1886. As had been anticipated by the press, it followed many of the precedents set by Gladstone's 1881 Irish Act, offering security of tenure, freedom of sale and the establishment of a 'Crofters' Commission' to set fair rents.[71] Davitt also visited Scotland in advance of the 1886 general election, speaking in Glasgow and Galashiels in order to promote the 'case of Ireland before the Scotch people'.[72] He appealed to the general 'democracy' of Great Britain, arguing that home rule could provide a firm base for all the other social reforms they desired. After taking part in many other home rule speeches prior to the general election, Davitt spent the second part of 1886 in America.[73]

He made two short visits to Scotland in early 1887, speaking in Edinburgh on home rule and a month later embarking upon a mini-tour of the Clyde area, intended initially to promote unity between the workers of Britain and Ireland.[74] In April 1887, Davitt and Angus Sutherland, a Glasgow-Highland radical who had been elected MP for Sutherlandshire in 1886, toured the crofting districts of Scotland, shadowing the fallen radical hero, Joseph Chamberlain.[75]

Although Chamberlain's tour had been a long time in the planning, his motives were rather vague. His stated aim was to improve the lot of the toiling crofter and to lead them into a constitutional agitation. Additionally, he seems to have been genuinely concerned that the

Highlands was becoming too influenced by Irish politics.[76] In addition to countering Chamberlain, Davitt remained keen to prevent Scotland settling, as he believed Ireland had done, for mere tinkering with the land laws. The 1886 Crofters' Act, if accepted without amendment, would have meant that more radical solutions would be thwarted once more.[77]

In the midst of rhetoric which emphasised the common cultural heritage of the Highland and Irish Gaels, and their shared struggle for the land, Davitt's first trip to Skye seemed to leave him with the impression that there was little desire on the part of the local crofters to go beyond the 1886 act: 'If they obtain a 30 per cent reduction from the Crofter Commissioners,' he wrote, 'you will hear no more of agitations on Skye.'[78]

Although these suspicions were well founded, they underestimated the genuine fervour with which Davitt was greeted on the island, and this may indicate that his own priorities remained, at least privately, with land and social reform.[79] The crofter representatives at Skye welcomed Davitt, the 'martyr patriot of Ireland', as a 'harbinger of a bright day for the sea-divided Gael', before resolving that 'we deeply sympathise with our long-suffering and much enduring brethren in Ireland.'[80] Transport problems prevented Davitt from speaking at Oban, which was supposed to host the tour's finale, but he promised to return at the earliest opportunity.[81]

The major event in Davitt's life between leaving Oban in May and returning in July was witnessing evictions at Bodyke, Co. Clare, in June 1887.[82] As a result of the evictions, he appealed for the support of the Scottish people for his revised call for 'rational resistance'.[83] After Oban, he headed for Glasgow and Dumfries to proclaim that passive resistance must give way to 'rational resistance'. Davitt then attended a miners' rally in Kirkintilloch, where Angus Sutherland condemned the 'present social arrangements by which the wages of such necessary and useful labour of miners are only 14s. per week, while a man who does no service to society, such as feudal owners of land and mines, are in receipt of £150,000'.

The invidious position in which Davitt found himself in 1887 – between Parnellites who could see no value in the developing labour movement and radicals who deprecated the narrow nationalism of the Irish parliamentarians – continued for several years. For the Glasgow radicals, though, new political developments provided a focus for their efforts. Miners' agent and journalist James Keir Hardie had announced that the miners were prepared to begin their own political organisation, and in 1888 a by-election in Mid-Lanark meant that he would have the chance to stand against the Liberals and Conservatives as an independent 'Labour' candidate.[84] As in 1885, the Irish Parliamentary Party rejected any suggestion of supporting the labour interest, but now demanded a strong vote for the Liberals, who promised home rule on their return to power. It has been argued that 'even if all of the Irish had voted for him he still would have come in third', but Hardie himself made a great – ultimately fruitless – effort to win Irish support in Mid-Lanark, and he did this through the HGB.[85] At this stage, he claimed that the interests of Ireland and Labour were one, and that he would vote with the Irish members on Irish issues even if they were against the Liberals.

The activities of HGB members, likewise, continued to focus much more on labour than nationalism.[86] Ferguson chaired the St Patrick's Day speech in 1888, accompanied by Davitt.[87] The chairman's address illustrated how far these men had diverged from mainstream nationalism, when he stated that 'St Patrick was a social reformer. He came to Ireland not to establish a nationality – there was a nation there when he came.'[88] Although home rule and coercion dominated the early parts of his keynote speech, Davitt returned to social themes:

> We demand the land of Ireland for the people of Ireland. We will have no peddling with this great social question … this Irish movement had precipitated a social as well as a political issue in the three countries … Does the Lanarkshire miner, who risks life and limb every day for a few shillings, get as fair or just a reward as does the nobleman who walks off with £100,000 a year without soiling a finger or risking a single hair of his ducal head?[89]

While the formation of the Scottish Labour Party (SLP) in the summer of 1888 was not without ideological problems for the radical home rulers, many of whom refused to accept the SLP as a final break from the Liberals, they increasingly became viewed as pariahs among the Glasgow-Irish for their advocacy of labour, either through the single tax or through socialism.[90]

During the spring and summer of 1889, speakers including R. B. Cunninghame Graham, Prince Kropotkin and Shaw Maxwell were invited to address the HGB.[91] Still nominally an Irish body, the main debate in the branch was over the best method of superseding peasant proprietorship – land restoration or communalisation of both land and capital – and the Parnellites were condemned in strong terms for their own timid solutions to the land question: 'They desired to abolish the present landlord system and for what? To establish a greedy, avaricious and reactionary class, who through time would prove as big a curse."[92]

In July 1889, when Parnell was granted the freedom of the city of Edinburgh, over 150 addresses of welcome were presented to the Irish leader.[93] Amid the general obsequiousness, the address from the SLRL struck a quite different tone:

> In later times, induced by your party politics and the idea of obtaining Home Rule from one or other of the two great parties that hitherto have controlled this Empire, you gave our 'Social Reform' some serious and most ungrateful blows. We hold that this was an error even in your party politics. It was the Democracy that compelled the Liberal Party to take a wise relation towards Ireland. It is the Democracy that will compel the full measure of your just demand. But we are aware this will not be so apparent to you as it would be to a more democratic leader; therefore we have no fault to find with those acts of yours which were injurious to Scottish Land Restoration and to Scottish Home Rule. As men of principle we help all reformers, whether they help us or no ...[94]

In the hope of clarifying some of the main issues, Glasier addressed the Scottish Socialist Federation on 'Irish Nationalists, Radicals, and Socialists: Where they agree and where they differ'.[95] Michael Davitt's short-lived newspaper, the *Labour World*, gave support to the crofters as part of a general workers' agitation.[96] George himself gave several 'sermons' in Glasgow, some of which were later published in pamphlet form by the SLRL. While the Georgites among the Glasgow-Irish had been marginalised, not least by the increasing antipathy shown towards them by the *Glasgow Observer*, they continued to speak out for their beliefs:

> The Home Government Branch of the Irish National League has in its time cut some strange capers. Its reputation for doing queer things should possibly protect it from the criticism which would apply to utterances or acts as a body composed of ordinarily sane men, and in treating it as being so composed we are perhaps laudably magnanimous, but rather unwise.[97]

It was hoped that George's tour of the industrial lowlands would build on Davitt's earlier work, and win groups of miners over to the cause by exposing the amount of money landlords made through royalties on the backs of the workers. The labour movement had already begun to crystallise its ideals along the lines of socialism, rather than Georgism, and so the hopes were not to be fulfilled.[98] Nevertheless, Glasgow remained a shining beacon to Georgites all over the world, especially after John Ferguson's election to the council on a land value taxation programme in 1893.[99]

CONCLUSION

The 'Father of the Land League' epithet which was given to Davitt even during his own lifetime certainly gave him a great amount of influence during his later career, but in the eyes of some Irish historians it referred to a golden age which he could never live up to again. As with some Irish nationalists in the late 1880s, who considered Davitt's later career 'one of disappointment', he has been seen as drifting, albeit sincerely, from one good cause to another. Away from the mainstream of Irish (or Parnellite) politics, it seems axiomatic that his importance diminished after 1882.

This perception also, perhaps, influenced the way Davitt's mission in Scotland and the Highlands has been portrayed. The fact that he arrived in Scotland in 1882, not long after Edward McHugh had been in Skye, means that the part he played in the Highland agitation has been seen as a continuation of his work in Ireland. This impression is compounded by Davitt's own pronouncements, along with those of John Ferguson, McHugh and others, in the nationalist press and especially the *Irish World*. Describing Skye as 'the Scotch Irishtown', for example, although clearly an attempt to stoke passions and raise cash in America, has led to over-simplistic interpretations of the relationship between Scotland and Ireland at the time.

Davitt is fêted for setting in train the events that led to the 1881 Irish Land Act, and – via the New Departure – the failed 1886 Home Rule Bill. By his own reckoning, however, the Irish land wars failed in that they brought about neither land nationalisation nor any real union of the workers of Ireland.[100] This is partly because his own philosophy on the land question developed over the period of the land wars, but it may nevertheless be recognised, as Moody has observed, that 1882 started a new era in Davitt's life. The 'Scotch Campaign', as Ferguson referred to it, was a part of the beginning of this new era, not a postscript to the old. Davitt's interest in the crofters was not to support a particular 'cause', as he did with the Boers or the Russian Jews, but to advance his theories of land nationalisation in a specific context.[101]

This reference to a 'Scotch Campaign' is also vital in understanding the roles of Davitt, Ferguson and McHugh, because in spite of their assertions of an oppressed, but doughty, Celtic population in the Highlands, they saw no real difference between rural and urban society in relation to the overall land question. They perceived the Highlands as part of a much wider agitation, and especially they saw the need, along with Henry George, to get city dwellers to understand the vital importance of land reform. In Glasgow in particular, these men realised the importance of breaking down prejudice against Ireland among Scots in order to popularise land reform, but they also recognised that the absence of a pressing national question made Scotland a perfect base from which to pursue their tactic of 'loyal opposition' against the Parnellites.

NOTES

1. Roy Douglas, *Land, People and Politics – A History of the Land Question in the United Kingdom, 1878–1952* (London, 1976), p. 64; James Hunter 'The Gaelic connection: The Highlands, Ireland and nationalism, 1873–1922', *Scottish Historical Review*, vol. 54 (1975), p. 187.
2. Andrew G. Newby, '"Scotia Major and Scotia Minor": The Glasgow-Irish and the birth of the Highland Land Agitation, 1878–1882', *Irish Economic and Social History*, vol. 31 (2004), pp. 23–40.
3. John F. McCaffrey, *Scotland in the Nineteenth Century* (Basingstoke, 1998), pp. 55–82; Colin Kidd, 'Race, empire and the limits of nineteenth-century Scottish nationhood', *Historical Journal*, vol. 46 (2003), pp. 873–92; William E. Vaughan, *Sin, Sheep and Scotsmen: John George Adair and the Derryveagh Evictions, 1861* (Belfast, 1983).
4. Theodore W. Moody, *Davitt and Irish Revolution* (Oxford, 1981), p. 548; Thomas M. Devine, *The Scottish Nation, 1700–2000* (Harmondsworth, 1999), pp. 304, 496; T. Christopher Smout, *A Century of the Scottish People* (London, 1986), p. 71.
5. This imbalance is now being redressed. See Carla King, *Michael Davitt* (Dublin, 1999); Carla King (ed.), *Michael Davitt: Collected Writings*, 8 vols (Bristol, 2001); Laura A. McNeil, 'Land, labor and liberation: Michael Davitt and the Irish Question in the age of British democratic reform, 1878–1906', PhD thesis, Boston College, 2002; Laurence Marley, *Michael Davitt: Freeland Radical and Frondeur* (Dublin, 2007); Andrew G. Newby, *Ireland, Radicalism and the Scottish Highlands, 1870–1912* (Edinburgh, 2007).
6. *Highland News*, 13, 20 August, 10 September, 1 October 1892.
7. Liam McIlvanney and Ray Ryan (eds), *Ireland and Scotland: Culture and Society, 1700–2000* (Dublin, 2005), p. 14.
8. *Scotsman*, 4 May 1874.
9. Máirtín S. Ó Catháin, *Irish Republicanism in Scotland, 1858–1916: Fenians in Exile* (Dublin, 2007), pp. 1–13.
10. *Highlander*, 7 June, 15 November 1873.
11. *Highlander*, 16 May 1873.
12. Hunter, 'The Gaelic connection', p. 182.
13. James Hunter, *For the People's Cause: Selections from the Writings of John Murdoch* (Edinburgh, 1986), pp. 70–5.
14. *Highlander*, 9 May 1874; William O'Brien and Desmond Ryan (eds), *Devoy's Postbag*, 2 vols, Dublin, 1953), vol. 1, p. 125.
15. Hunter, *For the People's Cause*, pp. 168–85.
16. *Connaught Telegraph*, 26 April 1879.
17. Andrew Newby, 'Edward McHugh, the National Land League of Great Britain and the "Crofters' War", 1879–1882', *Scottish Historical Review*, vol. 82 (2003), pp. 74–91.
18. Newby, *Ireland, Radicalism and the Scottish Highlands*, pp. 34–6; Elaine W. McFarland, *John Ferguson 1836–1906: Irish Issues in Scottish Politics* (East Linton, 2003), pp. 87–8.

19. Harold J. Hanham, 'The problem of Highland discontent, 1880–1885', *Transactions of the Royal Historical Society*, 5th series, vol. xix (1969), p. 62; John P.D. Dunbabin, *Rural Discontent in Nineteenth-Century Britain* (New York, 1974), p. 184; John R. Frame, 'America and the Scottish left: The impact of American ideas on the Scottish labour movement from the American Civil War to the end of World War One', PhD thesis, University of Aberdeen, 1998, pp. 77–118.
20. Moody, *Davitt and Irish Revolution*, p. 481.
21. Andrew G. Newby, '"Shoulder to shoulder"? Scottish and Irish land reformers in the Highlands of Scotland, 1878–1894', PhD thesis, University of Edinburgh, 2001, p. 43.
22. *Scotsman*, 2 December 1879.
23. Ibid.
24. James Hunter, *The Making of the Crofting Community* (Edinburgh, 1976), p. 141; Ian M.M. MacPhail, *The Crofters' War* (Stornoway, 1989), pp. 20–1.
25. Michael Davitt, *The Fall of Feudalism in Ireland, or, the Story of the Land League Revolution* (London & New York, 1904), p. 449; Moody, *Davitt and Irish Revolution*, p. 461; Arthur L. Morton and George Tate, *The British Labour Movement, 1770–1920* (London, 1956), p. 157.
26. Moody, *Davitt and Irish Revolution*, pp. 481, 497, 545; Davitt, *Fall of Feudalism*, p. 449.
27. *Irish World*, 10 September 1881.
28. *Irish World*, 17 September, 24 September 1881.
29. Newby, *Ireland, Radicalism and the Scottish Highlands*, pp. 54–5.
30. Ibid., p. 62.
31. Moody, *Davitt and Irish Revolution*, p. 539.
32. *Irish World*, 20 May 1882.
33. *Glasgow Herald*, 26, 27 October 1882; *Freeman's Journal*, 28 October 1882.
34. TCD, DP, MS 9535, Davitt's diary, 25 October 1882.
35. TCD, DP, MS 9535, Davitt's diary, 2 November 1882.
36. *Northern Chronicle*, 15 November 1882.
37. TCD, DP, MS 9535, Davitt's diary, 4 November, 9 November 1882.
38. *Irish World*, 2 December 1882.
39. Moody, *Davitt and Irish Revolution*, p. 547; TCD, DP, MS 9328, Davitt to McGhee, 22 May 1883.
40. NYPL, Henry George Papers, Henry George to Thomas F. Walker, 23 January 1884.
41. *Scotsman*, 5 June 1883; TCD, DP, MS 9521/5911, Davitt to McGhee, November? 1883.
42. *Freeman's Journal*, 5 February 1884; *Irish World*, 15 March 1884.
43. Pauric Travers, 'Davitt after the Land League', in Carla King (ed.), *Famine, Land and Culture in Ireland* (Dublin, 2000), pp. 86–8.
44. TCD, DP, MS 9536, Davitt's diary, 31 December 1883; Theodore W. Moody, 'Michael Davitt and the British labour movement, 1882–1906', *Transactions of the Royal Historical Society*, 5th series, vol. 3 (1953), p. 62; Frame, 'America and the Scottish Left', p. 98.
45. *Irish Times*, 12 January 1884; *Oban Times*, 19 January 1882.
46. TCD, DP, MS 9521/5912, Davitt to McGhee, c. 11 December 1883.
47. *Dundee Advertiser*, 2 February 1884; *Aberdeen Daily Free Press*, 5 February 1884.
48. Frame, 'America and the Scottish left', p. 93.
49. H. George Jr., *Life of Henry George* (New York, 1900), pp. 433–4.
50. TCD, DP, MS 9328/180/11, Davitt to McGhee, n.d., 1884.
51. *Freesoiler*, May 1884.
52. *United Ireland*, 19 April 1884; Francis S.L. Lyons, *Charles Stewart Parnell* (London, 1977), p. 258; Andrew Boyd, *The Rise of the Irish Trade Unions* (Tralee, 1972), p. 64.
53. TCD, DP, MS 9328, Davitt to McGhee, 15 April 1884; *The Times*, 10 April 1884; Fintan Lane, *The Origins of Modern Irish Socialism, 1881–1896* (Cork, 1997), pp. 86–8.
54. TCD, DP, MS 9375/992f. Davitt to Ferguson, 25 June 1884.
55. TCD, DP, MS 9521/5930–2, Davitt to McGhee, 11 January 1885.
56. *Exile*, 4 October 1884; McFarland, *John Ferguson*, pp. 148–9.
57. *Exile*, 15 November 1884.
58. *Scotsman*, 13 November 1884; Thomas Johnston, *History of the Working Classes in Scotland* (Glasgow, 1929), pp. 348–9.
59. *The Times*, 5 November 1884; *Exile*, 22 November 1884.
60. Newby, *Ireland, Radicalism and the Scottish Highlands*, pp. 117–37.
61. Lyons, *Charles Stewart Parnell*, pp. 283–6.

62. *Glasgow Observer*, 28 November 1885; Newby, *Edward McHugh*, pp. 81–4; Owen Dudley Edwards, 'The Catholic press in Scotland since the restoration of the hierarchy', *Innes Review*, vol. 29 (1978), p. 164.
63. TCD, DP, MS 9521/5941, Davitt to McGhee, 23 November 1885; *Scotsman*, 27 November 1885.
64. Moody, 'Davitt and the British labour movement', p. 64.
65. *Glasgow Observer*, 2 January 1886.
66. *Glasgow Observer*, 29 August, 12 December, 19 December, 1885, 2 January 1886.
67. See, for example, *Glasgow Observer*, 29 August 1885, in which John Ferguson is described as being 'disgusted' at William Forsyth's rejection of the need for Irish home rule. This did not stop 'Davitt and the land reformers' being condemned by the Govan branch of the Irish National League, a resolution that was swiftly counter-attacked by the HGB. *Glasgow Observer*, 12, 19 December 1885, 2 January 1886
68. Moody, 'Davitt and the British labour movement', p. 65.
69. Christopher H. D. Howard (ed.). *Joseph Chamberlain: A Political Memoir, 1880–1892* (London, 1953), p. 194.
70. Alvin Jackson, *Home Rule: An Irish History, 1800–2000* (London, 2003), pp. 53–4.
71. Smout, *Century of the Scottish People*, p. 73.
72. *Glasgow Observer*, 24 April 1886.
73. *Glasgow Observer*, 6 February, 13 February, 20 February, 5 June, 12 June, 3 July 1886; *The Times*, 22 February, 17 March 1886.
74. TCD, DP, MS 9612/8–8v; *Freeman's Journal*, 8 February 1887; *Scottish Leader*, 9 February 1887; *Scotsman*, 9 February 1887; *Glasgow Observer*, 12 February 1887.
75. Annie Tindley, '"The sword of avenging justice": Politics in Sutherland after the third Reform Act', *Rural History*, vol 19 (2008), pp. 181–7.
76. James L. Garvin, *The Life of Joseph Chamberlain*, 2 vols (London, 1932), vol. 2, p. 307; National Archives of Scotland, Ivory Papers, GD1/36/1/50, 10 May 1887, Chamberlain to Ivory; *The Times*, 19 April 1887; *Northern Chronicle*, 20 April 1887; MacPhail, *Crofters' War*, p. 181; Howard, *Joseph Chamberlain: A Political Memoir*, pp. 281, 284, 297.
77. *Scottish Highlander*, 28 April, 5 May 1887.
78. Máirtín Ó Catháin, 'Michael Davitt and Scotland', *Saothar*, vol. 25 (2000), p. 24.
79. Newby, 'Shoulder to shoulder', p. 273.
80. *Scottish Highlander*, 5, 12 May 1887; *Glasgow Observer*, 7, 14 May 1887; *Scottish Leader*, 9 May 1887.
81. Newby, 'Shoulder to shoulder', p. 284.
82. *North British Daily Mail*, 13 June 1887; Moody, *Davitt and Irish Revolution*, p. 547.
83. TCD, DP, MS9612/35v.
84. Kenneth O. Morgan, *Keir Hardie: Radical and Socialist* (London, 1975), pp. 27–43.
85. NLS, MSS 1809, f. 72, Keir Hardie to Secretary, Home Government Branch, 11 May 1888; Morgan, *Keir Hardie*, p. 27.
86. *Glasgow Observer*, 11 February 1888.
87. Newby, 'Shoulder to shoulder', p. 298.
88. *Glasgow Observer*, 24 March 1888.
89. Ibid.
90. Fred Reid, *Keir Hardie: The Making of a Socialist* (London, 1978), pp. 102–26.
91. *Glasgow Observer*, 16, 30 March, 20 April, 8 June 1889; *Standard* (New York), 22 June 1889.
92. *Glasgow Observer*, 11 May 1889.
93. *Highland News*, 17 July 1889; Adam C.I. Naylor, 'Scottish attitudes to Ireland, 1880–1914', PhD thesis, University of Edinburgh, 1981, pp. 35–45.
94. Naylor, 'Scottish attitudes to Ireland', p. 44.
95. *Scottish Leader*, 7 October 1889.
96. TCD, DP, MS 9545, 14 January 1888; *Labour World*, 27 September, 18 October 1890.
97. *Glasgow Observer*, 14 December 1889.
98. Frame, 'America and the Scottish left', p. 114.
99. McFarland, *John Ferguson*, pp. 247–9.
100. Although he later softened this position. Davitt, *Fall of Feudalism*, p. 317.
101. Moody, *Davitt and Irish Revolution*, p. 547.

CHAPTER TEN

'Bravo Benburb!':
John Ferguson and Michael Davitt

ELAINE McFARLAND

'In fullness of time ... I found myself in Glasgow, *and there I discovered not only Ireland, but that I was an Irishman.*'

John Ferguson (1903)[1]

This chapter will examine the points of connection and departure in the lives of John Ferguson and Michael Davitt, two of the most charismatic Irish leaders of their generation. In so doing, it will highlight the different routes that led individuals to embrace 'Irish identity' in the late nineteenth century. It will also underline the diversity that was implicit in the Irish experience of migration and settlement.

It is perhaps Ferguson who most needs introduction to a wider audience.[2] This would have surprised contemporaries, to whom he seemed a ubiquitous and enduring presence. For almost forty years, 'Benburb' was the public face and voice of the Irish home rule movement in Scotland.[3] Yet, far from being constrained by ethnic consciousness, he was also able to forge a personal bridge between Irish nationalism and progressive politics in his country of adoption. He was at the same time a leading Irish home ruler *and* a British democrat, a political activist *and* a self-made radical intellectual, present at the formation of the Reform League, the Irish Land League and the Scottish Labour Party. There was much in this substantial career that was fluid and volatile. Indeed, as an Irish Protestant, Ferguson consciously sought to build an image for public consumption, weaving together his activism with his religious and ethnic identity. However, one of the constants in this turbulent life was his friendship and collaboration with Michael Davitt.

EARLY LIFE

At first sight, the bond between the two men was not an obvious one. Indeed, Ferguson's boyhood and family antecedents could not have been more different from the bitter legacy of dispossession and dislocation that marked Davitt's early life. Ferguson was born in Belfast in 1836, the product of a 'mixed' marriage in Ulster Protestant terms – between a Presbyterian and an Episcopalian. His father, a provisions merchant, was a determined Presbyterian Conservative, vehemently denying his family's radical nationalist past, which included active participation in the 1798 rebellion. The family of his mother were prosperous Antrim tenant farmers and even more entrenched in the Orange yeoman tradition.

Ferguson's early years were spent in the commercial heart of Belfast, but following his father's early death around 1844, the family escaped to Glenavy, Co. Antrim. This prosperous village was an unlikely setting for a future land reformer. Towards the end of his life, he recalled an idyllic boyhood spent on the farm of his maternal grandfather. Cut off from daily contact with Catholic Ireland, he was also sheltered from the famine scenes that embittered many of his nationalist contemporaries. Instead, an older and more insistent collective memory among his family and friends was the massacre of Protestants in the 1641 rebellion. Raised in a culture of Tory Episcopalianism, his formal education and informal socialisation, as he later reflected, combined in short to create 'a loyal Protestant and Unionist'.[4]

Aged fourteen, he returned to Belfast to begin his working life as a stationer's apprentice. The new urban environment initially seemed unlikely to challenge his early upbringing, but it was here that the first stage of Ferguson's 'self making' would unfold. The 'inner-directed self' is a powerful Victorian motif, and both Davitt and Ferguson were indeed 'self-made men' in terms of their intellectual and social development.[5] However, if the prison library at Dartmoor became Davitt's university, for Ferguson it was the clubs and societies of Belfast, with their tradition of free public discussion, which provided an environment for learning. His early years were dominated by a restless sense of intellectual enquiry and a search for 'useful knowledge'. Devising a personal system of self-study, he consumed the classics of history, logic and political economy. The land question held an early fascination, drawing on the work of Professor T.E. Cliffe Leslie and the published letters of Dennis Holland on the plight of the rural poor in Donegal.[6]

However, rather than apply his broad and liberal education to the problems of Ireland in any systematic fashion, he remained constrained by the fervent conservatism of his family and social circle. The next stage of his intellectual and political development would be dependent on his migration to new surroundings.

John Ferguson arrived in Glasgow around 1859. Unlike the family of Michael Davitt, he left Ireland to improve his prospects for material advancement rather than to escape destitution. Initially, he clung to the familiar company of fellow Irish Protestant migrants, who comprised about a quarter of Scotland's Irish-born population.[7] He got a job as a traveller with a wholesale stationers and printers' firm, but within seven years had risen to a partnership in 'Cameron & Ferguson', soon to become a major purveyor of popular histories, patriotic literature and cheap song books to British, Irish and overseas markets. Although this migrant experience was far from remarkable, Ferguson's eventual destination was typically more idiosyncratic. Increasingly, the secure and culturally familiar rallying points of his Protestant circle in Scotland would be eclipsed by a newly acquired 'Irish' identity. This was an active and conscious process – a continuation of his 'self making'. Indeed, it was also through this medium that he began to make sense of his migration to Scotland. From the vantage point of over three decades later, Ferguson would present this development as a dramatic 'conversion experience', taking place in a Glasgow public hall. His account was that he was suddenly seized by an awareness of his ethnicity in the midst of an open debate in which the rights of Ireland and the Irish were being traduced.[8]

In fact, the process of 'becoming an Irishman', as he termed it, also had deeper intellectual roots in his continuing engagement with British radical philosophy and a personal credo that drew on Herbert Spencer and John Stuart Mill. This is an important facet of Ferguson's developing conception of nationalism. While some Catholic nationalist contemporaries in Britain grew conscious of challenges to their identity in their country of adoption, employing their embrace of the Irish national cause as a cultural defence mechanism, Ferguson's new 'Irishness' co-existed with a vigorous respect for what he considered to be intrinsically British values and ideologies.[9] Indeed, just as he represented a personal point of connection between Protestantism and nationalism, John Ferguson's public career, like Michael Davitt's, would continue to be grounded in reconciling other apparent opposites: the 'nation' and 'humanity'; 'capital' and 'labour'; 'town' and 'country'.

EARLY INTERACTIONS

Ferguson and Davitt met for the first time in London on 19 December 1877. Ferguson was one of a small reception committee of leading nationalists, previously active in the campaign to free political prisoners, who welcomed Davitt on his release from Dartmoor.[10] The contrast in their recent political experiences could not have been greater. As the returning hero, Davitt, with his soldierly appearance, cut an impressive figure; seven years of incarceration for treason-felony had underlined his moral authority even among constitutional nationalists. Ten years older than Davitt, but with an equally compelling physical presence, Ferguson's recent personal engagement with fenianism had been altogether more ambiguous.[11] While Davitt had been in prison, Ferguson had doggedly been building up his local power base in Glasgow, re-channelling the energies of the Irish community along firmly constitutionalist lines to match the realities of the 1870s.

Yet, despite this initial gulf, both men would be immediately drawn together by their joint credo of nationalism and agrarian radicalism. More than ideologies, these were the social languages of the day through which Ferguson and Davitt defined their personal identities and found meaning for their feverish political activism. Indeed, Davitt was already familiar with Ferguson's writings on the land question, which he had read while in prison.[12] Both men were also to find that they shared similar strengths and weaknesses of character: determination, probity, courage and idealism were tempered by pride and impulsiveness. Inevitably, differences were to reveal themselves over specific tactics over the years, but both remained acutely sensitive to changing political situations and willing to grasp new opportunities. Ferguson's eloquence could be overwhelming – even exhausting – while his tendency to act without consultation sometimes caused Davitt pained embarrassment.[13] These tensions aside, their friendship survived over thirty years. In *The Fall of Feudalism in Ireland*, published towards the end of his life, he paid a double tribute to Ferguson: he was described as a man of 'fearless nationalism', a connecting link in the roll call of Irish Protestant champions from Molyneux to Parnell, but Davitt also acknowledged him as an intellectual leader on land and social questions, who stood 'among the foremost thinkers and advocates in Great Britain'.[14] He once commented that finding something to say after a speech of John Ferguson was as difficult as picking up a crumb of bread in a Dartmoor cell.[15]

For his part, Ferguson could always guarantee his friend a sympathetic platform when the tide turned against his radicalism in the official Irish Party. Davitt became the darling of Glasgow Irish audiences, but always found a haven from his demanding touring schedule at Ferguson's home. His daughter, Anna, remembered the weary campaigner throwing himself into a seat at their fireside with a sigh of relief and contentment, before turning to gossip and plan with her father. Later, he would join the family group around the piano as they sung 'Dear Little Shamrock'.[16]

The meeting in 1877 then was to be an auspicious event for both of their careers. Typically, its first fruit was an invitation for the newest Irish hero to make a public appearance in Glasgow. In April 1878, Davit delivered an address in the City Hall on his prison experiences, but also took the opportunity to condemn sectional interests in Irish politics. This was to be the first of many visits to Glasgow and it is here we can already trace the impact of Davitt's tremendous moral leverage in encouraging practical cooperation between the local revolutionary and constitutionalist nationalist movements. On the very day of his release, Ferguson had prophesised that this was the man who would bring together the warring nationalist parties. The New Departure that Davitt now preached in Glasgow would soon become the accepted model for nationalist politics.[17] Davitt was also destined to play an important role in his colleague's broader educative mission among the Irish in Glasgow. To understand Ferguson's strategy here, it is essential to grasp the Irish community's situation in the last quarter of the nineteenth century. The fact that Irish Catholics had acquired such an unconventional leader as John Ferguson was testament in itself to the challenges that they faced locally. The community was a large one, frustrated at its political marginalisation and concentrated both in the poorest housing and in casual, low-wage employment.[18] Paralleling Ferguson's own journey, they were now embarked on a search for ethnic identity and communal self-worth.

Here, Ferguson's contribution as a driving political force was twofold. First, his close personal relations with major figures in the Dublin home rule leadership helped secure British-based home rulers – formerly distrusted for their lowly social origins – a voice in developing national policy. Second, his determination to cast Irish nationalism as part of a larger 'democratic alliance' helped shift community politics further into the Scottish mainstream. Essentially, his master plan was to educate, organise and persuade. In the first place, the Irish themselves, he believed, required to be schooled in an awareness of their civic rights and responsibilities. Next, the Scottish press and political establishment must learn to take the Irish seriously as a major interest group. In order to achieve this, the Irish vote had to be solid and uni-fied and deployed to the maximum tactical effect, but the home rule campaign must also gain support among the shapers of progressive opinion. 'Clansman nationalism', he argued, would only serve to fur-ther isolate the Irish: 'We shall thus make neither enemies or friends ... and we will have just as much, and no more, political power to serve Ireland or ourselves.'[19] This would be a highly public campaign fought on countless platforms with the weapons of rhetoric and a barrage of Ferguson's beloved social statistics.

Against this background, the visits of Davitt, like those of Isaac Butt's at the beginning of the decade, were intended to convince Glasgow nationalists that they were part of a larger national movement, while offering them the additional opportunity to display their numerical strength, responsibility and seriousness of purpose to sceptical Scottish observers.

LAND LEAGUE

However, the most decisive phase of Davitt's collaboration with John Ferguson was yet to come. For Ferguson, the formation of the Irish National Land League in 1879 was a defining historical moment, pro-viding a new junction point between radicalism and nationalism. As he expressed it:

> The banner of the rights of man was uplifted. The morning was as dreary as the nation's prospect; but men who believed in the immortality of Truth spread her light that day before the people, and a living blaze has been kindled over the island of which the whole world has heard. Doctrines hitherto known to be true in halls of learning only, became accepted in the cabins of Connaught, and the truths of Economic Science have given new hope to the Irish peasant.[20]

Characteristically, Ferguson grabbed the credit here, citing his speech to the Home Rule Confederation of Great Britain's convention in Dublin in October 1878. This had called for a root and branch reform of the land system, involving 'the disestablishment of the landlords and the return of the right of property to the peasant', but had also made land reform part of a wider call to national regeneration.[21] In Ferguson's later recollection, the greatest impact was on Davitt, who was then in America and still 'taking no part in constitutional action'. Reading the *Irish World* account, he suggested that 'the interest it excited in him and throughout the country suggested the formation of the Land League'.[22] In fact, a complex range of influences and personalities was at work on Davitt at this point, but whatever the precise truth of Ferguson's claim, he certainly was one of the first colleagues that Davitt turned to as he attempted to formulate a rapid response to the escalating agrarian crisis of the late 1870s.

The practical outcome was the historic meeting at Irishtown on 20 April 1879. It was Ferguson who represented Davitt, who had allegedly missed his train.[23] His platform performance stood out on two counts. First, he adopted a 'strictly economic treatment' of the land question. Peppered with references to John Stuart Mill, he emphasised that it was worthy of settlement on its own merits.[24] Secondly, he now set out his belief that land agitation was of universal significance to oppressed 'producers', arguing that the principle of solidarity should be extended beyond mere national boundaries. Indeed, Irishtown would set the pattern for Ferguson's future involvement in the land campaign. His expertise in land economics continued to inform the movement, but he was unwavering in his belief that the question was a social rather than an instrumental or political one. His influential role and his increasingly close relationship with Davitt were confirmed by his eventual membership of the league's enlarged Executive Council.[25]

Over the next two years, he concentrated his attention on the pressing task of rallying support for the Irish land agitation, touring the Irish counties in the company of an exhausted Davitt.[26] Both men, however, also remained anxious to broaden the struggle beyond Ireland, which meant first building solidarity with progressive forces in Scotland. Accordingly, during 1881 an increasing number of Scots radicals addressed Land League meetings in Glasgow. Anxious to reduce the 'otherness' of Irish agitation, Ferguson was indeed proud to boast that half the Glasgow Land League Council were 'Scotchmen', while the majority, including himself, were Protestants – a tribute to 'Irish Catholic chivalry'.[27] In one Scottish contemporary's view, this development reflected the prevalent 'anti-imperialist views' of the time and the tendency of some progressive Scots to regard the Irish question as 'an economic question', bound up with the current debates over land ownership.[28] More candidly, the radical land reformer J. Shaw Maxwell admitted that Irish meetings also had attractions often lacking in conventional Scottish politics:

An assemblage of Irish men and women forms perhaps the most
sympathetic audience a speaker could possibly have ... Less
phlegmatic than the Scots, and less emotional than the French,
the great mass of them are always in such accord with the hero
of the hour that every part of his speech is a 'palpable hit'.[29]

For Ferguson and Davitt, the mounting land crisis in the north
of Scotland, particularly in the north-west Highlands and islands, presented another opportunity to put this new democratic alliance into
practice. In response, Davitt toured Scotland during the autumn of
1882, with Ferguson in the role of 'impressario'.[30] In the lowland
towns, he was able to broaden his audience beyond the local Irish, but
it was the situation in the north that seemed particularly heartening.[31]As
he rested with the Ferguson family at Benburb, he was still intoxicat-
ed by the good work he had done in breaking down 'a good deal of
Scotch prejudice against the Irish land movement, and [carrying] the
banner of the land for the people into the Highlands'.[32]

'FREELANCE' NATIONALISTS

From the early 1880s, however, Davitt's and Ferguson's conception of
a 'common cause' between secular nationalism and other radical
political forces came under threat from two directions. First, the local
Irish community in Glasgow had rapidly developed in terms of ambition and social complexity since the original foundation of the Glasgow
Home Rule Association in 1871. Removed from the pioneering experiences of the early 1870s and more assertive in their Catholic identity, a
rising generation of 'new nationalists', increasingly chaffed under
Ferguson's individualistic leadership, protested that his predilection for
'peculiar movements' was dividing the community and scaring away
'the respectable Irishmen of the city and the clergy'.[33] Rejecting his
democratic vision, which claimed to hold 'humanity above the nation',
they were determined to operate in accordance with their own single-
minded conception of Ireland's destiny.[34]

Crucially, these local developments intersected with fundamental
shifts in the balance of power within the national home rule movement.
Maintaining his hold over Irish political organisation in Glasgow had
always been a delicate task for Ferguson, even with the support of the
parliamentary party. However, during 1883 and 1884, the latest New
Departure in Irish politics was already well underway, resulting in a
rightwards shift in politics and a more disciplined and centralised

organisation, now under Parnell's personal dominance. This left little room for unorthodox local experiments, especially those inspired by the agrarian left of the party. Not only was Parnell unwilling to maintain the momentum of Irish land agitation, he was also determined on a strategy of 'decontamination', of which Ferguson's and Davitt's 'great principle of Irish Democracy' would be an early victim.

Suddenly then, for both of these consummate activists the formal avenues for political work seem to narrow dramatically. In line with the energy and restlessness that characterised their personalities, their response was to go 'freelance', stretching beyond the constraints of party to deepen their engagement with the forces of social radicalism. For Ferguson, the 'land war' begun in Mayo still held the key for future political action. As he had written in his 1881 polemic *The Land for The People*, an unholy alliance of feudalism and capitalism had expelled the peasant from the countryside and sucked him into an industrial labour force, where man was bound to deteriorate 'under the urban conditions of life'. His conviction that the Land League's principles of social justice were of universal relevance was assisted by widespread economic depression that gripped Scottish commerce and industry in earnest by the mid-1880s. Political developments also widened his sphere of operations. The franchise reform of 1884 created a more varied and unpredictable electorate, while Gladstone's embrace of Irish home rule in 1886 further undermined traditional political alignments, while contributing to the increasing bitterness of political life in Scotland. The malleable new forces in society and politics presented both opportunities and challenges – not least over how the Irish should respond. As the Parnellites had captured the political machinery in Glasgow, Ferguson sought out a new audience: the majority of the Irish locally were still part of the urban working-class labour force who might be persuaded that the goal of legislative independence for 'the nation' need not be pursued separately from their immediate material needs. Meanwhile, he had drawn closer to an alternative democratic element in Glasgow politics which he believed could be usefully cultivated. These 'Home Rule Radicals', as he termed them, were young men, both native Scots and Irishmen. They were drawn together by similar social backgrounds as rural migrants and autodidacts, but they were also united in their admiration for Michael Davitt. They cited his record of leadership and self-sacrifice, but were also drawn by a more intangible quality, which one of their number, Bruce Glasier, called his 'moral grandeur'. The hero worship that Davitt inspired in these circles is well represented in

one of Glasier's own poems. Prompted by the fenian heckling of
Davitt at an Oldham public meeting in 1883, he wrote:

> They cannot bring his noble soul to bay;
> They cannot chain his fearless spirit down:
> But they can hiss at him, and yell like fiends, and drown
> In ghoulish clamour what his speech would say:
> ... a war of ignorant and recreant rage
> Against the truest heart they have today.
> ... at what – at England? No! But at the man,
> The best of Ireland's sons, the first in Freedom's van.[35]

The remainder of the decade, with its ferment of ideas and political
dislocations, would raise a series of more prosaic dilemmas that continued to complicate the pattern of Ferguson's and Davitt's political
allegiances. At their heart was the question of how to square demands
for independent labour representation with Irish dependence on the
Liberal Party to deliver home rule. This was most eloquently witnessed
in a series of electoral contests in Scotland into which the unfortunate
Davitt was dragged by Ferguson as a talisman of probity. At the Mid-
Lanark by-election of 1888, for example, they were united in support
for the independent candidature of Keir Hardie, but even Davitt's
personal intervention could not rescue a hopeless cause once the
national leadership of the Irish party backed the official Liberal.[36] Yet
it is a mark of Davitt's popularity in Scottish progressive circles that
his reputation was undiminished by these electoral expeditions.
Significantly, he retained tremendous drawing power as a public
speaker, addressing audiences estimated at 20,000 at the end of the
1880s.[37]

Given this sort of momentum, victory for the Irish home rule movement at last seemed at hand. Soon, however, the wreckage of the
Parnell divorce crisis in late 1890 would strike not only at the heart of
Davitt's and Ferguson's mission, but also at the hopes of a generation
of nationalists. Both men had grown impatient for home rule to be
speedily 'settled', so that they could focus on issues of social reform;
now this seemed further away than ever. Arguably, in his self-appointed
role as 'a patriot of no party', Ferguson sensed the ideological complexities of the resultant split in the Irish Party more perceptively than
the fervent anti-Parnellite Davitt.[38] While Davitt intervened early, then
faded from the brutalising struggle as it dragged on relentlessly
through the 1890s, it was Ferguson who quietly concentrated his
energies at a local level, protecting the infrastructure of nationalist

politics from the worst effects of internecine warfare and lifting his colleagues' eyes to the 'the revolt of labour'.

By the 1890s, home rule could no longer set the boundaries of political debate for the Irish in Britain as it had in previous decades. While Davitt turned to radicalism on an international stage, Ferguson at first sight turned inwards, finding new battleground in Glasgow municipal politics. His business interests had always kept him rooted in Glasgow, frustrating any ambitions to become an MP. Instead, in 1893 he became a Glasgow councillor. His reincarnation as a municipal politician was partly an escape from political paralysis, but this new role also offered a positive route for his struggle to link ethnic consciousness with a broader progressive spirit. The corporation chamber offered a fresh setting in which he could recast the 'democratic alliance' largely on his own terms. Furthermore, Glasgow's peculiar historical position, with its relatively small area of fiscal jurisdiction, high urban values, extreme deprivation and scarce and expensive building land provided the perfect laboratory for the land taxation theories he had nurtured for over twenty years. Here, like Davitt, he drew heavily on the messianic 'single tax' doctrine of the American radical, Henry George. This stated that land should be taxed to its full value, exclusive of improvements, thus obviating the need for all other taxes. The landlord's unearned increment would be abolished, along with speculation in land, and absolute free trade would reign. This was more than a matter of fiscal readjustment, but offered a message of spiritual rebirth, for the tax on rent would ultimately reverse urbanisation, end man's alienation and inequality, and bend human nature towards nobler vistas.[39]

Within months of his election, Ferguson had already won a vote to investigate the 'unearned increment' of the city and how this could be tapped for municipal purposes.[40] 'Bravo Benburb!' was Michael Davitt's reaction to a step which, he believed, showed the enormous strides that Georgite teachings had made since 'Philosopher John' entered the council.[41] Over the next decade, Ferguson was to turn the city into a land tax bastion, signalled by its hosting in October 1899 of the 'National Conference to Promote Land Values', attended by over 600 delegates from across Britain and the empire.[42] Again, Davitt continued as an adviser and collaborator, helping to draw in the Irish municipalities into his friend's schemes.[43] Ferguson now came to assume the mantle of national leader of the land taxation movement, chairing a series of conferences after 1904 and pressing his case on the new Liberal administration following their landslide general election of 1906. However, this new beginning was cut short. Overburdened with campaigning work and suffering from the effects of a tramcar accident, his health collapsed completely. He died at his home in Lenzie, near Glasgow, on 22 April 1906. The news of his death dealt a grievous blow to Michael Davitt, himself recovering from an operation.[44] Their careers had been intertwined for over thirty years. He followed Ferguson to the grave within weeks.

CONCLUSION

How do we finally sum up the achievement of these veteran campaigners? Certainly, despite their different backgrounds and early experiences, there seems more in common at the end of their lives than separating them. For those left behind at their passing, there was the sense of a real void. While neither was an original thinker, both men grasped the linkages and complexities in Irish politics where others saw only absolutes. They were also practical men – theorists *and* activists. Together they helped to build successive popular movements in Ireland and Scotland, encouraging their countrymen in political organisation and bringing them into contact with broader democratic forces. While many of their Irish parliamentary colleagues remained bound by the frustrations of opposition politics at Westminster, these two figures were energetic in finding alternative outlets for talents, whether in municipal government or in international radicalism. Above all, Michael Davitt and John Ferguson emerge as *leaders*. Whether as resident philosopher and teacher of the Glasgow Irish or as a frequent guest on home rule and radical platforms, both had the stature and the charisma to keep alive the self-belief of a migrant community during its critical formative years, when it faced exclusion from Scottish society and politics.

NOTES

1. John Ferguson, 'Incidents of my life', *Irish Packet*, 14 November 1903.
2. For a full discussion of Ferguson's life and times, see E.W. McFarland, *John Ferguson 1836–1906: Irish Issues in Scottish Politics* (East Linton, 2003).
3. He shared the soubriquet with his villa 'Benburb' in Lenzie. The reference was to his favourite battle, 'Red Benburb', at which the Covenanting army were defeated in 1646.
4. *Glasgow Star*, 28 April 1906.
5. See Patrick Joyce, *Democratic Subjects: The Self and the Social in Nineteenth-Century England* (Cambridge, 1994).
6. Originally published in *The Ulsterman* during 1857 and 1858, Holland's notes were republished as *The Landlord in Donegal: Pictures from the Wilds* (Belfast, n.d.).
7. Graham Walker, 'The Protestant Irish in Scotland', in Thomas M. Devine (ed.), *Irish Immigrants in Scottish Society* (Edinburgh, 1990), p. 49.
8. *Glasgow Echo*, 1 September 1894.

9. See Liam Harte, 'Immigrant self-fashioning: The autobiographies of the Irish in Britain, 1856–1934', in Oonagh Walsh (ed.) *Ireland Abroad: Politics and Professions in the Nineteenth Century* (Dublin, 2003), pp. 47–61.

10. For Ferguson's prominent role in Davitt's official reception committee in Ireland, see *Freeman's Journal*, 14 January 1878.

11. While sympathetic to their cause – his firm published cheap editions of patriotic songs – he probably did not take the fenian oath: *Special Commission*, vol. 3, p. 285. *Special Commission Act 1888: Report of Proceedings before the Commissioners appointed by the Act. Reprinted from The Times* (London, 1890), vol. 3, p. 285.

12. *Special Commission*, vol. 3, p. 285.

13. In his diary, Davitt confided his lack of excitement at another 'eternal verities speech' from his colleague: TCD, DP, MS 9535, Davitt's diary, 25 October 1882. On another occasion, Ferguson attempted to organise a national subscription on Davitt's behalf in the belief that he was about to leave Ireland through lack of money. In fact, he was only embarking on an extended lecture tour: *Tipperary Herald*, 9 May 1884, in TCD, DP, MS 9603.

14. Michael Davitt, *The Fall of Feudalism in Ireland, or, the Story of the Land League Revolution* (Shannon, 1970), p. 714.

15. *Glasgow Herald*, 26 October 1882.

16. *Glasgow Observer*, 15 March 1913. A signed copy of the *Fall of Feudalism* would remain one of her cherished possessions.

17. *Glasgow Star*, 14 April 1903.

18. See Iain G.C. Hutchison, 'Politics and society in mid-Victorian Glasgow 1846–86', PhD thesis, University of Edinburgh, 1975, pp. 270–8; James E. Handley, *Irish in Modern Scotland* (Cork, 1947), pp. 122–63.

19. *The Nation*, 6 January 1877.

20. John Ferguson, *The Land for the People: An Appeal to All who Work by Brain or Hand* (Glasgow, c.1881), p. 17.

21. *Irish World*, 16 November 1878.

22. *Glasgow Observer*, 22 December 1894.

23. Ibid., Alexander M. Sullivan, *New Ireland* (Glasgow, 1877), p. 434. The latter account is, however, disputed by Theodore W. Moody in his *Davitt and Irish Revolution* (Oxford, 1982), pp. 288–9. Ferguson's own version shifted over time. In 1903, he claimed to a Glasgow audience it was Parnell who had telegraphed him to attend with the message, 'You are to open the ball at Irishtown on Monday morning': *Glasgow Star*, 11 April 1903. See also Davitt, *Fall of Feudalism*, p. 147.

24. Davitt, *Fall of Feudalism*, p. 148.

25. Ibid., p. 240.

26. *Irish World*, 27 March 1880. See also *Special Commission Act 1888: Report of Proceedings before the Commissioners appointed by the Act. Reprinted from The Times* (London, 1890), vol. 3, pp. 286, 290–1.

27. *Glasgow Herald*, 13 June 1881; *Irish World*, 10 September 1881.

28. James Mavor, *My Window on the Street of the World* (London, 1923), vol. 1, p. 164.

29. *Voice of the People*, 10 November 1883.

30. He also acted as Davitt's publisher, rushing out two pamphlets, based on his original Manchester land nationalisation speech and on the lectures from his Scottish tour: *The Land League Proposal: A Statement for Honest and Thoughtful Men* (Glasgow & London, 1882); *Land Nationalisation or National Peasant Proprietary: Michael Davitt's Lectures in Scotland* (Glasgow & London, 1882).

31. *Glasgow Herald*, 26, 28, 30 October, 1 November 1882.

32. *Glasgow Herald*, 6, 7, 9 November 1882; see also TCD, DP, MS 9602.

33. *Glasgow Herald*, 12 February 1881.

34. Ferguson, *Land for the People*, p. 20.

35. John B. Glasier, *On the Road to Liberty: Poetry and Ballad* (Manchester, 1920), p. 36.

36. For background of this contest see, for example, William Stewart, *J. Keir Hardie* (London, 1921), pp. 35–45; James G. Kellas, 'The Mid-Lanark by-election (1888) and the Scottish Labour Party', *Parliamentary Affairs*, vol. 17 (1964–5), pp. 318–29; Kenneth O. Morgan, *Keir Hardie: Radical and Socialist* (London, 1975), pp. 23–43; Fred Reid, *Keir Hardie: The Making of a Socialist* (London, 1978), pp. 110–15. Even Davitt's last-minute telegram of support for Hardie went astray. See *Archives of the Independent Labour Party. Series III: The*

Francis Johnson Correspondence, 1888–1950 (Brighton, 1980), J. Ferguson to Keir Hardie, 17 May 1888.

37. *Glasgow Observer*, 14 July 1888. In comparison, a 'monster' anti-coercion meeting addressed by Ferguson attracted 4,000, *Glasgow Observer*, 23 April 1887.

38. Davitt, *Fall of Feudalism*, pp. 642–5.

39. Henry George, *Progress and Poverty: An Inquiry into the cause of Industrial Depressions and of Increase of Want with Increase of Wealth: The Remedy* (London, 1883). For Ferguson's application of these principles see his pamphlet, *Glasgow: The City of Progress* (Glasgow, 1900).

40. *Single Tax*, August 1894.

41. TCD, DP, MS 9556, Davitt's diary, 1 August 1894.

42. See City of Glasgow Archives, Glasgow Corporation Minutes, 5 October 1899 for debate over the corporation's role in the conference.

43. TCD, DP, MS 9447/3571, J. Ferguson to M. Davitt, 10 October 1904.

44. F. Sheehy-Skeffington, *Michael Davitt: Revolutionary, Agitator and Labour Leader* (London, 1967), p. 211.

CHAPTER ELEVEN

Anomalous Agitator?
Defining and Remembering Davitt

LAURENCE MARLEY

Scholarly research in recent years has made considerable headway in redressing the serious neglect of Davitt as a political thinker and activist, and in correcting the view, implicit in the rather breathless epilogue of T.W. Moody's study, *Davitt and Irish Revolution*, that his political career after the 'Kilmainham treaty' of 1882 was something of a post-script to the 'land war'.[1] Davitt remains principally remembered as the 'father of the Land League'. Yet the range of commemorative events during 2006 which marked the centenary of his death was testimony to a growing interest in viewing him through a wider lens, beyond his role in the Irish agrarian revolution. For most of the twentieth century his political ideas and his later career after the 'land war' – a career which spanned almost a quarter of a century – were largely overlooked. The treatment of his reputation in the recent centenary year differed markedly, for instance, from the way in which he was viewed in 1946 during the centenary of his birth. He always remained a committed Irish nationalist. Ultimately, though, the nature of his radicalism, and his particular preoccupation with a broad international agenda, ensured that he was effectively ignored by the main political traditions in twentieth-century Ireland. There were often ritual genuflections in honour of the 'father of the Land League'; but beyond that, Davitt's 'ghost' could never be comfortably invoked. Indeed, the evolution of his political thought, and the trajectory of his activism after the 'land war', reflected a complex political figure whose ideas, some of which betrayed inconsistencies and contradictions, were essentially eclectic.

DAVITT AFTER THE LAND LEAGUE

In the political fallout after the Kilmainham accord, Parnell remarked to his eager young acolyte, William O'Brien: 'If I were Davitt, I should never define; the moment he becomes intelligible, he is lost.'[2] This was a direct reference to the land nationalisation policy which Davitt championed after his discharge from Portland prison, Dorset, in May 1882. Having been denied access to news reports during his fifteen months' imprisonment, Davitt was ignorant of the terms of his release when it eventually came. Yet he was confident that on his return to Ireland he would find seditious fervour in the countryside still sufficiently strong to advance a radical agrarian, and political, agenda. In reality, as Paul Bew has observed, the peasants by now had the 'whiff of property in their noses' following Gladstone's 1881 Land Law (Ireland) Act,[3] and the subsequent Arrears Bill (passed in August 1882) which promised to satisfy still further what Davitt himself was reluctantly forced to identify many years later as 'the strong human desire or passion to hold the land as "owner" which is so inherent in Celtic nature'.[4]

Parnell, for his part, was satisfied that the historic work of the Land League had been enough to lay a foundation for the advancement of legislative independence for Ireland. At least until the mid-1880s, he and his lieutenants had to be mindful of Davitt's considerable standing among Irish nationalists, on both sides of the Atlantic. However, as his comments to O'Brien indicated, Parnell viewed Davitt's alternative land policy as extremist folly, which would ultimately be lost on the Irish peasantry. Davitt's ideas were not only challenged by Parnell and his coterie of parliamentarians, but also by other former Land League colleagues, including neo-fenian associates John Devoy and Matt Harris.[5] His proposal for state ownership of the land was viewed as tantamount to inviting the British state to consolidate its hold over Ireland.[6] His critics particularly focussed on his relationship with the American radical social reformer, Henry George, whose acclaimed work, *Progress and Poverty* (1879), had had a major influence on him when he read it thoroughly during his time in Portland. Davitt differed with George on the details of a definitive land settlement formula, but he was, certainly by the time of his release from prison in May 1882, taken by the basic Georgite argument that land monopoly was the root cause of extremes of wealth and poverty, not just in Ireland but also internationally. This view, however, rankled with most Irish nationalists who were focussed exclusively on the injustice of the Irish land system.[7]

The effective settlement of the Irish land question by the end of 1882 (through Gladstone's land acts), and the development of the Irish Parliamentary Party along conservative lines, meant that the old left-wing of the Land League became emasculated and effectively dispersed. Davitt's closest radical colleagues, Patrick Egan and Thomas Brennan, left for America in 1882–3.[8] Through political expediency, Davitt himself maintained his links with the constitutional nationalist movement, but he was now a diminished political figure on the margins of mainstream nationalism. With the formation of the Parnellite Irish National League as a successor to the Land League, he assumed the role of a freelance radical and turned his attention to land and labour politics in Britain, where he expected the Georgite reform gospel to have a far-reaching impact. His involvement in radical politics in Britain was encouraged and supported by three prominent Irish immigrants in Scotland: John Ferguson, an old Land League colleague, Richard McGhee and Edward McHugh, all of whom remained life-long friends who worked closely with him as political allies in attempting to radicalise the British working class, particularly on the Irish question.[9]

It is important to point out, however, that Davitt himself was always a natural loner, without a political faction of his own. Indeed, his radical activism not only straddled both the Irish and British political scenes, but also eventually led to his involvement in international issues and causes, from Indian nationalism to the second Anglo-Boer war,[10] and later to the debate on Zionism and the plight of the Russian Jews.[11] He did, it is true, have a close association with the anti-Parnellites in the 1890s; and he even sat, briefly, as an anti-Parnellite MP, albeit reluctantly.[12] However, despite his prominent role in the bitter divisions of the Irish Party split in 1890–1, he never quite viewed himself as an anti-Parnellite. He was always a political maverick, once aptly described by William O'Brien as a 'born *frondeur*'.[13] In the final months of his life he openly clashed with the Catholic Church on the controversial question of denominational education, much to the frustration of Dillon and John Redmond, both of whom apparently appealed to him directly to refrain from giving public vent to his views on the matter.[14] As Patrick Maume has observed, Davitt's death, when it came, 'saved the Irish Party from considerable embarrassment'.[15]

LATER POLITICAL CAREER

During his later political career, Davitt relied heavily on his pen to articulate his own eclectic views. In fact, his journalism served as an essential political platform. His first biographer, Francis Sheehy-Skeffington, captured this point well when he wrote of the importance Davitt had attached to the *Labour World*, the radical paper he launched in September 1890:

> The man who writes primarily to express the ideas that are in him, and only in a secondary degree to make a living, must [Sheehy-Skeffington wrote] always feel a craving for an organ of his own, wherein he can say precisely what comes to mind, unhampered by any restrictions.[16]

Sheehy-Skeffington had had an editorial venture of his own with a short-lived paper, the *Nationalist*, in 1905.[17] Later, shortly after Davitt's death, he launched another, the *National Democrat*, in which he attempted to advance many of the causes on which Davitt had latterly campaigned, including non-denominational education.[18] The title of the paper was taken, by way of tribute, from an article Davitt had written in 1905 on an imagined future Irish national assembly, in which a radical party, the 'National Democrats', would have come to power by 1910.[19] The young Sheehy-Skeffington was enamoured of Davitt and his politics. In his hagiographical biography, published in 1908, he identified Davitt as the 'greatest Irishman of the nineteenth century'.[20]

Davitt, undoubtedly, was widely celebrated for his role in the 'land war'; but, other than that, his political ideas, which so stirred Sheehy-Skeffington, enjoyed no significant appeal among the main political and cultural movements in early twentieth-century Ireland. As we have seen, he was even a difficult figure for the leadership of constitutional nationalism. His piece on the future national assembly was, as it happens, crafted as a deliberately provocative attack on the politics of Redmond and William O'Brien.[21] Yet it was Davitt's own connections with conservative nationalism – especially with a clericalist, anti-Parnellite strain in the early 1890s – and his preoccupation with the interests of the British working class, that led him to fall foul of many within the Irish labour movement.[22] He himself acknowledged privately that the Irish Party split had dealt a 'death-blow' to the *Labour World* in 1891.[23] After the publication of Sheehy-Skeffington's biography, James Connolly was quick to respond to its assessment of Davitt. In an editorial in *The Harp*, Connolly acknowledged Davitt's place in Irish history as the 'father of the Land League', but he criticised him for aligning himself (as Connolly saw it) with the political interests of the Catholic Church in Ireland, and for neglecting the interests of the Irish proletariat by involving himself too much in English party politics.[24]

Davitt did indeed spend much of his later career in Britain, where he attempted to build an alliance between Irish nationalism and British democracy.[25] This proposition had been rejected by Parnell in the early 1880s, and in his later years Davitt also drew criticism from other quarters for his role in Britain, notably from sections of the Irish-Ireland movement. In an editorial in the *Nationist* in February 1906, he was accused of having ignored the 'battle for the [Irish] language, Irish industries, and all things that will save, inspire and develop' Ireland, and was attacked in particular for having proposed that, under home rule, Ireland would establish standing trade links with Britain.[26] Davitt was a free trader in principle, and was critical of the economic policies of self-sufficiency and protectionism, such as those espoused by Arthur Griffith's Sinn Féin.[27] In a letter of reply to the *Nationist*, Davitt defended himself by pointing to his own contribution to reviving Irish industries, through his writings and also through a number of practical interventions in the 1880s which included a glass bottle industry and an Irish Woollen and Manufacturing Company, all 'before the advent of the Gaelic League, the Irish-Ireland Movement and the *Nationist*'. He envisioned an Ireland, he explained in his letter, that was politically independent and economically outward-looking, and whose people were well educated 'in Gaelic and in English, and in as many other languages as they wish to learn'.[28]

Davitt himself spoke Irish fluently and celebrated the language as part of his cultural heritage. Growing up in his native Mayo and later in the Irish immigrant community in Haslingden, Lancashire, he absorbed the language from his parents. He certainly recognised the importance of a new generation's efforts to revive Irish,[29] but he did not attach the same importance to it as did revivalists such as Douglas Hyde, first president of the Gaelic League. For Hyde, language did not simply express thought; it gave it form. To speak English, then, was not merely to *use* a different language but to adopt an entirely new mode of thought, and in doing so to disconnect from the Gaelic past. In a celebrated lecture before the National Literary Society in Dublin, in November 1892, on 'The Necessity for De-Anglicising Ireland', Hyde lamented the decay of the Irish language, the adoption of

English dress and habits, and the spread of English materialist culture in Ireland. It was, he argued, simply 'anomalous' to resist English rule while 'copy[ing] England in every way'. In condemning the 'vile habit' of Irishmen who dropped the 'O' and 'Mac' from their surnames, he made reference to 'Mr Davitt'.[30] Davitt was in fact sensitive about his name and its pedigree, and insisted that the Davitts had come 'from the O'Doherty's, all black Celts'.[31]

In 1882, shortly after his release from Portland, Davitt included a proposal for the cultivation of the Irish language as part of the agenda of a new 'National Land Reform and Industrial Union of Ireland', which he hoped would succeed the Land League.[32] Parnell rejected the draft proposals for the new organisation; and when the Irish National League was established in October 1882, many of Davitt's objectives were omitted from its programme, including the revival of the language.[33] That is not to say that there was no interest in the language among nationalist parliamentarians. Dillon had shown an early interest, and later went on to join the Gaelic League.[34] Indeed, the Irish Party was sympathetic to the language movement and gave practical support to enhancing the position of Irish within the education system.[35] The party publicly expressed what Gearóid Ó Tuathaigh has described as general 'good will' towards the Gaelic League and the early efforts to secure 'a real "option" for the survival of Irish'.[36]

The question of viable options for the preservation of the language arose controversially in 1908 when the Gaelic League campaigned vigorously to have Irish adopted as a compulsory subject for entry to the new National University of Ireland. The campaign was ultimately successful, but the debate on the matter caused divisions within the nationalist movement. J.P. Boland and Thomas O'Donnell, MPs for South Kerry and West Kerry respectively, were prominent in supporting the campaign, but Redmond and Dillon, and most of the leadership, were opposed.[37] The leadership wanted Irish to be elevated to a position of dignity in schools and universities, but the demand that the language should be a requirement for matriculation was, in their view, a step too far. Some years later, Dillon remarked in the House of Commons that if a policy of compulsion were to be introduced in a parliament in Dublin, most nationalist members would convert to unionism.[38] Davitt, had he lived to contribute to the debate in 1908–9, would not perhaps have felt as strongly as Dillon. Yet there is nothing in his earlier pronouncements on the revival of Irish to suggest that he would have identified with the more inflexible language activists, many of whom would later naturally gravitate towards 'advanced' nationalist groups such as Sinn Féin and the Irish Republican Brotherhood (IRB). According to Tom Garvin, indeed, the Gaelic League 'was in many ways the central institution of the development of the Irish revolutionary élite'.[39]

By the turn of the twentieth century, after resigning from parliament in protest against the Boer War, Davitt, as Donal McCracken has observed, 'found himself on the periphery of both nationalist movements', the Irish Party and the 'advanced men'.[40] He was always a reluctant parliamentarian, and less than a year after taking his seat as MP for South Mayo, to which he was elected in 1895 while in Australia, he expressed a desire to retire 'altogether'.[41] While he was genuinely outraged by the Boer War, its outbreak in 1899 also provided him with the perfect opportunity to extricate himself from what he had once called 'parliamentary penal servitude', and to step back from his responsibilities to the Irish Party.[42] He was uncomfortable in party politics, and was drawn back to the role that was most natural to him, that of *frondeur*. Significantly, after his parliamentary resignation he attempted to establish areas of co-operation between the IRB and constitutional nationalists. The Dublin police observed that 'he never fails to do anything he can to attract the extreme party and constitute himself a connecting link between the two parties'.[43] His activism in these years serves, indeed, to illustrate Maume's point that, in the period between the fall of Parnell and the demise of the Irish Party in 1918, constitutionalism and physical-force separatism shared a 'common discourse'.[44] His efforts to forge alliances between members of the IRB and constitutionalists were undermined, however, by the fact that there were some fenians, 'old Parnellites', who retained vivid memories of him as a leading anti-Parnellite strategist and propagandist during the Irish Party split.[45] Griffith was critical of him because of his role in the split, and because he had, as far as Griffith was concerned, betrayed his IRB oath.[46]

Certainly, by the end of the 'land war', Davitt had distanced himself from the political violence of the separatist tradition, and subsequently hitched himself to the constitutional wagon. Yet he never abandoned his republican ideals. During a public meeting in Limerick in 1887 to commemorate the Manchester Martyrs, he stated that in the political and ideological alignments in a future home rule Ireland, he expected the interests of the bourgeoisie and the main Churches to be represented by a Parnellite 'Conservative Nationalist Party', and working-class interests to be advanced by a 'Democratic' or 'Radical Nationalist Party', which would also have a separatist agenda.[47] His decision to take a parliamentary seat in Westminster in the 1890s had never been an easy one. In 1896, only months after assuming his position as the MP for South Mayo, he told the prominent English journalist, W.T. Stead, that he was 'a republican by creed and conviction'.[48] However, in his post-Kilmainham alignment with constitutionalism, and particularly by sitting in Westminster, he paid a price. In 1898, shortly before resigning from his South Mayo seat, he reminded Dillon that he had 'all but alienated *almost all* my staunch American friends through entering the British parliament'.[49]

Davitt once described himself as 'the most radical "revolutionist"' produced by the fenians, 'if by revolutionist we are to understand one who goes in for fundamental change and in war against the older order of things'.[50] In this, he was alluding to the broad political agenda that not only included the cause of Irish self-government but which also involved challenging structures of power and privilege at an international level. In the summer of 1882, when he first began preaching land nationalisation, he was attacked by Matt Harris for attempting to spread 'cosmopolitan' ideas in Ireland. In a broadside against Davitt, Harris stated: 'Is it time for any Irishman, except one who has lost himself in dreams of world reform, to float a new agitation? I say no whoever says yes [sic].'[51] For the fenian John O'Leary, Davitt had become 'not a nationalist at all in any intelligible sense to us [fenians], but only some sort of internationalist or socialist, in some sense not intelligible even to himself'.[52] To the next generation of republicans, Davitt clearly remained just as unmanageable. Indeed, it is significant that when Patrick Pearse was later writing his short essay, 'Ghosts', Davitt's name did not suggest itself; instead, in the pantheon of inspirational fathers of the nation, it was the 'pale and angry ghost of Parnell' who was given a place alongside Theobald Wolfe Tone, Thomas Davis, James Fintan Lalor and John Mitchel.[53]

DAVITT AND THE INDEPENDENT IRISH STATE

In the independent Irish state from 1922, Davitt's 'ghost' did not prove serviceable in the contested public histories of the main political traditions, as represented by Cumann na nGaedheal (later Fine Gael) and Fianna Fáil. Nor was he embraced by the left in Ireland. He was, of course, invoked as the Land League founder, even by the extreme right. Eoin O'Duffy, leader of the Blueshirts in the 1930s, and Fine Gael's first president, actually laid claim to the Land League tradition: 'If Parnell or Davitt were alive today they would lash those who are driving the Irish farmers into a destitution greater than slavery.'[54] In August 1934, O'Duffy, himself from a rural background in Monaghan, promised farmers the support of the Blueshirts in a campaign, involving direct action, against land annuities and agricultural rates.[55] Two of the leading intellectuals of Fine Gael in its early days were Michael Tierney, a classics professor at University College Dublin and the son-in-law of Eoin MacNeill, and James Hogan, professor of history at University College Cork and brother of Patrick Hogan, minister for agriculture in the Cumann na nGaedheal government. Both were staunch advocates of the corporate state, and proved major influences on thinking within the Blueshirts. They paid lip service to Italian fascism, largely as a reaction against 'the growing menace of the Communist-IRA'.[56] The contents of Hogan's 1935 tract, *Could Ireland become Communist? The Facts of the Case*, actually prevented the socialist republican, Peadar O'Donnell, from gaining entry to the United States in the late 1940s during the 'red scare' there.[57]

However, the violent tactics employed by the Blueshirts in the anti-annuities campaign in 1934 alarmed Tierney, Hogan and others within Fine Gael, and by September of that year O'Duffy's resignation was forced. Fine Gael subsequently reverted to the parliamentary politics which Tierney and Hogan had effectively disavowed.[58] The Catholic Emancipation centenary celebrations had been organised by the Cumann na nGaedheal government in 1929, and after Fine Gael distanced itself from O'Duffy and the Blueshirts from the mid-1930s, the strongly Catholic, parliamentary democracy of Daniel O'Connell was again embraced by party intellectuals as a safer ideological space to occupy. In an essay written to mark the O'Connell centenary in 1947, Tierney attempted what was clearly a rehabilitation of O'Connell's reputation. Against Tone and the physical-force tradition, O'Connell, with his 'doctrinal belief in the efficacy of moral agitation', was elevated as a pioneer of the concept of home rule, Dáil Éireann and land reform legislation.[59] Davitt's own family had connections with Cumann na nGaedheal. His son, Robert Emmet, was in fact elected as the Cumann na nGaedheal TD for Westmeath in 1932.[60] However, Davitt himself did not sit well alongside O'Connell. Moral force was, of course, central to the land campaign of 1879–82, but Davitt, even during his later career, understood the power of the implied threat of violence, and ultimately upheld the right to resist oppression by force.[61] One of the chief weaknesses he identified in O'Connell was 'his truly ridiculous contention that liberty was not worth the shedding of human blood'.[62]

The merger which gave birth to Fine Gael in 1933 was a reaction against the electoral rise of Fianna Fáil and the perceived threat the party posed to political liberty and free market economics. However, Fianna Fáil was actually determined to consolidate political stability and win the favour of the Catholic hierarchy, particularly given the opportunity provided by the spectacle of the Eucharistic Congress in 1932. On the economic front, Éamon de Valera was gradually forced to depart from his fundamental belief that tillage farming created more jobs, and to acknowledge the importance of the cattle economy. In 1935 the coal-cattle pact, which signalled the relaxation of the 'economic war' with Britain, marked, as J.J. Lee has noted, 'a recognition by de Valera that historical illusion must sometimes succumb to economic reality'.[63] Land redistribution was, therefore, jettisoned, rendering the Fianna Fáil rhetoric of agrarian radicalism increasingly redundant, particularly after the emergence of Clann na Talmhan in 1939, the party that appealed to the interests and frustrations of small farmers, and which posed a significant electoral threat to Fianna Fáil in the west during the 1940s.[64]

In 1946, during the centenary of Davitt's birth, the Fianna Fáil government could still appeal to his memory; it even commissioned a stamp to mark the occasion.[65] Davitt was, predictably, generally remembered at this time for his achievements during the 'land war', although de Valera interestingly referred to one aspect of his wider, international interests. At an event in the Mansion House, Dublin, in March, the taoiseach, in the presence of members of the Davitt family, paid tribute to Davitt for having given 'the land of Ireland to the people of Ireland'.[66] De Valera avoided complicating matters with any reference to land nationalisation, the policy to which Davitt remained wedded after the 'Kilmainham treaty'. Indeed, there were fundamental differences in economic policy between de Valera and Davitt: the latter was ideologically predisposed to free trade and would not have countenanced Fianna Fáil protectionism. He, too, had a scheme for encouraging self-sufficiency among the poorer sections of the peasantry,[67] but not one based on the isolationist premise of de Valera's vision.[68]

In his Mansion House speech, de Valera alluded to Davitt's support for Indian nationalism: 'Nothing would have given [Davitt] greater satisfaction than what happened a few days ago when a British Prime Minister told the Indian people that they could have whatever independence they wanted.' He presented Davitt as a model 'before our nation', along with Thomas Davis.[69] Yet it was the ecumenical Davis who was more serviceable to Fianna Fáil at this time. Only months earlier, de Valera had laid a tablet at the site of the new statue of Davis to be erected in College Green, Dublin.[70] Significantly, as reflected in the *Irish Press* coverage, the government gave greater time and effort to the 1945 commemoration of Davis's death than it did to Davitt's the following year.[71] De Valera did, however, express an interest in the fact that T.W. Moody had the Davitt papers in his possession with a view to producing an authoritative work on Davitt.[72] As it happens, in 1946 Moody resigned from an academic project, partly conceived by de Valera in 1943 or 1944, which aimed to produce a substantial history of the Great Famine. Instead, Moody concentrated his time on the Faber & Faber 'Studies in Irish History'.[73] By the time of the centenary of Davitt's birth, he had written a number of articles on Davitt for academic journals,[74] and would later write his particularly important piece for the *Transactions of the Royal Historical Society* on Davitt and the British labour movement.[75] Yet it is significant that even he did not see fit to commit himself totally to producing a major work on the complete Davitt and his relevance to modern Ireland.

Davitt's last major written work, *The Fall of Feudalism in Ireland* (1904), was a celebration of the agrarian revolution and the transfer of land ownership, which by the early twentieth century had effected the demise of ascendancy landlordism in Ireland. Paradoxically, he himself always held 'fondly and firmly to the great principle' that a finite resource such as land could never be owned privately, not in any 'absolute sense'.[76] Ultimately, however, he accepted and acknowledged, albeit in a heavily qualified manner, the benefits accruing from the various pieces of land reform legislation, even those brought about through constructive unionist policies in the late nineteenth and early twentieth centuries, because he believed that they hastened the decline of what he called the 'landlord garrison'.[77] Due, then, to his celebration of the settlement of the Irish land question, he could be invoked, as he was by de Valera, as the champion of the land-owning farmer.

By the early twentieth century, the radicalism of the 'land war' had long given way to the status quo of the conservative farmer, and Davitt, notwithstanding his principled commitment to land nationalisation and his identification with the small farmer, was retrospectively viewed by the Irish left as having acted as the midwife of a land settlement that had satisfied the interests of the petit bourgeoisie from the early 1880s.[78] Moreover, despite the tenacity of labour support among the residuum of agricultural labourers, the rhetoric of the strong labour movement that emerged after Davitt's death was concerned with urban structures and challenges, precisely the arena in which James Larkin's syndicalism operated. In any case, Davitt generally did not address urban audiences in Ireland during his later political career. His engagement with industrial workers was instead concentrated in the more industrialised Britain, much to the chagrin not only of Connolly but also to earlier socialists, who had attempted to enlist Davitt's support in spreading 'new unionism' in Ireland. Davitt's decision to base the *Labour World* in London rather than in Dublin certainly did not ingratiate him with the Irish left.[79] In the 1890s, he himself had actively worked to advance the cause of labour in Ireland, and he emphasised the importance of an all-Ireland trade union. But he was also extremely wary of militant trade unionism; he much preferred arbitration as a means of resolving industrial disputes.[80]

ANOMALOUS AGITATOR?

The difficulty for many of Davitt's contemporaries, and indeed for later generations, was that, after the 'land war', he appeared as something of an anomalous agitator. It was not just that he never quite became a party man, or that he never immersed himself in politics at an organisational level; rather, he was particularly difficult to classify because of the sheer breadth of his interests in international issues and causes, and the fact that his radicalism, the impulse behind his engagement with these various causes, did not easily conform to an ideological paradigm. His radicalism was underpinned by two basic ideas. One was that the land and labour questions were inextricably linked, given that landlords and employers were in much the same position vis-à-vis their tenants and industrial workers respectively. The other was that resistance to oppressive social and political structures could never merely be parochial; it had to be identified with the much broader, global interests of humanity. He always had a passion for travel, but his interest in land reform, prison reform, educational systems, 'new' societies (such as those 'embryonic' communities in the Canadian provinces at the end of the nineteenth century), cultural diversity, minorities, human rights and anti-imperialism brought him on various travels throughout Europe, Palestine, Egypt, North America, Australasia, South Africa and Russia, sometimes as a political activist, sometimes as a freelance journalist, often simply as a silent witness.[81] Three of his six main published works were based on his international travels, and one of the others, his first, *Leaves from a Prison Diary*

(1885), was, as he told Henry George, written as 'a kind of politico-socialist manifesto in Gt. Britain . . . My object, of course, is to "get at" the democracies of England and Scotland in view of their coming enfranchisement so as to incline them towards justice for Ireland.'[82]

For Matt Harris in the early 1880s it was precisely Davitt's cosmopolitanism that was his undoing. Interestingly, similar points were later made by a variety of political and literary figures. For the historian of the Irish Parliamentary Party, F.H. O'Donnell, Davitt was 'a mere Lancashire radical compounded of Chartism and the French Revolution'.[83] In an obituary to Davitt in 1906, the English radical figure, Wilfred Scawen Blunt, stated that he was 'always too much of a theorist . . . in some ways . . . less Irish than cosmopolitan'.[84] W.B. Yeats felt that Davitt had 'wrecked his Irish influence by international politics'.[85] And the British socialist, H.M. Hyndman, whom Davitt actively supported in Burnley during the 1906 general election campaign, commented that Davitt 'had a Utopia of his own for Ireland and other countries'.[86] For some, the course of Davitt's political career could be explained by his apparent political naivety. Harris, again, maintained that by supporting land nationalisation Davitt had not taken an independent line on the Irish land question but had effectively become George's 'latest acquisition'.[87] Connolly, of course, later deprecated Davitt's involvement in British politics, and could only conclude that he 'became the tool of political crooks and social reactionaries'.[88]

In fact, Davitt was not as pliable as Harris and Connolly suggested. He always remained a strongly independent figure; even in his journalism, there is no evidence that he ever towed a particular editorial line against his better judgement. Nor was he a political anomaly. While the Irish national question was always central to his political agenda, his politics bore the influences of both that strain of radical Irish republicanism which identified with 'the men of no property' and the tradition of English radicalism represented by the Chartists in the 1840s. Irish immigrants had played a hugely important role in the development of British working-class radicalism in the 1840s.[89] Davitt, by his own admission, was heavily influenced by Chartist thinking in his formative years in England.[90] It is significant, indeed, that the most enduring of Chartist sentiments was internationalism,[91] for this probably explains something of Davitt's interest in issues of justice and liberty in an cosmopolitan context. The *Labour World* aimed, for example, to unite in 'the bonds of human brotherhood' the workers of all nations.[92] There was no Marxist connotation to this language; its broad, egalitarian sentiments were based, rather, on the principle of democratic-republican liberty. Despite Davitt's associations with British democracy and with an international agenda, he was as much an Irish nationalist and republican at the end of his days as he had been as an active fenian. In 1893, he himself remarked that he was 'more a revolutionist than I was 30 years ago'.[93] In a sense, internationalism, understood in a broad, egalitarian sense rather than a strictly ideological one, is a useful prism through which to view Davitt. In his own view, there was nothing paradoxical at all about his nationalism and internationalism. In 1884, he wrote: 'The cause of labour, like that of religion, can be international without being unpatriotic.'[94]

CONCLUSION

At a conference in Mayo in 2006 to mark the centenary of Davitt's death, the Fianna Fáil senator, Martin Mansergh, remarked that Davitt was 'difficult to classify'.[95] Yet the elusiveness of Davitt is not now so problematic, and the lens has discernibly widened on him since the early 1990s. At an academic level, this has had much to do with the fact that, after the death of T.W. Moody in 1984, a younger generation of Irish scholars was given access to the Davitt papers and the neglect of Davitt's later career could therefore be rectified and viewed in a new, revised context. By the time of the centenary, Davitt had also become much more accessible at a political or popular level. With the erosion of essentialist ideological positions in the 1990s, there appeared to be much less need to view him as a class crusader or to shoe-horn him into a rigid ideological position. With the Northern peace process and social partnership structures in the Republic, he was also much more amenable to the reformist discourse of accommodation and consent. Furthermore, Mary Robinson's redefining of the function of the Irish presidency in the 1990s recharged a recognisably Irish humanitarian rhetoric, in which the Irish experience of famine and exile resonated with international humanitarian crises of the late twentieth century. In this context, Davitt could easily be invoked as a symbolic figure, both because of his early life experiences and his wider engagement with issues of justice and liberty. In recognition of the scope of Davitt's political life, President Mary McAleese, Robinson's successor, concluded during the centenary commemorations of 2006: 'May those who drink the water never forget the debt they owe to those who dug the well.'[96] Davitt has therefore become much more serviceable and current. It should also be remembered, however, that in his political activism he could be guilty of double standards and inconsistencies, such as his support for the Boers and his almost wilful neglect of the plight of native South Africans during the Anglo-Boer wars of 1899–1902. This is also part of the complexity of his life and politics, and by acknowledging it we can more fully understand him as an historical figure and indeed the complexities of the political world which he inhabited.

NOTES

1. Theodore W. Moody, *Davitt and Irish Revolution, 1846–82* (Oxford, 1981). Moody did address aspects of Davitt's later political career in a number of short publications, the most notable of which was on Davitt's involvement in British labour politics; see Theodore W. Moody, 'Davitt and the British labour movement, 1882–1906', *Transactions of the Royal Historical Society*, 5th series, vol. 3 (1953), pp. 53–76. However, by framing his biographical study of Davitt largely within the context of the subject's earlier personal and political life, up until 1882, Moody diminished the importance of the post-Kilmainham years. The biography certainly made a major contribution to Irish historiography, but it has fallen to a new generation of scholars to give Davitt's later career the attention it deserves. See John Slatter, 'An Irishman at a revolutionary court of honour: From the Michael Davitt Papers', *Irish Slavonic Studies*, no. 5 (1984), pp. 32–42; Carla King, 'Michael Davitt and the Kishinev Pogrom, 1903', *Irish Slavonic Studies*, no. 17 (1996), pp. 19–43; Carla King, *Michael Davitt* (Dundalk, 1999); Carla King (ed.), *Michael Davitt: Collected Writings, 1868–1906*, 8 vols (Bristol, 2001); Carla King, 'Michael Davitt, Irish nationalism and the British empire in the late nineteenth century', in Peter Gray (ed.), *Victoria's Ireland? Irishness and Britishness, 1837–1901* (Dublin, 2004); Laura McNeil, 'Land, labor and liberation: Michael Davitt and the Irish Question in the age of British democratic reform, 1878–1906', PhD thesis, Boston College, 2002; Elaine W. McFarland, *John Ferguson, 1836–1906: Irish Issues in Scottish Politics* (East Linton, 2003); Andrew G. Newby, *Ireland, Radicalism and the Scottish Highlands, c. 1870–1912* (Edinburgh, 2007); Laurence Marley, *Michael Davitt: Freelance Radical and Frondeur* (Dublin, 2007).
2. William O'Brien, *Recollections* (London, 1905), p. 445.
3. Paul Bew, 'Parnell and Davitt', in George D. Boyce and Alan O'Day (eds), *Parnell in Perspective* (London, 1991), p. 46.
4. Michael Davitt, *Some Suggestions for a Final Settlement of the Land Question* (Dublin, 1902), p. 6.
5. *Connaught Telegraph*, 1, 8 July 1882.
6. Paul Bew, *Land and the National Question in Ireland, 1858–82* (Dublin, 1978), pp. 230–1.
7. Fintan Lane, *The Origins of Modern Irish Socialism, 1881–1896* (Cork, 1997), pp. 67–8; see also Matt Harris's letter to *Connaught Telegraph*, 1 July 1882.
8. Bew, *Land and the National Question*, pp. 238–40; Joan Haslip, *Parnell: A Biography* (London, 1936), p. 244.
9. For more on Ferguson, McGhee and McHugh, including their relationship with Davitt, see McFarland, *John Ferguson*; Andrew G. Newby, *The Life and Times of Edward McHugh (1853–1915): Land Reformer, Trade Unionist and Labour Activist* (New York, 2004); Eric Taplin, 'Richard McGhee (1851–1930)', in Joyce M. Bellamy and John Saville (eds), *Dictionary of Labour Biography*, vol. vii (London, 1984).
10. Marley, *Michael Davitt*, pp. 226–31, 240–52.
11. King, 'Michael Davitt and the Kishinev Pogrom', pp. 19–43.
12. Davitt was elected MP for North Meath in 1892 but was quickly unseated on the grounds of clerical interference in his election campaign. He was elected for North-East Cork in

1893, but the same year was disqualified due to bankruptcy. Later elected for South Mayo in 1895, he famously resigned four years later in protest against the second Anglo-Boer war.

13. O'Brien, *Recollections*, p. 418.
14. Alfred Webb, *Alfred Webb: Autobiography of a Quaker Nationalist*, edited by Marie-Louise Legg (Cork, 1999), pp. 74–5.
15. Patrick Maume, *The Long Gestation: Irish Nationalist Life, 1891–1918* (Dublin, 1999), p. 83.
16. Francis Sheehy-Skeffington, *Michael Davitt: Revolutionary, Agitator and Labour Leader* (repr. London, 1967), p. 148.
17. Roger McHugh, 'Thomas Kettle and Francis Sheehy-Skeffington', in Conor Cruise O'Brien (ed.), *The Shaping of Modern Ireland* (London, 1960), pp. 128–9.
18. *National Democrat*, February 1907.
19. Davitt, 'The Irish National Assembly (Session of 1910)', *Independent Review*, vol. v (April, 1905).
20. Sheehy-Skeffington, *Michael Davitt*, p. 215.
21. Davitt, 'The Irish National Assembly', pp. 284–5.
22. See Lane, *Origins of Modern Irish Socialism*, pp. 168–9; also James Connolly, editorial in *The Harp*, August 1908.
23. TCD, DP, MS 9556, Davitt's diary, 25 December 1894.
24. *The Harp*, August 1908.
25. Erich Strauss, *Irish Nationalism and British Democracy* (London, 1951), p. 188.
26. *Nationist*, 1 February 1906.
27. Marley, *Michael Davitt*, pp. 148–53.
28. *Nationist*, 8 February 1906. For Davitt's ideas on Irish economic development, and his own interventions in reviving Irish industries, see Marley, *Michael Davitt*, pp. 153–64.
29. Marley, *Michael Davitt*, p. 5.
30. Douglas Hyde, 'The necessity for de-Anglicising Ireland', in Breandán Ó Conaire (ed.), *Language, Lore and Lyrics: Essays and Lectures – Douglas Hyde* (Dublin, 1986), pp. 154, 164–5.
31. TCD, DP, MS 9553, Davitt's diary, 24 January 1890.
32. TCD, DP, MS 9398.
33. F.S.L. Lyons, *Charles Stewart Parnell* (Suffolk, 1978), pp. 235–6.
34. F.S.L. Lyons, *John Dillon* (London, 1968), p. 20.
35. Lyons, *John Dillon*, pp. 304–5.
36. Gearóid Ó Tuathaigh, '"Designs for Living": National identity, state and nation in Ireland, c. 1880–1932', unpublished paper delivered at Canadian Association of Irish Studies conference, Toronto, March 1990.
37. Maume, *The Long Gestation*, pp. 98–100. See also Gearóid Ó Tuathaigh, 'The position of the Irish language', in Tom Dunne, John Coolahan, Maurice Manning and Gearóid Ó Tuathaigh (eds), *The National University of Ireland, 1908–2008: Centenary Essays* (Dublin, 2008).
38. Lyons, *John Dillon*, pp. 305–7.
39. Tom Garvin, *Nationalist Revolutionaries in Ireland, 1858–1928* (Oxford, 1987), pp. 78, 96. This suggestion has been subjected to some qualification more recently by Gearóid Ó Tuathaigh, who points out that the number of those within the Irish political establishment between the 1920s and the 1950s who were resolutely committed to the project of cultural change, '(or, more crucially, perhaps, who had any clear idea of what such a project might mean in practice)', is probably significantly lower than is generally supposed; see Gearóid Ó Tuathaigh, 'Cultural visions and the new state: Embedding and embalming', in Gabriel Doherty and Dermot Keogh (eds), *De Valera's Irelands* (Cork, 2003), p. 173.
40. Donal McCracken, *Forgotten Protest: Ireland and the Anglo-Boer War* (Belfast, 2003), p. 89.
41. TCD, DP, MS 9407/1733, Davitt to John Dillon, November 1896.
42. TCD, DP, MS 9554, Davitt's diary, 30 March 1893.
43. Quoted in Matthew Kelly, 'The end of Parnellism and the ideological dilemmas of Sinn Féin', in D. George Boyce and Alan O'Day (eds), *Ireland in Transition, 1867–1912* (London, 2004), p. 149.
44. Maume, *The Long Gestation*, p. 2.
45. Kelly, 'The end of Parnellism and the ideological dilemmas of Sinn Féin', p. 149.

46. Maume, *The Long Gestation*, p. 51.
47. *Freeman's Journal*, 17 November 1887.
48. TCD, DP, MS 9459/[3753/15], Davitt to Stead, 4 April 1896.
49. TCD, DP, MS 9409/1766, Davitt to Dillon, 29 October 1898.
50. TCD, DP, MS 9377/1063, Davitt to R. Barry O'Brien, 6 December 1893.
51. *Connaught Telegraph*, 1 July 1882.
52. Quoted in Moody, *Davitt and Irish Revolution*, p. 521.
53. Patrick Pearse, *The Murder Machine and other Essays* (Dublin, 1986), p. 39.
54. Quoted in Fearghal McGarry, *Eoin O'Duffy: A Self-Made Hero* (Oxford, 2005), p. 236.
55. McGarry, *Eoin O'Duffy*, p. 262.
56. Ibid., pp. 205–6, 223.
57. Donal Ó Drisceoil, *Peadar O'Donnell* (Cork, 2001), p. 114.
58. McGarry, *Eoin O'Duffy*, pp. 223, 263–5.
59. Michael Tierney, 'Repeal of the union', in Michael Tierney (ed.), *Daniel O'Connell: Nine Centenary Essays* (Dublin, 1949), pp. 151–70.
60. Bernard O'Hara, *Davitt* (Castlebar, 2006), p. 106.
61. See Marley, *Michael Davitt*, pp. 88–90.
62. Michael Davitt, *The Fall of Feudalism in Ireland, or, the Story of the Land League Revolution* (London & New York, 1904), p. 36.
63. J. Joseph Lee, *Ireland, 1912–1985: Politics and Society* (Cambridge, 2001), p. 201.
64. Lee, *Ireland, 1912–1985*, pp. 239–40.
65. Orla Hearns, 'Stamp of approval for Davitt', *Western People*, 16 November 2006.
66. *Irish Press*, 26 March 1946.
67. Michael Davitt, 'Remedies for Irish distress', *Contemporary Review*, vol. 58 (November 1890), pp. 625–33.
68. Lee, *Ireland, 1912–1985*, p. 186.
69. *Irish Press*, 26 March 1946.
70. Ibid., 13 September 1945.
71. Ibid., 10, 11, 12, 13 September 1945; 25, 26 March 1946.
72. Ibid., 26 March 1946.
73. Cormac Ó Gráda, *Ireland's Great Famine: Interdisciplinary Perspectives* (Dublin, 2006), pp. 234–8.
74. Theodore W. Moody, 'Michael Davitt in penal servitude, 1870–77', *Studies*, 30, 120 (December 1941), pp. 517–30; 31, 121 (March 1942), pp. 16–30; Theodore W. Moody, 'Michael Davitt and the "Pen" letter', *Irish Historical Studies*, 4, 15 (March 1945), pp. 224–53.
75. As above fn. 1. Much of this was later reproduced in Theodore W. Moody, 'Michael Davitt', in John W. Boyle (ed.), *Leaders and Workers* (Cork, 1966), pp. 47–55.
76. Davitt, *Some Suggestions for a Final Settlement*, pp. 6–7.
77. Davitt, 'Retiring the landlord garrison', *Nineteenth Century*, vol. 27 (March 1890), pp. 357–83.
78. See Brian O'Neill, *The War for the Land in Ireland*, with an introduction by Peadar O'Donnell (London, 1935), p. 187.
79. Lane, *Origins of Modern Irish Socialism*, p. 167.
80. Marley, *Michael Davitt*, pp. 185–91.
81. See Marley, *Michael Davitt*, pp. 78–89, and Chapter 6, *passim*.
82. NYPL, Henry George Papers, Michael Davitt to Henry George, 8 August 1884. His other works, in chronological order of publication, were *The Times-Parnell Commission: Speech Delivered by Michael Davitt in Defence of the Land League* (London, 1890), *Life and Progress in Australasia* (London, 1898), *The Boer Fight for Freedom* (New York & London, 1902), *Within the Pale: The True Story of Anti-Semitic Persecutions in Russia* (New York & London, 1903), and *Fall of Feudalism*, as above fn. 62.
83. Frank H. O'Donnell, *The History of the Irish Parliamentary Party* (London, 1910), vol. 1, p. 367.
84. *The Speaker*, 9 June 1906.
85. W.B. Yeats, *Autobiographies* (London, 1970), p. 140.
86. Henry M. Hyndman, *Further Reminiscences* (London, 1912), p. 53.

87. *Connaught Telegraph*, 1 July 1882.
88. *The Harp*, August 1908.
89. See Christine Kinealy, '"Brethren in Bondage": Chartists, O'Connellites, Young Irelanders and the 1848 Uprising', in Fintan Lane and Donal Ó Drisceoil (eds), *Politics and the Irish Working Class, 1830–1945* (Basingstoke, 2005), pp. 88–90.
90. Davitt, *The Times-Parnell Commission*, p. 30.
91. John Newsinger, 'Old Chartists, Fenians and New Socialists', *Éire-Ireland*, vol. 17 (1982), p. 26.
92. TCD, DP, MS 9422/2270.
93. TCD, DP, MS 9377/1063, Davitt to R. Barry O'Brien, 6 December 1893.
94. TCD, DP, MS 9540/76, Davitt's diary, 1884 (no precise date).
95. *Western People* ('Davitt: A Centenary Tribute' supplement), 16 November 2006.
96. *Western People*, 16 November 2006.

CHAPTER TWELVE

Dissecting Davitt: (Ab)using the Memory of a Great Irishman

LAURA McNEIL

On 24 September 1907, a little more than a year after Michael Davitt's death, a ceremony was held in Roscommon to dedicate a life-size oil portrait of Davitt, which was to be placed on display in a local court-house. To mark the occasion, Roscommon County Council invited various Irish MPs and labour leaders to address the dedication gathering. One Irish parliamentarian, J.P. Hayden, unveiled the portrait and in his speech celebrated Davitt as a reformed revolutionary, one who turned away from violence in favour of constitutional agitation as the most effective means of achieving Irish self-government. 'Davitt retired from the Irish Party because he thought he could do more useful work outside,' Hayden concluded, 'but he did not – like some cranks and critics – occupy his time in abusing Parliamentarianism.'[1]

After Hayden had finished, John McGreevy, a prominent labour organiser and member of Roscommon Trade and Labour Association, addressed the crowd and dismissed his fellow speaker's claims that Davitt was a constitutionalist, instead insisting that he had abandoned Westminster because of grave flaws within the Irish Parliamentary Party and the parliamentary process. McGreevy's speech became a diatribe against Irish participation in a London parliament and the Irish Party as a whole, which he denounced as a political machine, a 'penny in the slot' business 'of which the Directory in Dublin held the key'. An offended Hayden made a point of order, stating that in making these accusations McGreevy was desecrating the reputation of Davitt, who had been a member of the Irish Party; a scuffle then erupted between Hayden and McGreevy, each flanked by their numerous supporters. The speakers were shoved from the stage and the brawl spread into the audience, involving various councillors, labourers and much of the general public. It was only after nineteen policemen were dispatched to break up the disturbance that the meeting briefly resumed, with the chairman denouncing McGreevy and his followers as 'Sinn Féiners' who 'were disturbing the memory of a great Irishman'.[2]

Across the Atlantic, a similar controversy arose after Davitt's death, this time in response to a series of articles written by John Devoy, a one-time New Departure colleague of Davitt's and later a relentless enemy. The articles, written in Devoy's *Gaelic American* newspaper, focused mainly upon Davitt's life prior to his split with the fenian leadership, roughly around 1882. Devoy concluded that, despite his estrangement from revolutionary nationalist circles, in his later years Davitt was in fact 'drifting back to his old Fenian ideas'.[3] This assertion provoked a bitter controversy with John O'Callaghan, national secretary of the United Irish League of America, who wrote lengthy denunciations of Devoy in the *Irish World* newspaper, rejecting the suggestion that Davitt died a fenian at heart.[4]

The months and years following Davitt's death were filled with accusations from all sides regarding the perceived misuse of his memory for the purpose of political gain. Various constitutional and revolutionary nationalist groups, as well as labour and land reformers, claimed Davitt's reputation for their own, suggesting that he represented and embraced their often opposing political agendas. Why and – more especially – how this happened is the subject of this chapter. The question of *why* this happened should be fairly self-explanatory. After all, one of the things that was readily apparent in the many presentations at the Davitt Centenary Conference in 2006 was that he was a man of high principles and humanitarian concerns, which he applied generously, not only to the people of Ireland but throughout the world. His reputation as a defender of the vulnerable made him a beloved public figure and popular platform speaker worldwide. In this sense, it should not be terribly surprising to modern observers of the incident in Roscommon or the Devoy/O'Callaghan squabble that such a disparate variety of political organisations and personalities wished to associate themselves with Davitt's memory. What is perhaps more perplexing is the question of *how* it is that his lasting memory was apparently so pliable that it could be reshaped to fit any number of different agendas.

AN OUTSIDER

Looking at Davitt's political identifications and reputation with contemporary politicians and activists, we can see that he remained something of an outsider for most of his career and, in fact, he took pride in his reputation for intellectual and political independence. Davitt rarely fully backed any party or organisation and, even when he did, more often than not he refused to sacrifice his own idealism for the sake of diplomacy. In fact, he fought with most of the leaders of those organisations that subsequently publicly promoted their association with him. Contemporaries had often criticised Davitt for his obstinacy, accusing him of being headstrong and irrational because of his unwillingness to offer unequivocal support. In his memoirs of late nineteenth-century Irish politics, for example, William O'Brien patronisingly recalled Davitt as an incorrigible revolutionist, 'ever liable to an occasional lovable rebellion against the realism of earthy politics'.[5] Davitt and O'Brien took opposing positions on the Wyndham Land Act in 1903 and their friendship never fully recovered. Thereafter, O'Brien dismissed Davitt as hopelessly contentious, promoting an idealistic political agenda that scorned realpolitik. And yet, after Davitt's death, even O'Brien had to acknowledge his enduring popularity, something bordering on a reverence that many Irish people attached to Davitt's memory:

> [H]e was a born *frondeur*, bound to be in opposition to every concrete proposal of action in hours of emergency, but, unlike the *frondeurs*, too generous not to admit his mistakes with an almost childlike simplicity as soon as his anticipations had been refuted by results. For that reason, his colleagues had come to regard their great countryman with less confidence in his advice in practical affairs than affection for his charming personality ... There is the man in a lightning flash: the sharp word of a moment forgotten, and the sure reaction to a large-hearted generosity ... hence the undying popularity of his name with a race for whom, in a famous French phrase, the heart hath reasons which mere Reason knoweth not.[6]

Similarly, T.P. O'Connor, who also had fought bitterly against Davitt over his land nationalisation programme, recalled that 'in spite of his hot temper' and an 'almost insane' attachment to his radical land platform, Davitt inspired 'a very warm affection' from both his parliamentary colleagues and the general public.[7] Frank Hugh O'Donnell, in his reminiscences of the parliamentary party, referred to Davitt as a 'very popular incendiary'.[8] But O'Brien, O'Connor and O'Donnell essentially suggest that Davitt was valued more for his personal magnetism than his political agenda, that his radical politics were received, as one obituary noted, with a 'good-humoured indifference to his philosophising'.[9]

Davitt was 'an irreconcilable',[10] not only towards the landed interests, British imperialists and unionists he so vehemently opposed, but also often towards Irish Party leaders such as Parnell and Redmond, fenian leaders such as Kickham and Devoy, labour leaders such as Keir Hardie, land reformers such as O'Brien, and sometimes even the Irish Catholic Church, to which he remained a devoted adherent throughout his life. Davitt was a perpetual member of the opposition, firmly committed to promoting what he believed to be the best interests of those who remained powerless and underrepresented in political decision-making. His enduring popularity in Ireland and among the Irish communities of Britain, the United States and elsewhere was an irritation to those who held political power, adopted political expediencies or promoted merely modest reforms. He frustrated those who deeply desired his support, or at least his silence. In one alleged exchange between Davitt and Parnell, Davitt asked the great Irish leader what he would do if suddenly he was made Irish prime minister. 'I think, Davitt,' was Parnell's alleged reply, 'I should begin by locking you up.'[11]

Davitt took pride in his reputation as an outsider and a defender of the working man against all forms of elitism. One story exists in which Davitt, when he first became a member of parliament, was approached by a titled courtier and given a special invitation to join the queen for tea at Windsor, as the queen desired to meet him and to assure him of her goodwill. Davitt replied to the invitation by inquiring: if he took tea with the queen, would she also come and take tea with Mrs Davitt and himself at his residence? 'Oh no,' the emissary answered. 'You know she could hardly do that.' 'Very well,' said Davitt, 'and I cannot go to Windsor.'[12] Later in his life, he was asked by Lady Gregory to assist her in soliciting financial contributions from wealthy Irish-Americans for her proposed modern art gallery in Dublin. Davitt gave her the names of several prominent Irish-Americans, but he also cautioned her: 'Don't mention my name if you write to these people. I am not *persona grata* with rich people anywhere.'[13]

Davitt took great pride in his reputation as an outsider, and his career as a public figure was defined by this independence or, as some would suggest, this irreconcilability. He was deemed a firebrand by some, a nuisance by others. The great American land reformer Henry George supposed him to be a 'bull in a china shop',[14] while Conservatives, too, gloated about his potential for destruction in Liberal, Radical and home rule circles.[15]

A COMPLEX NATIONALIST

During his lifetime, Davitt did not fit into neat compartments of nationalist or labour political circles. Like many others, he straddled the line among various movements and parties, denying his unequivocal support to any of them but lending a helping hand when he saw that his efforts would be useful to obtain the goals he set himself. In terms of the Roscommon debacle or the Devoy/O'Callaghan squabble, each of these adversaries had some validity behind their assessments of Davitt, but by the same token they were all stretching the truth. Davitt differed from all of them.

A brief look at Davitt's most public pronouncements on constitutional and revolutionary nationalism shows the complexity of his approach. For example, in 1886, when Parnell was concerned that the Irish National League of America was becoming too militant, he dispatched Davitt to their national convention in Chicago to steer them back towards constitutionalism. There, Davitt beseeched his Irish-American audience to support the parliamentary party in its continuous efforts to achieve self-government in Ireland through 'peaceful and constitutional' means, as, to that point, revolutionary violence had not won any victories.[16] On that occasion and several subsequent ones, Davitt's defence of parliamentary efforts was both sincere and forceful. In later years, he joined the parliamentary party and, in fact, remained a member of its directory to his dying day because he genuinely believed that progress was possible without young Irish men needlessly sacrificing their lives and freedom. As he suggested in a letter to Parnell's biographer, Barry O'Brien, shortly after having obtained a seat in the Irish Party, 'I believe that constitutional media is infinitely more effective in these countries for real revolutionary work than conspiracy or secret societies ...'[17]

And yet, Davitt's choice of terminology in this letter and many other pronouncements suggests that, while he viewed constitutionalism as the most viable medium, he never fully discounted the appropriateness of revolutionary action under certain circumstances. In other words, he was never fully won over to constitutionalism as the only means for achieving Irish self-government. In fact, on those occasions when

Davitt received the maximum exposure he went on the record declaring, at the very least, some sympathy and compatibility with the old fenian agenda. For example, in October 1889 Davitt testified before the Times-Parnell Commission, refuting charges that he was directly connected to agrarian outrages during the 'land war'. In doing so, Davitt explained his own revolutionary past and connections with the IRB and Clan na Gael, but neither apologised for nor distanced himself from any of his past actions or associations. Instead, he expounded at length upon the political and economic conditions in Ireland that precipitated revolutionary vengeance, explaining that 'historically and politically considered, the Fenian movement had some justification for its existence ... after peaceful demands had been refused again and again when put forward by constitutional endeavour.'[18] Similarly, his resignation speech in the House of Commons in October 1899 made it clear that he was not opposed to a revolutionary response to what he deemed British tyranny in South Africa: 'I have been some five years in this House, and the conclusion with which I leave it now is this, that no cause, however just, no right, however pressing or apparent, will find redress here unless backed up by force.'[19] Even in his most celebrated book, *The Fall of Feudalism in Ireland*, he lamented the possibility that reform for Ireland might not be possible without 'insurrection, illegality, and the general warfare of "righteous violence"'.[20]

In other words, on these extremely prominent occasions, Davitt went on the record declaring, at the very least, that he had some sympathy and compatibility with the old fenian agenda. In short, he pursued constitutional reforms and lent support to non-violent efforts – and repeatedly condemned senseless agrarian outrages and dynamite campaigns – but he never discounted the appropriateness of armed revolt in Ireland given the right circumstances.[21] His independence as a nationalist concerned constitutionalists and annoyed revolutionaries all at once.

AN INDEPENDENT ADVOCATE OF LABOUR

Similarly, Davitt was an 'irreconcilable' within labour circles and his advocacy was, like his brand of nationalism, extremely independent. Much has been written about Davitt's efforts in the general election of 1906, in which he was influential in getting the Irish Party to support many Labour candidates in contests throughout Britain. In his final years, Davitt expended great efforts to get some Labour candidates into office, especially after his resignation from parliament.

However, for most of the preceding decades, he had resented and sometimes even opposed organised labour efforts in parliament, throwing his support – like most anti-Parnellites – behind the Liberal alliance. Davitt's commitment to the labour cause was unquestionable, but he feuded at length with James Keir Hardie and rejected the direction of the Independent Labour Party in the 1890s. In short, he believed that Irish nationalist efforts should be geared toward influencing Liberal Party policy on Irish home rule and labour reform issues because he believed this stood the best chance of success.[22]

While he was estranged from sections of the labour leadership in parliament, Davitt instead turned his efforts towards supporting trade unionism. To encourage this, he helped bring the American union, the Knights of Labor, into the British Isles, founded a short-lived newspaper, *Labour World*, and even helped to initiate his own general labour union, the Irish Democratic Labour Federation.[23] Nevertheless, while Davitt clearly was supportive of this form of activism, he was also, at the same time, very wary of union actions, especially those that threatened individual freedom, had little chance of success, or imposed hardships upon the poorest classes. For these reasons, though Davitt was an unflinching supporter of trade unionism and lent support to striking workers when he could, he also, more often than not, discouraged and sometimes condemned the aggressive strike policies often associated with the 'new unionism'.[24] Again, he could be counted upon to have sympathy for the workers, but could not be counted upon to provide his uncompromising support for aggressive union tactics.[25]

CONCLUSION

So how do we assess the importance of a man who was apparently both charming and difficult? Davitt cannot be lauded as an activist or parliamentarian who obtained the legislation and reforms he sought. His politics were usually too radical to be adopted by the Irish or Liberal parties, or, for that matter, by large sections of the Irish population; his role, inside parliament and out, was often polemical. Davitt's importance as a public figure lay in his willingness to engage in this polemical role, regardless of the unlikelihood, even impossibility, of achieving the goals he set. As a parliamentarian, he spoke out against any legislation that he deemed too moderate, condemning, time and again, legislation that he believed bailed out the landlord interests at the expense of the Irish or British working classes. His goal was not simply to prevent the passage of otherwise useful land and labour reform legislation; it was to raise awareness of the inadequacies of the reforms offered to the working classes, despite the hopelessness of achieving his own programmes in their stead. Perhaps his radicalism allowed people, inside and outside parliament, to recognise moderation for what it was. And though many would deem him an extremist, few doubted the sincerity behind his desire to represent the interests of those who held little political authority themselves.

Michael Davitt's reputation as a 'man of the people' appealed to a diverse following of nationalists and reformers, as well as large sections of the general public who admired (if nothing else) his independence, dedication and integrity. His lasting image was as a man who – as one of many obituaries noted – devoted his life 'to the service of the poor and oppressed of all lands'.[26] Contrary to James Connolly's famous assessment of him, as an idealist who 'gave his name and his services freely at the beck and call of men who despised his ideals',[27] Davitt showed tremendous integrity and remained steadfast to his own moral compass throughout his lifetime. For this reason he was constantly at odds with constitutionalists as well as revolutionaries, Tories as well as labour and land reform leaders, socialists and radicals alike. However, after his death, when he could no longer defend his independence, many of these groups could finally claim this 'man of the people' for themselves, using – and sometimes abusing – his reputation, harnessing his support after his death, because in life he was rarely so pliable.

NOTES

1. *The Times*, 24 September 1907.
2. *Irish Times*, 24 September 1907.
3. *Gaelic American*, 18 July 1906.
4. *Irish World*, 11 August 1906.
5. William O'Brien, *Evening Memories* (Dublin, 1920), p. 13.
6. Ibid., pp. 299–301.
7. T.P. O'Connor, *Memoirs of an Old Parliamentarian* (New York, 1929) vol. 1, pp. 127–8, 163–4.
8. Frank Hugh O'Donnell, *A History of the Irish Parliamentary Party* (London, 1910), p. 166.
9. *Plymouth Western Mercury*, 1 June 1906.
10. *Evening Times* (Glasgow), 31 May 1906.
11. O'Brien, *Evening Memories*, p. 65; *Lancaster Post*, 31 May 1906.
12. *Irish Independent*, 17 August 1908.
13. NLI, MS27826, Davitt to Lady Gregory, 10 May 1905.
14. Thomas Brown, *Irish-American Nationalism* (Philadelphia, 1966), p. 126.
15. Conor Cruise O'Brien, *Parnell and his Party* (Oxford, 1957), pp. 103–4; L.G. Redmond-Howard, *John Redmond* (New York, 1911), p. 108.
16. Brown, *Irish American Nationalism*, pp. 161–4; John E. Redmond, *The Irish Question: The Chicago Convention* (London, 1886), p. 4.
17. TCD, DP, MS 9377, f. 1063, Davitt to Barry O'Brien, 6 December 1893.

18. Michael Davitt, *The 'Times'-Parnell Commission Speech delivered by Michael Davitt in Defence of the Land League* (London, 1890), p. 14.

19. *Dublin Evening Telegraph*, 26 October 1899.

20. Michael Davitt, *The Fall of Feudalism in Ireland, or, the Story of the Land League Revolution* (London & New York, 1904), p. 301. Also see L. Perry Curtis Jr, 'Moral and physical force: The language of violence in Irish nationalism', *Journal of British Studies*, vol. 27 (1988).

21. James Winder Good, *Michael Davitt* (Dublin, 1921), p. 13.

22. TCD, DP, MS 9521, f. 5979, Davitt to Richard McGhee, 12 March 1892. For more on Davitt's estimation of Keir Hardie, see TCD, DP, MS 9521, ff. 5988 and 6001, Davitt to Richard McGhee, 7 August 1892 & 30 August 1895.

23. Arthur Mitchell, *Labour in Irish Politics, 1890–1930: The Irish Labour Movement in an Age of Revolution* (Shannon, 1974), pp. 16–17; Emmet O'Connor, *A Labour History of Ireland, 1824–1960* (Dublin, 1992), p. 53; Davitt, *Fall of Feudalism*, p. 636.

24. John Cunningham, *Labour in the West of Ireland* (Belfast, 1995), pp. 17–18; TCD, DP, MS 9556, f. 263, Davitt's diary, 13 July 1894; TCD, DP, MS 9328, f. 180/39–40, Davitt to Richard McGhee, 20 May 1890.

25. See also NLI, MS18563, Davitt to Michael McKeown, 10 February 1891; Cunningham, *Labour*, pp. 22–4.

26. *Bristol Evening News*, 8 June 1906.

27. James Connolly, 'Michael Davitt: A text for a revolutionary lecture', in Owen Dudley Edwards and Bernard Ransom (eds) *James Connolly: Selected Political Writings* (New York, 1974).

Index